Obscurity's
Myriad Components

Photograph of Faulkner taken in Nagano, Japan, August 1955. Inscribed by Faulkner: "To Mr and Mrs Jelliffe, William Faulkner, Nagano 13 Aug 1955." By permission of the Faulkner Estate

Obscurity's Myriad Components

The Theory and Practice of William Faulkner

R. Rio-Jelliffe

Lewisburg
Bucknell University Press
London: Associated University Presses

Associated University Presses
440 Forsgate Drive
Cranbury, NJ 08512

Associated University Presses
16 Barter Street
London WC1A 2AH, England

Associated University Presses
P.O Box 338, Port Credit
Mississauga, Ontario
Canada L5G 4L8

The paper used in this publication meets the requirements of the American National Standard for Permanence of Paper for Printed Library Materials Z39.48-1984.

Library of Congress Cataloging-in-Publication Data

Rio-Jelliffe, R., 1922–
    Obscurity's myriad components : the theory and practice of William Faulkner / R. Rio-Jelliffe.
        p. cm.
    Includes bibliographical references and index.
    ISBN 0-8387-5462-7 (alk. paper)
    1. Faulkner, William, 1897–1962—Technique.   2. Faulkner, William, 1897–1962—Aesthetics.   3. Narration (Rhetoric)   4. Fiction—Technique.
I. Title.
PS3511.A86 Z955   2001
813'.52—dc21   00-065137

To
Angela Jelliffe, Cynthia Rio Brown,
Amy and David Brown
—my joys

Contents

Preface and Acknowledgements

I MET AND HEARD WILLIAM FAULKNER IN AUGUST 1955 AT NAGANO, Japan, where for ten days he conversed with Japanese and American professors at a seminar on American Literature. He addressed every kind of question on his art, his country and people, and humankind. His responses were extensive and thorough, but what re-echoed through the sessions were his affirmations of the high purpose of art and the human capacity for good. The positive notes struck me, for they sounded unlike the somber tones for which he was reputed. Faulkner's gentle voice somehow made me perceive in darkness the possibility of hope. I wondered then which Faulkner spoke in his fiction, the "nihilist" readers and critics often disparaged, or the voice at Nagano that recognized the force of evil yet kept faith with good. That hint of Faulkner's binary mind proved years later to be the distinctive mark of his theory and art. Contradiction or paradox governs his theory of language and form, and shapes the elements of technique and structure in fiction; while meaning and theme often materialize in polar images, like the frozen but renascent redworm that reify hope for Mr. Compson in *Absalom, Absalom!* or, in *As I Lay Dying,* Darl's water bucket, a "nothingness" with "a star or two" glimmering in it.

My initial interest in theme shifted to language and form when Professor J. Hillis Miller, Chair of the Department of English at Yale University and Director of the NEH Summer Seminar I attended, invited me to be a Postdoctoral Fellow of the Department. My research at Yale and at Virginia and writing for five years under the direction of Professor Miller uncovered in the Faulkner nonfiction materials, both published and unpublished, a set of congruent ideas predicated on the writer's view of his duplicitous but potent medium of language that form must overcome. The paradox shapes Faulkner's artistic principles that, applied in practice, overturn conventions of fictive technique and structure so as to surmount the word. The iconoclast who believed in hope I heard at Nagano, the

9

antithetic language and form, and the antonymous substance and
theme of the fiction were all of a piece, analogues of the writer's
bisected view of the universe. Technique and structure naturally en-
tail content and theme, but this study observes Faulkner's fundamental artistic credo: the sources, substance, and theme of narrative
are incidental to language, technique, and structure that embody
sense. Faulkner contrives of language a form that signifies more
than it denotes, and thus transcends the word.

Various theoretical articles shape the six novels in this study—
*Light in August, Absalom, Absalom!, The Sound and the Fury, As I
Lay Dying, The Unvanquished,* and *Go Down, Moses*—but all exemplify two central tenets on time and structure in the two primary
components of Faulkner's form: the diverse linguistic simulations
of synchronic time that fragment narrative and the contrary operation of dispersal and counterpoint that organize disjunct narratives.
The emergence of Faulkner's theory admits more precise assess-
ments of Henri Bergson's influence on the novelist's thought and
art, the nature and quality of his work, and his place in the history
of the theory of language and narrative.

I take pleasure in acknowledging my indebtedness, foremost to
Professor Miller, who encouraged and guided the beginnings of this
study. I must remark the largeness of mind of this prominent mem-
ber of the "Yale mafia" (from NEH seminarians awed/daunted by
deconstruction), who never, through the five years I worked with
him, suggested any approach to Faulkner but my own. I also grate-
fully acknowledge the generous help of the late Professor Cleanth
Brooks, who was intrigued with the way the theory illuminated
Faulkner's language, in particular, the power of the word converted
to voice. I value our conversations about Faulkner, his comments
and letters on the works, and his wise counsel on the manner of
presenting one's ideas. I thank Professor and Mrs. Thomas Whi-
taker and the late Professor Michael Cooke and his family for their
welcome and support of my work at Yale, and to Professor Cooke
in particular for his advice to conceive each chapter as a whole,
from the beginning through each point to the end.

I thank Professor James B. Meriwether for his encouragement
and instructive reading of some early versions of this work, and
other unknown readers of journals and presses who helped me resolve problems of thought and expression. Above all, I acknowledge a great debt to Professor Dennis Baumwoll, whose meticulous

and perceptive readings helped to clarify the focus and style of this
study during its final stages.

I am grateful for the research grants from the National Endow-
ment for the Humanities and the University of Redlands; and for
permission to do research at the Sterling Library at Yale University
and the Special Collections at the Alderman Library of the University of Virginia.

I thank the Alderman Library for permission to quote from the
following materials: Taped Interviews with William Faulkner for
Faulkner in the University (MSS 6187), Special Collections Department, University of Virginia Library; Papers Relating to William Faulkner from Harold Ober Associates Inc. (MSS 8969),
Special Collections Department, University of Virginia Library;
and The Faulkner manuscripts. I also thank the University Press of
Virginia for permission to reprint material from *Faulkner in the
University;* Random House, Inc. for permission to quote from six
Faulkner novels and from *Faulkner at West Point;* Kenkyusha Publishing Co., Ltd. for permission to quote from *Faulkner at Nagano;*
the Peters Fraser and Dunlop Group Ltd, on behalf of Michael Millgate, for permission to reprint material from *Lion in the Garden;*
The Journal of Narrative Technique for permission to use parts of
my essay on *Absalom, Absalom!,* published in the spring of 1981;
and Rowman and Littlefield Publishers for permission to quote
from *A Study in Metaphysics: The Creative Mind* by Henri Bergson.
I also thank Bucknell University press for permission to quote from
the reader's reports.

A survey of Faulkner criticism through seven decades provides
the background for this study of his poetics and art. Among the
many Faulkner scholars who illuminated the way for us who follow
after them, I take special note of Cleanth Brooks for his valuable
insights into Faulkner's background and work; John T. Matthews
for his study of Faulkner's language; Michael Millgate for his in-
vestigations into the genetic history of Faulkner's fiction; Stephen
M. Ross for his systematic examination of the nature of voice in
Faulkner; Hugh M. Ruppersburg for his exploration of point of
view; and Olga Vickery for her incisive reading of the novels. To
the other scholars and critics, including those writing on the theory
of language and narrative, who facilitated this study of Faulkner's
language and form, some of whom I cite and many more I do not,
I acknowledge my immense debt.

Through the years, Professor Bruce McAllister gave support and wise direction; Mrs. Laura Vroman, faithful friend and patient typist, gave both encouragement and emendation; and Mr. Hung Ma did invaluable research on references. The staff of the University of Redlands Armacost Library facilitated my work, with special thanks to Ms. Sandy Richey and Ms. Trisha Aurelio, and to my assistant, Mr. Nathan Thibodeaux. I acknowledge the sustaining presence of my daughters, Professor Angela Jelliffe, who stayed with me through years of conversation about Faulkner and music, and Ms. Cyndy Rio Brown, who always had the right word and touch.

Abbreviations

Listed below are abbreviations for works by William Faulkner cited or consulted.

NOVELS

AA   *Absalom, Absalom!* (New York: Random House, 1936/1964, facsimile of first edition). The second page cited in this study is from the Corrected Text (New York: Vintage International, 1990).

AILD *As I Lay Dying* (New York: Vintage Books, 1930/1964, collation of first edition and original manuscript and typescript). The second page cited is from the Corrected Text (New York: Vintage International, 1990).

F   *A Fable* (New York: Vintage Books, 1950/1978).

FD   *Flags in the Dust*, ed. Douglas Day (New York: Vintage Books, 1974).

GDM *Go Down, Moses* (New York: Modern Library, 1942). The second page cited is from the Corrected Text (New York: Vintage International, 1990).

H   *The Hamlet* (New York: Vintage Books, 1940/1958). The Corrected Text (New York: Vintage International, 1991).

ID   *Intruder in the Dust* (New York: Modern Library, 1948). The Corrected Text (New York: Vintage International, 1991).

LIA   *Light in August* (New York: Modern Library, 1932/1968, copy of the first printing). The second page cited is from the Corrected Text (New York: Vintage International, 1987).

TM   *The Mansion* (New York: Vintage Books, 1955/1965).

MA   *Mayday* (Notre Dame, IN: University of Notre Dame Press, 1976).

M   *Mosquitoes* (New York: Boni and Liveright, 1927).

P   *Pylon* (New York: Smith and Hass, 1935).

R   *The Reivers* (New York: Vintage International, 1962/1992)

RN   *Requiem for a Nun* (New York: Vintage Books, 1951/1975).

S   *Sartoris* (New York: Random House, 1929/1956).

SP   *Soldier's Pay* (New York: Boni and Liveright, 1927).

SF   *The Sound and The Fury* (New York: Modern Library, 1929/1956, copy of the first printing). The second page cited is from the Corrected Text (New York: Vintage International, 1990).

T   *The Town* (New York: Random House, 1957/1961).

U   *The Unvanquished* (New York: Vintage Books, 1938/1965, photographic reproduction of the first printing). The second page cited is from the Corrected Text (New York: Vintage International, 1991).

WP   *The Wild Palms* (New York: Vintage Books, 1939/1964).

Short Stories and Nonfiction

CS   *Collected Stories of William Faulkner* (New York: Vintage Books, 1977).

CWF   *Conversations with William Faulkner*, ed. M. Thomas Inge (Jackson: University Press of Mississippi, 1999).

EPP   *William Faulkner: Early Prose and Poetry*, ed. Carvel Collins (Boston: Little, Brown, 1962).

ESPL   *Essays, Speeches, and Public Letters*, ed. James B. Meriwether (New York: Random House, 1965).

FB   *Faulkner: A Biography*, 2 vols., Joseph L. Blotner (New York: Random House, 1974).

FB1   *Faulkner: A Biography*, 1 vol., Joseph L. Blotner (New York: Vintage Books, 1991).

FCF   *Faulkner-Cowley File: Letters and Memories, 1944–1962*, ed. Malcolm Cowley (New York: Viking, 1966).

FM   *A Faulkner Miscellany*, ed. James B. Meriwether (Jackson: University Press of Mississippi, 1974).

FN   *Faulkner at Nagano*, ed. Robert A. Jelliffe (Tokyo: Kenkyusha, 1956).

FU   *Faulkner in the University*, eds. Frederick L. Gwynn and Joseph L. Blotner (Charlottesville: University of Virginia

Press, 1959). Reprinted with permission of the University Press of Virginia.

FWP   *Faulkner at West Point*, eds. Joseph L. Fant III and Robert Ashley (New York: Random House, 1964).

LG   *Lion in the Garden: Interviews with William Faulkner, 1926–1962*, eds. James B. Meriwether and Michael Millgate (New York: Random House, 1968).

LF   *William Faulkner: Letters and Fictions*. James G. Watson (Austin: University of Texas Press, 1987).

NOS   *New Orleans Sketches*, ed. Carvel Collins (New York: Random House, 1968).

SL   *Selected Letters of William Faulkner*, ed. Joseph L. Blotner (New York: Random House, 1977).

TH   *Thinking of Home: William Faulkner's Letters to His Mother and Father, 1918–1925*, ed. James G. Watson (New York: Norton, 1992).

TWF   *Talking About William Faulkner: Interviews with Jimmy Faulkner and Others*, eds. Sally Wolff and Floyd C. Watkins (Baton Rouge: Louisiana State University Press, 1996).

US   *Uncollected Stories of William Faulkner*, ed. Joseph L. Blotner (New York: Vintage Books, 1981).

UV   William Faulkner Collection at the Alderman Library, University of Virginia. File name or number cited in text. Materials from:

1. Taped Interviews with William Faulkner for *Faulkner in the University* (MSS 6187), Special Collections Department, University of Virginia Library. Quotations only from unprinted segments of the tapes.
2. Papers relating to William Faulkner from Harold Ober Associates, Inc. (MSS 8969), Special Collections Department, University of Virginia Library.
3. The Holograph and Typescript manuscripts of William Faulkner.

WFO   *William Faulkner of Oxford*, eds. James W. Webb and A. Wigfall Green (Baton Rouge: Louisiana State University Press, 1965).

The works of Henri Bergson, cited or consulted, include the following (first dates indicate French editions):

CE   *Creative Evolution,* trans. Arthur Mitchell (New York: Holt, 1907/1911).

CM   *An Introduction to Metaphysics: The Creative Mind*, trans. Mabelle L. Andison (Totowa, NJ: Littlefield, Adams 1903–23/1965).

INP   *The Introduction to a New Philosophy*, trans. Sidney Littman (Boston: Luce, 1903/1912).

L   *Laughter*, trans. Cloudesley Brereton and Fred Rothwell New York: Macmillan, 1911/1928).

MM   *Matter and Memory*, trans. Nancy Margaret Paul and W. Scott Palmer (London: G. Allen & Unwin, 1896/1911).

TFW   *Time and Free Will*, trans. F. S. Pogson (New York: Harper, 1889/1960).

MR   *The Two Sources of Morality and Religion*, trans. R. Ashley Audra and Cloudesley Brereton (New York: Doubleday, 1932/1935).

Obscurity's
Myriad Components

Introduction

WILLIAM FAULKNER PRODUCED A LARGE NUMBER OF LITERARY works, but not a single essay in "defense" of his art. The subject, however, engrossed him. He spoke or wrote extensively on the source, language, form, and purpose of fiction in interviews and dialogues, speeches and letters, topical essays, sketches, and reviews. Readers have drawn from this large mass a passage or two to support one or another critical view, but the pronouncements of a writer notorious for willful distortion and inconsistency remain suspect. Unlike the finely articulated theory of Henry James or T. S. Eliot, Faulkner appears to have left nothing but incoherent commentary.

A comprehensive study of the nonfiction materials, however, discloses their common ground, the view that language, the writer's essential medium, "kill[s]" experience while recording it (*ESPL* 187).[1] The word mediates but also obstructs thought, art, and human relating. Yet the writer has no other means to conquer his enemy but language itself. That paradoxical premise underlies Faulkner's theory of language and narrative, whose primary articles address the problem of giving voice to the imagination with the duplicitous word. He overturns canons of narrative to convert language into word-transcending form. The writer's distrust of language is widely noted, but the solution he expounds in theory and practices in fiction is generally unnoted. Faulkner overcomes the word, not in wordlessness, as it is often denoted, but in silence where the word resonates beyond discourse.

To subdue the word so "the thunder and the music of the prose take place in silence" (*LG* 248), Faulkner finds he must subdue time. "There isn't any time. . . . I agree pretty much with Bergson's theory of the fluidity of time. There is only the present moment, in which I include both the past and the future, and that is eternity. In my opinion time can be shaped quite a bit by the artist; after all, man is never time's slave" (*LG* 70). Faulkner shapes time in myriad simulations of "true duration," Henri Bergson's term for "moments inside one another," or "time perceived as indivisible" (*TFW* 232, *CM* 149, see Abbreviations for the list of Bergson's works). The "integration of past, present, and future which defies successive time" is "the kind of time known by books" where "a moment has endless perspectives of reality," Frank Kermode declares.[2] Faulkner encapsulates in a "moment of action" the "sum of [a man's] past" and "of his future too" (*FU* 84, 48), fusing at once cause and effect and thus inscribing in technical form a moral pattern. Synchronic condensations of diachronic time distinguish the language of Faulkner's major works. Since Jean-Paul Sartre's famous essay on Faulkner's time,[3] the novelist's handling of time has intrigued readers, but its formative effects on language and form, as well as the substance and theme of story, deserve a more thorough study.[4]

Time fused in layered voices, points of view, styles, concentric images, and other elements of technique breaks the sequential flow of narrative and causes discontinuity. Unlike the "simple direct line" of traditional narrative, his fiction, Faulkner admits, constitutes a "series of pieces" and, in a work like *Absalom, Absalom!,* the "inchoate fragments" may fail to "coalesce" (*FU* 45, 76). The seeming absence or the uncertainty of structural form in other narratives like *As I Lay Dying, Go Down, Moses, Light in August, The Sound and the Fury,* and *The Unvanquished* has preoccupied readers, who generally adduce patterns of action or theme to authenticate coherence in these disjunct novels. Faulkner himself, apparently obsessed with the problem of organizing his fragmented works, reiterates over the decades his solution: entwine antithetic elements and processes in the language and form of fiction, and coincidentally, the content and theme as well. He fuses time and meaning at a point latent with possibilities, whose variant but counterpointed unfoldings become essential components of the whole. Conversely, he splinters technical and structural elements to bring about the "contrapuntal . . . integration" of discrete parts, a procedure that projects sense past the word. Faulkner's primary artistic principle of "contradiction" or "antithesis," operating with the other principles of "condensation," "repetition," and "counterpoint," generates a converging-expanding-converging process that disjoins/conjoins narrative.[5] Robert Scholes thinks "design" in fiction or the "meaningful pattern" that frames "the whole work" is static.[6]

Faulkner's idea of "pattern" entails the metamorphic transformations of heterogeneous components, an evolving formal design.
Resonating inside one another, the antonymous parts sound past
the word a silent tale that recasts the discursive surface of narrative.

Readers harp on the discontinuity in Faulkner's works, but few
detect the counterforces to dispersal built into his antithetic form.
The following passage surfaces everywhere, but the structural pattern of source and variant amplifications encoded in it remains un-
detected:

> Not only each book had to have a design but the whole output or sum
> of an artist's work had to have a design. . . . Beginning with *Sartoris* I
> discovered that my own little postage stamp of native soil was worth
> writing about and that I would never live long enough to exhaust it, and
> by sublimating the actual into apocryphal I would have complete liberty
> to use whatever talent I might have to its absolute top. It opened up a
> gold mine of other peoples, so I created a cosmos of my own. I can
> move these people around like God, not only in space but in time
> too. . . . Time is a fluid condition which has no existence except in the
> momentary avatars of individual people. There is no such thing as
> *was*—only *is*. . . . I like to think of the world I created as being a kind
> of keystone in the Universe; that, as small as that keystone is, if it were
> ever taken away, the universe itself would collapse. (*LG* 255)

The "design" of each book and of the "sum" of his work is not the
Yoknapatawpha theme, as it is generally assumed, but a pattern of
multiple yet correlated unfoldings from a concentric point.[7] The
"little postage stamp of native soil" generates inexhaustible variations on a "cosmos" of "peoples." "Sublimating" the insignificant
"actual" to the multivalent "apocryphal" opens diverse angles on
the subject. "Fluid" time, precipitated in the "*is*" of individual
"avatars," produces variant modulations. The "keystone" analogizes the "small" source or germ that engenders and holds together
the multifarious "Universe" of a book or of "an artist's work."
The passage itself exemplifies the source-unfolding pattern it
sketches. It encodes embryonic ideas on technique and structure
amplified for decades in discourse and in many works of fiction.
That structural design of germ or source and separate but affiliated
unfoldings distinguishes Faulkner's theory of structure and his
practice in multipartite narratives.

Antithetic condensation, counterpoint, and repetition shapes language and form, as well as the substance and theme of fiction. Repetition by contrast highlights without overt explication the import of a unique gesture. Caddy Compson's affection for her idiot brother Benjy, unmatched among the members of an unloving family, or Isaac McCaslin's unprecedented repudiation of property in a dynasty founded on ownership stipulates the theme of each work. Mirroring its equivocal medium, Faulkner's equilibrated technique seldom poses what Paul de Man calls "mutually self-destructive" oppositions. Rather, antinomies deconstruct then reconstitute each other and achieve "an alterity even more irreducible than that of opposition," or what Ralph Flores, echoing Derrida, labels the "nonoppositional play of opposites." Paradox in Faulkner's practice signifies not an erasure, but essential mutuality. Robert Penn Warren, back in the sixties, labeled Faulkner's art a "perilous balance."[8] Meaning emanates from the "reciprocal friction" of antinomies (Bergson's phrase, *INP* 102; see Abbreviations), and irony recasts a story constituted of the splintering and layering of difference (adapted from Roland Barthes's "layering of significance"[9]).

Recent criticism certifies Faulkner's "modernism" with what it labels his "subversive" language.[10] The subversive quality stems in great part from the interplay of diffusion and confluence, of opposition and mutuality in a self-denying narrative that transgresses the rules so as to empower the word to speak beyond itself.

The challenge of his double-edged medium may have led Faulkner to valorize form over subject and theme. His own repeated references to his "country," the South, and the pervasive attention to that background give the general impression of a writer engrossed with his subject.[11] The theory denies that assumption. The most familiar of Faulkner's pronouncements reiterate "the same point" to which the works are "basically directed," the writer's "faith in man and his ability to always prevail and endure over circumstances and over his own destiny," and to say "No to death" (*LG* 113, 221; *ESPL* 181). But those statements consistently bond the subject of "universal truth" with the most "moving," "important," "memorable," "beautiful," "passionate," "terrible," or "effective" "method" (*LG* 113, 201, 203–4; *FU* 160). Faulkner deliberately secures content with "style" (*FN* 94, 152–53). Three months before his death, he recapitulates the writer's aim, to tell a "story in the most moving and dramatic way" and "to use the best method he possibly can find" (*FWP* 56–57, 59). The core of his discourses addresses the central question of "technique," "pattern," "design," "shape," or "structure" by which art embodies and organizes the subject. The "craft," the "artificial means," the "ordered words," or the "new way" (*ESPL* 153, *LG* 253, *FM* 165, *FCF* 14) enunciated in theory and practiced in fiction converts language to "form" which, in Tzvetan Todorov's terms, "signifies" more than it "designates,"[12] and thus transcends the word. The reader of *Absalom, Absalom!* must hear past the words a speaking silence that recasts and completes the literal story.

Substance and theme naturally inhere in form; but shifting the critical focus from the content to the language, technique, and structure of a fractured but polyphonic tale may assess more precisely the quality of Faulkner's art. The diverse linguistic formulations of "indivisible" time and the perpetual interplay of heterogeneous elements of form and sense distinguish Faulkner from modernists like Marcel Proust, Joseph Conrad, and James Joyce, who sought as he did to conquer time and the word. Challenged by his recalcitrant medium, Faulkner deconstructs and reconstructs language and form so "the thunder and the music of the prose take place in silence" (*LG* 248).

Applying Faulkner's poetics to the fiction would be a circular exercise if the theory were nothing but a defense of practice, and the fiction simply illustrated and confirmed the poetics. That danger remains, but self-justification seems less likely when praxis overrules or transcends theory, and art once more eludes intention. In theory, the structural design of a "germ" or "center" and its conjoined unfoldings appears simple. In practice, a novel may pose an apparent "source," then proceed to decenter itself with other time/meaning condensations that supplant one another as the work's axis. True to his antonymous "method," Faulkner's practice exemplifies, but also counters his theory.[13]

The purpose of this study is to bring to light material hitherto considered nonexistent, William Faulkner's theory of language and narrative, founded on the writer's belief in the bisected nature of language, of human beings, and of the universe (chapter 1); and to examine the relation of theory to practice, the translation of creed to fictive technique, structure, and theme (chapters 2–7). The main doctrines, which remain consistent from their tentative beginnings to the latest enunciation,[14] combine precepts from classical thought and modern theory, and the practice prefigures antinovelistic fiction in America. The theory throws light on the way Faulkner reinvents language into word-transcending form. Each of the six novels applies different theoretical articles for its own distinct purpose, but all of them exemplify the two ruling components of Faulkner's narrative: the language of synchronic time that overcomes the intractable word and the contrapuntal structure the writer contrives for his discontinuous narrative.

The preeminence of synchronic time in Faulkner's concept of form and in his fiction calls for a reappraisal of the influence of Bergson on his thought and art. Bergson celebrates the power of literary tropes to surpass the limits of language and tell a truer tale, while Faulkner seeks to forge a language of consonant time that tells more than it states. Their parallel theories clarify the scope and function of Faulkner's linguistic delineations of "true duration" and its effects on the technique, structure, and theme of *Light in August* (1932, chapter 2) and other novels. In *Absalom, Absalom!* (1936, chapter 3), layered voices fuse time and tell a silent tale that completes the improbable, literal story. Four fractional novels, *The Sound and the Fury* (1929, chapter 4), *As I Lay Dying* (1930, chapter 5), *The Unvanquished* (1938, chapter 6), and *Go Down, Moses* (1942, chapter 7), illustrate the operation of counterprocesses that frame a modulant structure. Elements of form and sense splinter and fuse at points of converged time that, like the "germ," reproduce diverse but correlated unfoldings, or, like a later "moment," interconnect segments before and after it. Faulkner's revisions in several major works, particularly in *Light in August, The Unvanquished,* and *Go Down, Moses,* show his increasing reliance on the language of synchronic time to structure each work and to expand sense beyond the word. The writer's view of an incongruent universe materializes in the interplay of antinomies in his fiction.

A prominent writer's poetics has intrinsic significance, although after De Saussure and his followers, Faulkner's concept of a self-negating medium may appear less distinctive. In the twenties and thirties, however, the strategies he devised against the unstable word were revolutionary, and their manifestation in literary form changed the direction of American fiction. The leap from Henry James and Ernest Hemingway to Faulkner charts the evolution to "new" fiction, a genre that self-consciously questions its duplicitous means and fictional status, but obtains its being with the very word it seeks to surmount. Faulkner has been labeled an uncon-scious artist, something in the order of an unschooled genius. The theory proves he is a knowledgeable artisan who reinvents fictive form and verismilitude to overcome the killer word. More than a casual commentator on his art, Faulkner, whose influence has been acknowledged by writers worldwide, points fiction to new direc-tions.

The literary work ultimately surpasses the author's conception and intention. That transcendence reveals the "inextricable[,] com-positeness" of "*obscurity's myriad components*" with which a writer would burst the limits of language (*LIA* 465/491, *AA* 143/ 115).

1

Theory of Language and Narrative

I. LANGUAGE AND "METHOD"

WILLIAM FAULKNER, WHO IS UNIVERSALLY HONORED FOR HIS LITERary art, held in profound distrust his medium of language. Three months before his death in 1962, he reflects on over four decades of working with a potent but treacherous "tool." The writer "wants to make it on paper as startling, as comic, anyway as moving, as true, as important as it seems in the imagination. And in the process of getting it into cold words on the paper, something escapes from it. It's still not as good as when he dreamed it. Which is the reason that when he finishes that to the best of his ability, he writes, tries again—he writes another one. He is still trying to capture that dream, that image of man, either victorious or defeated, in some splendid, beautiful gesture inside the dilemma of the human heart" (*FWP* 112).[1] The valedictory reprises Faulkner's lifelong distrust of a medium that subverts its function to express or communicate. Imagination transforms experience to something more than it is: comic, moving, true, significant; but the "cold words" blight the "dream," and the foiled writer "tries again" to contain his "image of man" in one "splendid, beautiful gesture." "Repetition" and "condensation," two of Faulkner's primary artistic principles, may enkindle the "cold" word so it speaks past itself the language of the imagination.

About a decade earlier, Faulkner defines the problem and its solution. The writer "discovers pretty soon in his career that having nothing to his hand but language, he is doomed to about the damndest clumsiest frailest awkwardest tool he could have been given. But it also proves that if you just keep on trying to say a thing long enough and hard enough, it will emerge; someone will hear it; . . . it's a good workable excuse for Faulkner's writing style" (*SL* 296–

97). Chained to his "curse" (*SL* 424), the "clumsy method of speech, of writing" (*FWP* 50), he will continue the round of attempt and failure: "I'll keep on writing. Because as I see it one never does tell the truth as he views it. He tries and each time he fails. And so he tries it again. He knows the next time will not be good, either, but he tries it again" (*LG* 93). Repeated trials may subdue the clumsy, frail, awkward tool of language, but there remains something a writer "alone feels" that "never quite gets into the actual words" (*SL* 63).

As early as 1931, Faulkner expresses his misgivings over the power of language to stifle rather than give life to thought. "Authentic experience transferred to paper word for word" does "not make a book. No matter how vivid it be, somewhere between the experience and the blank page and the pencil, it dies. Perhaps the words kill it" (*ESPL* 187). The idea of the killer word reechoes through the fiction, from *Mosquitoes* (1927) to *A Fable* (1954), including among others, *Absalom, Absalom!*, *The Sound and the Fury*, and *As I Lay Dying*. Human beings are like the novelist whom Dawson Fairchild classifies as "that species all of whose actions are controlled by words." But words are "a kind of sterility" that displace ideas: "You start right off to think in words. And first thing you know, you don't have thoughts in your mind at all: you just have words in it." Words also "substitute" for "things and deeds," and "pretty soon the thing or the deed becomes just a kind of shadow of a certain sound you make by shaping your mouth a certain way" (*M* 130, 210, 231). Faulkner ranks words and their sounds the least reliable modes of expression. When a well-intended but ill-worded tribute infuriates Ernest Hemingway, Faulkner concludes one ought not "depend on words" to "communicate" (*FWP* 118). Addie Bundren, who recapitulates the author's strictures on language, mocks Cora Tull's doubly debased language where "the high dead words in time seemed to lose even the significance of their dead sound" (*AILD* 167/175).

The word and its empty sound obstruct communication, but voice and silence facilitate it. Words converted to "voice speaking the speech" compress "observation, experience, and imagination" and, fusing "image" and "sound" (*FU* 181), tell past the word in silence. Faulkner identifies fiction writing with oral storytelling, and narrative with voice recounting "in the tongue of the human spirit" (*ESPL* 143). To the last recorded talks three months before his death, Faulkner equates writing with speech (*FWP* 50). His acknowledged master, Joseph Conrad, offers a paradigm of narrator and passive but formative listener who jointly affect the course of narrative. Faulkner alters the model when, with some exceptions (like the exchanges in *Absalom, Absalom!* or Ratliff telling Varner the Pat Stamper story in *The Hamlet*), he omits the audience. The reader becomes the surrogate listener, her constitutive role made difficult by the multiple narrators and layered points of view displacing Conrad's single voice and point of view.[2] The Bundren story splinters into fifteen voices and viewpoints, unmediated by a focal narrator or consciousness. Faulkner thinks Quentin Compson's voice (his bitterness) and angle of vision (his "hatred" of the South) raise *Absalom, Absalom!* above a "historical novel" (*SL* 79); but numerous voices in fact stratify in Quentin's voice, creating possibly the most convoluted permutation in the canon. Intermeshed voices and points of view are among the main devices to compress time in the major works.

The tone of voice calibrates dramatic intensity, as the rise and fall of variant voices in *A Fable* (1954) heighten the conflict, while the comic interlude of the "horse piece" remains a "monotone, sustained on one note." A "gentle story" ought "to be told gently," but "a story of violence" requires a matching tone in the "way it is told" (*SL* 259, 351). Each person's distinctive tone and style in *The Sound and the Fury* represent a linguistic equivalent of being. Jason Compson's bitter tone sounds his malevolent nature and silently elicits judgment on his character. Benjy's voice does not tell about Benjy; it *is* Benjy. Voice and tone amplify sense past the word and thus overcome it.

Voice used for wrongful ends causes the "evil and grief of this world" and "all human ills" and becomes "mankind's curse." A Hitler or Mussolini speaking to a "captive audience" brings out the "worst of both" (*SL* 424–25, 252). But the human voice also helps to "assimilate and endure" experience (*ESPL* 60) and to withstand wrongdoing. "Anyone can save anyone from injustice if he just will, if he just tries, just raises his voice" (*LG* 130). "Never be afraid to raise your voice for honesty and truth and compassion, against injustice and lying and greed" (*ESPL* 123–24). A "single voice always somewhere" calling us to be "braver," "more compassionate," "more truthful" than we are, always elicits a response, "Yes, I will!" That's how "we get rid of the tyrants" and human "misery" (*LG* 109). The child and the old lady who save the black man in *Intruder in the Dust* (1948) are such voices. The poet's voice, Faulkner declares in his Nobel Prize speech, should enable human beings to "endure and prevail" (*FN* 206). Like the writer who pursues a round of attempt and failure with the word, the individual fails to match vision with action, but "tries again" until some good does "emerge." Faulkner closely affiliates artistic creativity with moral endeavor (see IV).

Above the word, sound, and voice, Faulkner elevates silence: "I like silence . . . Silence and horses. And trees" (*LG* 64). Like his characters, Quentin Compson (*SF*), Addie and Darl Bundren (*AILD*), the author identifies the truest form of speech in the stillness past the word: "I prefer silence to sound, and the image produced by words occurs in silence. That is, the thunder and the music of the prose take place in silence" (*LG* 248). This "silence," generally identified with the "wordless," signifies for Faulkner not an absence of words, but a "speaking" silence beyond the "cold words" empowered to tell an "implied story" (UV 8969 Ober-Faulkner 1942–1943).[3] Fiction then becomes a language function whose aim is to overpass the very medium that gives it life. An unvoiced but requisite tale evoked through and past the word distinguishes Faulkner's narrative.

The writer, Faulkner admits, "can't do anything but use words" (*F:B* II.1143) for his "very great responsibility" to "record man's endeavor" against "suffering, injustice," and to hold out to man the hope that his condition "can be improved" by "his own efforts" (*LG* 201, 178). The writer's dilemma of having only the inadequate word to overcome itself actuates the search for form that exceeds the word. Faulkner is reported to have said, "Sometimes the meaning of a word in its context transcends the dictionary definition" (*WFO* 133). The comment gives a clue to his strategy against the word: create a "context" that sets the word resonating beyond itself. "A balance, a counterpoint" (*LG* 132) of discords and incongruities provides that context in fiction. Faulkner's capacity to "assume two contrary points of view at the same time" that are irreducible to "two antagonistic concepts," as Henri Bergson characterizes the deeper mental states (*INP* 47; see Abbreviations for the list of Bergson's works), imprints his theory and fiction. The resulting equivocal narrative presents itself as self-contradictory and implausible, yet seeks belief for its truth/lie. It gains credibility with double tales, the worded and the unworded, that contravene and, at the same time, complement one another. Meaning or theme lies on neither side of opposites, but in counterpoised polarities. Faulkner's people wrestle with both fate and free will. Causality, though inexorable, leaves choice open to each person, who becomes responsible in part for his or her destiny.

The "new way" Faulkner prescribes to make the word speak beyond itself materializes in the language, technique, and structure of six novels (chapters 2–7). The "method" he outlines in theory involves a course of transformation, first in the mind, where the raw materials of experience are refined through a hierarchy of faculties (see II); and in art, where language shaped into form comprised of diametric elements and counterprocesses imparts not a single story but its variant "mutations" (*FU* 132) (see III). A metaphysics of duality underlies the antithetic theory of language and narrative (see IV). Faulkner's poetics illuminates the complex nature of his art and should redirect critical attention from the source and substance of fiction to the language and form that surmounts the treacherous word.

II. THE ALEMBIC OF MIND AND THE SUBJECT OF ART

Although aware of the wide interest in the source and background of his fiction, Faulkner maintains: "My material, the South, is not very important to me. I just happen to know it, and dont [*sic*] have time in one life to learn another one." Of the thematic thread Malcolm Cowley detects in the canon, Faulkner contends: "I don't see too much Southern legend in it" (*FCF* 14–15, 78); and claims he "wasn't writing sociology at all," but about the "human heart," which is the "important thing" (*FU* 10). Talk about the "sociological picture" in "something like *As I Lay Dying*" amuses him, although he admits "a certain sociological importance" to a story like "Was," where he tries to show his "country as it really was in those days" (*LG* 220, *FU* 131). That background, though, is a "little warped for emphasis," and "incidental" to the writer's aim, "to talk about people in conflict" (*LG* 187). The subject of art is less than its transmutations in mind and "method."

The writer draws from an "environment which he knows," his "heredity" which includes "the language of a people" with its "poetry" and "folklore" and "important traditions" (*LG* 248, 203, 208). The language "spoken in America" is "the lustiest language of modern times," although converting it to literature is as difficult as slaying a hydra (*EPP* 95–96). But the "locale" the writer is "most familiar with" (*FU* 168) and all "materials at hand," including those from "books, plays, films, anything," are "just incidental" to "writing about truth" (*LG* 277, 202). Yet when queried about his portrait of the South, Faulkner avows that "truth" interests the storyteller less than contriving an untrue but pleasing fabrication. A "writer is congenitally incapable of telling the truth about anything. He has got to change it. He has got to lie. That's why they call it fiction, you see" (*FWP* 116). "I don't claim to be truthful," he continues. "Fiction is fiction—not truth; it's make-believe." Thus I stack and lie at times, all for the purposes of the story—to entertain." The "novelist does not want truth: he wants to create a story, with his imagination and facts helping of course" (*LG* 277–78). It is his "prerogative" to "emphasize, to underline, to *blow up facts, distort facts in order to state a truth.*" Like Dickens, he "over-emphasized, burlesqued" his characters, the Snopeses, for a "valid . . . reason," to "tell a story in an amusing, dramatic, tragic, or comical way" (*FU* 282, italics added). With variant repetition, fabulation ("stack and lie"), and sustained contraries like true/false, he sublimates the "actual into apocryphal" (*LG* 255).

Faulkner, however, may not disavow the significance of the "environment" he made famous and which has inspired studies on Southern history and culture. The works do record his "grief" for a "tragic" land that, "despite its faults" (*F:B* II, 1588), he values for the "deep indestructible bond" that "still exists between man and his environment" (*LG* 72, see also *FN* 26, 125–26). The subject the author disparages assumes a decisive place in his readers' experience—a classic discrepancy between intention and achieved form. The gap underscores Faulkner's elevation of artistic form over subject matter. "Locale," "symbolism," "message," "violence," "evil," and other elements of content are simply what the artist recasts to make them appear "as though they'd never happened before" (*FU* 239).[4]

The transmutation of fact into art begins in the mind where raw experience gained from observation evolves through remembrance and memory, reason and intellect, and the highest faculties of imagination and intuition, to something "a little different, which wasn't here yesterday" (*FU* 258). This taxonomy of mental faculties reappears in fiction as a formula for storytelling and for compressing time. It charts the development of characters like Joe Christmas (*LIA*), Bayard Sartoris (*U*), and Isaac McCaslin (*GDM*), who progress from uncomprehending experience to understanding through memory and reason, and finally to higher or spiritual cognition and moral action. In *The Unvanquished*, Bayard grows through bewildering experiences during the Civil War and, aided by reason and intuition, gains moral understanding and the courage to act on it.

Faulkner rehearses these stages of assimilation when talking about his most prolific source, the country folk: "I like these people, that is, I like to *listen* to them, the way they talk or the things they talk about. . . . I have *known* them in farming and in dealing with horses and hunting," though at the time he had "no intention to put it down, . . . just to *remember*." The Snopes story undergoes a similar evolution: "I had *thought* of it, had *remembered* it, and *planned* to write it so long before I got to it" (*FU* 233, 107, italics added). Fact thus refined is no longer "catalogued into the mind," but in the "muscles of the human spirit" (*FU* 203), Faulkner's metaphor for the creative imagination, which may supplant other faculties. "The poet is capable in his imagination alone of all grief and degradation and valor and sacrifice" (*SL* 279–280). The characters in *As I Lay Dying* "are people that I have known all my life" says Faulkner. Their "separate actions, I may have seen, remembered. It was the imagination probably that tied the whole thing together into a story" (*FWP* 96). Imagination, the faculty of magical changing, converts "fact" to art's enduring "lie."

But typically, Faulkner contravenes himself when he claims the imagination produces what is "moving and true" (*FWP* 116). The inconsistency marks a fundamental doctrine. The writer's effort to "distort facts in order to state a truth" distinguishes one kind of "truth" from the other: the fictive truth/lie which he values over "ideas and facts" (*FU* 282, *LG* 252). "Fact and truth have very little to do with each other" (*WFO* 134). "Maybe the imbecile [Benjy] should have that quality [of perception]. That's what I mean by truth. He probably hasn't, which is the fact, but maybe he should, which is the truth" (*FWP* 116). The writer aims not to reproduce reality, but to contrive a representation of "truth," what "man knows is right" (*LG* 145). With fabulation or exaggeration and repetition by difference, he obtains the end of story, to entertain. Faulkner, to whom "a balance" of opposites frames the "complete picture" (*AA* 111/88), deploys falsehood to tell a plausible tale of human beings.

Closely affiliated with the imagination, "intuition" or "instinct" drives the creative demon, intensifies the writer's "capacity for delusion or mysticism" (*FU* 160), and produces "symbols and images" that arise from "old dreams" or "blood" and "bones" (*LG* 61, 126). The language of the imagination and intuition straddles the rational and irrational, like Quentin Compson's monologue in *The Sound and the Fury*. The refining process culminates in the subconscious, where experience and ideas become "new" (*FU* 238) and enter the story "a little warped for emphasis" (*LG* 187); or, in the case of the "historically" based "locale and contents" of *A Fable,* turned "*fabulous* and *imaginary.*" The author hopes the book will "be accepted as fable, which it is to me" (*SL* 247, italics added). He confesses he reads the records of the Civil War and World War I, not "for information," but "exactly as I do fiction because it's people, man, in motion" (*FU* 251).

Events in Faulkner's own life mutate into "fiction," like the now demythicized foreign service and war wound. In story, history turns "fabulous." The dog he knew when he was young Ike McCaslin's age, a "tremendous big brute," never did anything heroic. For this "sorry, shabby world," he contrives one where Lion is a "little braver than he was," the "bear a little more of a bear than he actually was." The short story, "Death Drag," goes back to his barnstorming days after the war, but nothing in his experience "was specifically like this." For Colonel Sartoris, he "drew from family annals" a few parallel incidents, like the regiment he raised and his death (*FU* 59, 68, 254). The rest is fact blown up and distorted "in order to state a truth" (*FU* 282, see also *LG* 277–78). The "memoirs" he proposes modulate from fact to "half fiction" to "fiction": "It will be a book in the shape of a biography but actually about half fiction, chapters resembling essays about dogs and horses and family niggers and kin, chapters based on actual happening but 'improved' where fiction would help, which will probably be short stories" (*SL* 320–21). History or the "actual" converted into the "apocryphal" or "fiction" (*LG* 255) releases it from the constraints of reality to freedom from time and space of the imaginary or "make-believe."

The materials of experience, having been refined in the mind, undergo the next stage of alteration in the "form" that embodies it. Faulkner, like the earlier organicists, correlates form with substance: "The moment in the book, the story, demands its own style . . . as natural as the moment in the year produces the leaves" (*FU* 56). Intuition and intellect jointly create form. A "novel compels its own form," or "invents its own style, its own method"(*LG* 132, 204), but the story has to be done "as much as possible mentally until it begins to sound right" before the writer can "put it down" (*FU* 55). Faulkner's prescriptions for converting language to word-transcending form provide a clue to the technique, structure, and substance of his fiction.

III. FORM: TECHNIQUE AND STRUCTURE

Technique

"Contradiction" and the counterprinciples of "condensation" or epitome and "repetition" or dispersal shape Faulkner's technique. A story must be told with "mutations," but "never" tell it "the same way twice" (*FU* 132, *WFO* 26). Repetition causes discontinuity, the necessary condition for counterpoint to coalesce the "pieces." Against the drive to repeat, multiply, and fragment is the "compulsion to say everything in one sentence because you may not live long enough to have two sentences," the "desire to put all that experience into one word" (*LG* 141, *FWP* 95), to contain "truth in a chalice" or "one single urn or shape," images that in theory and fiction signify a totality (*FU* 56, 65). In unpublished segments of tapes at the University of Virginia, Faulkner reports, " 'The Bear' is probably a summation of my whole experience from the first time I was big enough to go into the woods . . . until I became a man" (UV T-144); and "Like a flash of lightning . . . I saw the whole story . . . as soon as I thought of Flem Snopes" (UV T-117). Shortly before his death Faulkner recapitulates the artist's desire to syncretize, "to take all of the experience" and "reduce that to one single color or tone or word, which is impossible . . . , but he is still going to try" (*FWP* 95). A condensation of heterogeneous elements and ideas or a distillation of the past that promises the future reproduces a series of discrete but contrapuntally integrated unfoldings. That germ-expansions design lies at the heart of Faulkner's concept of structure (see Structure).

The Charles Bon–Sutpen relationship is a "manifestation of a general racial system in the South which was *condensed* and *concentrated* as the writer has got to do with any incident or any character," that is, "*epitomize* a constant general condition in the South" (*FU* 94, italics added). Epitome turns upon metonymy and synecdoche, which subserve the end of narrative, to tell past the word a larger tale. Faulkner sets the measure of aesthetic value in the small that signifies the vast, or a part that intimates the whole. A "word or phrase or the shape of her wrist, her hand" may evoke a woman's beauty. It is "best to take the gesture, the shadow of the branch, and let the mind create the tree" (*LG* 127–28). Spellbound "under the curse of words," Faulkner explains in the preface to *Sartoris* (1929), he wants "to recreate between the covers of a book the world" he would soon "lose and regret." He fails to "capture" that world, but a "kernel" of it may signify the whole, as "the evocative skeleton of the dessicated leaf" may "indicate the lost forest."[5] Metonymic contraction, which denotes not a presence but an absence, discharges above the word a nimbus of meaning and promotes the end of Faulkner's art, to overpass the word.

Faulkner's hero, the poet, may not "say it in one word," but renders in fourteen lines the "picture of all human passion" (*FWP* 122, see also 118). The novelist, a "failed poet" (*LG* 238), strives "to reduce the sum of all experience" in "one absolute word" (*FWP* 78, UV T-145). He fails when instead of putting "all mankind's history in one sentence," he produces "long clumsy sentences and paragraphs" (*FCF* 17, *FN* 81); but "the obscurity, the involved formless 'style,' endless sentences" (*FCF* 14) embody his desire "to crowd and cram everything" into "each paragraph, to get the whole complete nuance of the moment's experience, of all the recaptured light rays" (*FN* 37). The nuance of a moment distilled or splintered light rays converged hypostatize the counterprocess forging Faulkner's art.

When the word or image renders the "whole complete nuance" of experience, time, the paramount technical element in the fiction, appears with a kind of transparency. "My ambition," Malcolm Cowley reports the author to have said, is "to put everything into one sentence—not only the present but the whole past on which it depends and which keeps overtaking the present, second by sec-

ond." The "prodigious sentences" try "to convey a sense of simultaneity, not only giving what happened in the shifting moment but
suggesting everything that went before and made the quality of that
moment" (*FCF* 112). "A character in a story at any moment of
action is not just himself as he is then, he is all that made him, and
the long sentence is an attempt to get his past and possibly his future into the instant in which he does something." "There is no
such thing really as was because the past is. It is a part of every
man, every woman, and every moment." The future as well is "inherent in that man." The novelist strives to "freeze a picture, an
image" of what the "man will be doing in 2057," and also to "capture and fix the light rays showing what he was doing in B.C. 28"
(*FU* 84, 139). Time, Faulkner concludes, is a "fluid condition
which has no existence except in the momentary avatars" (*LG* 255)
of human consciousness or willed action.

Statements like, "Time *is*, and if there's no such thing as *was*,
then there is no such thing as *will be* " (*FU* 139); or, Benjy's time
"was not a continuation, it was an instant, there was no yesterday
no tomorrow, it all is this moment, it all is [now] to him" (*FN* 106),
if taken to imply the "timeless," the usual label, seem to contradict
the earlier formulations. In the context of the whole theory, such
statements denote not an *absence* of time, but the *copresence* of
all time, that is, the "timefull." Faulkner attributes his "sense of
simultaneity" to "Bergson's theory of the fluidity of time. There is
only the present moment, in which I include both the past and the
future" (*LG* 70). Bergson, however, distinguishes simultaneity, a
combination of distinct periods, from "real duration," when temporal planes interpenetrate like "moments inside one another" (*TFW*
232; see Abbreviations for the list of Bergson's works). The labels
differ, but their ideas match. Faulkner contrives in fiction dense
compressions of "all time" (*LIA* 266) whose unfoldings interpermeate like "moments inside one another."

Synchronic time, when the past yields its secrets in the present
which is its future, counters the diachronic tendency of language
and narrative. "Simple chronicity" is "disorganized" and "empty,"
Frank Kermode claims, but the "integration" of past, present, and
future assaults "temporality in fiction" and charges it with significance. At those points, cause and effect fuse. Critics like Jean-Paul
Sartre and Jean Pouillon think Faulkner has "decapitated" time and
"taken away its future," that is, "the dimension of free choice and

act."[6] Faulkner's time, in fact, projects toward the future when the past unveils its full import, and where choice and possibility remain open. A future-oriented time embodies the metaphysical ground of Faulkner's thought and art (see IV).

Formulas like flashback and foreshadow appear in the novels, but the myriad linguistic representations of "true duration" distinguish Faulkner's work from writers like Marcel Proust, Joseph Conrad, and James Joyce, who also sought to conquer time and language. Faulkner, in addition, sets antinomies inside one another and entwines counterprocesses. He splinters so as to converge and cause resonances among unlike voices, viewpoints, styles, stages of knowing, and even resorts to deviant grammar and typography to merge temporal planes. Notable among the synchronic formations are the flashforths that bring the future to bear on the past and present, and, most powerful of all devices, the image enclosing past/present/future and multiple significations. Faulkner's revisions in several works attest to his increasing compulsion to convert the word into voice that speaks the language of "indivisible" time (Bergson's term, *CM* 149).

The "best point of view" (*SL* 350) and voice in the great works tend to be plural. Embedded in one another, distinct points of view and voices fuse time. The child narrator, a favorite device used in early sketches like "Shingles for the Lord" (*CS* 27–43) and "Two Soldiers" (*CS* 81–99), through the final work, *The Reivers* (1962), admits the interplay of variant tones and angles. The "innocence of a child that knew what he was seeing but had no particular judgment about it" induces corrective or ironic supplements. "Someone that don't know he is telling something funny" accents the humor in *The Town* (1957). The blend of voices and viewpoints turns intricate when Charles Mallison, a "mirror" of "truth" (*FU* 116, 140), recounts directly the stories he heard from his uncle Gavin Stevens and his friend Ratliff, as though their experiences were his own; or retells sources several degrees removed, as though he himself had heard them. Charles's bisected voice further complicates the splintering-stratifying process when he relates events seen through his boy's eyes, but constantly interjects into the present the maturer perceptions and tone of the youth and man. Time coalesces as the distinct styles, marking the stages of his development, interpermeate. The same kind of layering converges time in *The Unvanquished* (see chapter 6); and in the story "Barn Burning" two distinct voices intertwine, one recounting the ten-year-old Sarty Snopes's present life, and the other, his perspective on past events from a distant future. The fusion delineates the boy's moral dilemma, to remain loyal to his erring father or to assert his growing sense of right and wrong. Multiple voices and angles, converging like splintered light rays in works like *Absalom, Absalom!, As I Lay Dying*, and *The Unvanquished*, uncover depths of inner being and shift the focus from an event to its ongoing reverberations through past and future in "avatars" of human consciousness.

Stratified voices and angles embody the author's view that no one comprehends truth "intact." Someone sees "one phase of it," another, a "slightly awry phase of it. But taken all together, the truth is in what they saw." "Quentin's father saw what he believed was truth, that was all he saw." "A little too big" for most people "to see all at once" (*FU* 273–74), Sutpen requires variant angles, each one a necessary component of the "complete picture" (*AA* lll/88). If the self-obsessed Quentin alone told the Sutpen story in *Absalom, Absalom!* "it would have become completely unreal . . . , vanished into smoke and fury." Appending an objective commentator like Shreve "held the thing to something of reality . . . believable, creditable" (*FU* 75). In *The Town*, Charles's innocence juxtaposed with the people's knowing, or the reader's knowledge of Rider's inner life set against the town's ignorance in "Pantaloon in Black" (*GDM*), or Christmas's subjective life contrasted with the people's false conjectures (*LIA*), discharges an "implied story" that modifies and completes the literal one (UV 8969 Ober-Faulkner 1942– 1943). Interpermeating distinct viewpoints sound a voiceless, ironic dialogue.

More potent than layered voices and mental stages, the "mediating *image*" that encompasses "matter" and "mind," as Bergson puts it, distills cause and act and consequence in "a single identical time" (*CM* 118, 150). Fusing a "thousand sensations, feelings or ideas," "comparisons and metaphors . . . suggest what cannot be expressed," Bergson claims (*TFW* 18, *CM* 42). For the writer who, Faulkner says, is driven to "epitomize," the concentric "gesture," "picture," or "symbol" encloses potentialities that unfold in diverse but affiliated expansions. Wishing to reduce "all the passion and the beauty of being alive . . . into something concrete" (*FWP* 78), the "failed poet" renders Christmas's being in the angle of his cap and his moral history in the circle he runs, which, at the end, he bisects with a straight line to his death. Then the multivalent "image produced by words occurs in silence."

Faulkner recognizes his "method" overturns conventions of verisimilitude, yet he insists on the "truth" of fiction. The writer wants to hold to a "concept of what is true," to tell about "authentic, credible, . . . flesh-and-blood, living, suffering, anguishing human beings" in "credible moving situations in the most moving way" (*FU* 120, 47, *LG* 248). But he often locates them in incredible "situations." A mute idiot sets the touchstone of veracity in *The Sound and the Fury*, and in "Barn Burning," the ten-year-old narrator's experience blends with the grown man's interpretation of it. Darl in *As I Lay Dying* speaks his country dialect, but reflects in ornate rhetoric and relates events he cannot see. Faulkner uses the generic term, "novel," but he tends to identify his fiction with the nonrealistic modes of "allegory" and "fable," or even "fantasy." Allegory after all equivocates, fable stratifies narrative, and disjunctive form obscures sense. Works like *The Sound and the Fury* and *Absalom, Absalom!* explore the dilemma of fiction that defies the rules of plausibility yet seeks to gain credibility.

The young Faulkner's review of an Erich Maria Remarque novel defends what will become the mature writer's practice: "It is a writer's privilege to put into the mouths of his characters better speech than they would have been capable of, but only for the purpose of permitting and helping the character to justify himself or what he believes himself to be" (*ESPL* 186). Years before he fashions his unorthodox form, the budding novelist locates verisimilitude within the operation of the dissembling word. A character who describes the unseen or tells the unheard conforms to no measure of external reality, but only to the word's contrived deception. The same unreliable word with which Addie decries language renders as well the essence of her life and of the whole work. As "fluid" time precipitates in human consciousness, the ten-year-old Sarty Snopes may comprehend the future. To skeptics who say a child "couldn't express this idea this way," Faulkner defends the writer's privilege to "distort" fact "to get a story told in a moving, dramatic way" (UV T-144). Truth thus transformed turns into what Miss Rosa calls a *"might-have-been which is more true than truth"* (*AA* 143/115), and gains belief. Benjy may be an idiot in fact, but in "truth" could be perceptive. Even typographic conventions give way when a printed dialogue depicts an unspoken exchange; but the abrogation of typographic, syntactic, and other rules in an incredible narrative attains the writer's purpose, to manifest the inner being and "truth" concealed behind the deceitful word.

In 1931 Faulkner is reported to have declared, "the novel form as we know it" will "break down completely." "Straight exposition" will give way to "objective presentation, by means of soliloquies or speeches of the characters." Something like the "play technique" will "eliminate much of the author from the story" (*LG* 17–18). Faulkner describes his own practice in works written by 1931, including *The Sound and the Fury* and *As I Lay Dying*, and in later works, most obviously *Requiem for a Nun* (1951). Eliminating the author and the mediating viewpoint or narrator, the dramatic mode lays the burden of revelation on the characters and erodes the operation of sequence or logic in narrative form. Faulkner prefigures in theory and practice the turn in America from the traditional narrative to "new" fiction that subverts established canons of language and form.

Although in interviews that provoke his flippant tone, Faulkner disavows any interest in "form" or "style," his extended discourses on the "way" to write a story that "compels its own form" or "invents its own style, its own method" attest to his preoccupation with fictive technique and structure. Even after the major works, he confesses, "I'm still having trouble reconciling method and material," and doubts he would ever find a "happy balance" between the two. He blames the problem partly on his "refusal to accept formal schooling (I am an old 8th grade man)," but mostly "on the heat" in which he writes. "I have written too fast, too much," driven by the notion that "something worth saying" is "better said poorly" than not at all. "And besides," he adds, reaffirming his faith in iteration, "there would always be a next time" (*SL* 142–43). The achievement proves those doubts unwarranted.

Structure

Faulkner acknowledges the fragmenting effect of his antithetic technique: "Unless a book follows a simple direct line such as a story of adventure, it becomes a series of pieces." To counter the disjunction, he organizes the "different pieces" (*FU* 45) around a "source" or a "center." "With me, a story usually begins with a single idea or memory or mental picture," and writing it "is simply a matter of working up to that moment, to explain why it happened or what it caused to follow" (*LG* 248). Three months before his death, he recapitulates a lifetime practice of setting discrete pieces about a nucleus: "The stories with me begin with an anecdote or a sentence or an expression, and I'll start from there and sometimes I write the thing backwards" (*FWP* 80–81). That compression-expansion design, regulated by counterpoint, underlies Faulkner's concept of structure. The "germ" or "moment," a point of temporal convergence, is that "speck of fire, that coal, from which a book or picture should burst almost of its own accord" (*SL* 187). In fiction the "germ" usually denotes an initial "seed" that embeds the past in the present and reproduces in the future distinct but correlated mutations. The "moment," a condensation of time and meaning later in the work, conjoins events leading to and from it. When asked how he shapes his novels, Faulkner describes precisely that counterspiraling process: "There's always a moment in experience—a thought—an incident—that's there. Then all I do is work up to that moment. I figure what must have happened before to lead people to that particular moment, and I work away from it, finding out how people act after that moment. That's how all my books and stories come" (*LG* 220).

Saxe Commins, who helped Faulkner revise *A Fable,* describes his structural method: "Bill wraps a scene around him and lets it unravel. . . . He allows it to rise out of the unconscious and get itself written down, without censorship, but with a general plan improved upon as the details are improvised."[7] Commins's "general plan" appears to be the "source" or "moment" that unravels in a network of "improvised" parts. The two terms become synonymous when a dense "moment" displaces the initial "germ" as the work's source or axis and reinforces the concentering-uncoiling process that coheres the "pieces."

Faulkner apparently took pleasure in identifying the "center" or "seed" of his works, inviting a comparison of conception with achieved form in the fiction. The "germ" of a story may be an image, or an idea of man "acting in that gallant way in spite of his fragility," or "a character who has in himself the seed of tragedy" (UV T-145). "Was" goes back to "one of the three oldest ideas that man can write about, which is love, sex," but converted to a comedy of accidental engagement (*FU* 131). If, however, the "source" encases and generates a significant portion of the work, then the true germ of *Go Down, Moses* lies encoded in an abstract of Isaac McCaslin's life that Faulkner composed for the novel and set at the head of the first story, "Was" (see chapter 7). *The Sound and the Fury*, his "most gallant failure" (*LG* 180), centers on the "symbolical" "picture" of the "muddy seat" of a "doomed little girl" whose bravery none of her brothers could match, and the children's "innocence" about death (*LG* 245, 146; *FWP* 111). In the novel, those images and actions simply merge with others denoting loss of innocence and decay. What infuses the segmented work is not the symbolic stained backside, but Caddy's singular tone of voice that offsets the many voices of indifference or cruelty or lovelessness. That initial germ and other germs of character and action expanded through the work confirms the author's assertion, "The story, the book is all there in that first section" (UV TS of "Introduction to *The Sound and the Fury*," p. 5). Whether a synopsis of theme in *The Wild Palms*, or the portrait of a black man accused of murder, who has "to be his own detective" in *Intruder in the Dust* (*FU* 142), each "seed" holds a "moment of time" when "the direction of things is about to change."[8] Such a synoptic/prophetic node, like the section in *A Fable* that encapsulates "what caused a man to do" a "single act which carries on the story" (*SL* 254), conjoins discrete parts leading to and issuing from it.

Faulkner declares at times, "I have no order" (*FWP* 80, see also UV T-117), but contradicts himself when he repeatedly insists art requires "an integrated form," or "some order, some unity," or "some shape" or "pattern" (*SL* 273, *FWP* 99, *FU* 52). "Even to a collection of short stories, *form, integration*, is as important as to a novel—an entity of its own, single, set for one pitch, *contrapuntal in integratio*n, toward one end" (*SL* 278, italics added). "Played . . . against each other . . . contrapuntally," the "inchoate fragments" may "coalesce" (*LG* 36, *FU* 76). Counterpoint, which for Faulkner always involves the "nonoppositional play of opposites" (Ralph Flores's term),[9] operates even in the most severely fractured narrative. For *The Wild Palms* (1939), he composes a "complete antithesis" to "counterpoint, to sharpen" the river story, that in turn, would "lift" the love story "like counterpoint in music" (*LG* 132, *SL* 106, *LG* 247; see also *FU* 171, 176, 178). He needs "the counterpoint, a fugue . . . to *underline* the other story," he maintains in an unpublished segment of tapes at the University of Virginia (T-144, italics added). He balances the "tragic view of life" of Christmas, who "didn't know what he was and so he deliberately repudiated man," with Byron Bunch and Lena Grove who "had a very fine belief in life, in the basic possibility for happiness and goodness" (*FU* 97). The "truly innocent" idiot in *The Sound and the Fury* offsets the "vicious" Jason, who also provides a "counterpoint" to the "protagonist," Quentin (*FN* 103–4). The "contrapuntal effect which comes in orchestration" of the dialogues against the "mystical" interludes in *Requiem for a Nun* creates a "sharper, more effective" story (*FU* 122). In *Go Down, Moses,* he finds it "necessary to break the story of the bear at one point and put something else in," as a musician might say, "Now at this point I will need counterpoint. I will need discord. Or I will suspend this theme for another." Part 4 of "The Bear" is therefore a "necessary portion" of what "was not a collection of short stories, but a novel" (*FWP* 102). The "petty comedy" of Boon at the conclusion of "The Bear" makes "the heroic tragedy of the bear and the dog" a "little more poignant" (*FU* 60). Faulkner conceives of design less in patterns of action or theme often traced in a composite like *Go Down, Moses,* but more in terms of the "reciprocal friction" (Bergson's term, *INP* 102) of heterogeneous elements of form; in other words, a *formal* organization. "Music would express better and simpler, but I prefer to use words," he declares (*LG* 248). Like a musician, however, the writer needs "counterpoint" or "fugue" or "discord" to "balance" or "underline" discrete parts and make them cohere not by the "simple direct line" of logic or causality, but the echoic entwining of unlike parts. A "new pattern" (*FU* 52) of fragments embedded in one another organizes the works with indeterminate structural form.

Faulkner's design for disconnected narrative matches the contrapuntal technique and fugal structure in classical music. Counterpoint sounds simultaneously two or more parts or voices, each of which retains its individual character while it weaves with the others a "coherent texture," according to *The Concise Oxford Dictionary of Music.* The "essence" of fugue is the "interweaving of melodic strands," with each "episodic material . . . brought into an opposing or contrasting context," *The New Harvard Dictionary of Music* adds. The fugal structure entails the "continuous expansion" of a given theme or motif from which "all subsequent materials derive organically." In fiction, the variant but entwined strands issuing from the "continuous expansion" of a germ or moment and the interweaving of distinct voices match the developments in contrapuntal music. "Language is my music,"[10] the author declares, and the contrapuntal design of language rather than pitched tones in his work sets resonances beyond the word in silence.

Faulkner outlines in theory the simple uncoiling of a germinal nucleus with counterpoint to "coalesce" the "series of pieces." In practice, the structural pattern becomes involute when temporal condensations displace the germ as "source" and restart at various points the countermovements of expansion and fusion. A fluctuating "source" deconstructs the concept of a "center." The germs of character of the brothers, Darl and Jewel, initiate conflict and action, but the more potent Addie "moment" in the second half of *As I Lay Dying* supplants them as the work's axis. Her belief in the power of the duplicitous word to damage people and their relationships sets the ground of Bundren life and generates their story backward and forward. The Darl sections, which probe into the motivations of the family, realign the segments in yet another pattern. *As I Lay Dying*, the author maintains, is about people subjected to "simple universal natural catastrophes" while pursuing their "simple natural motive" (*LG* 244); and some readers, anxious to establish "order" or sequence in a journey tale, extrapolate a chronology of events *outside* that fictive world. *Inside* the novel, however, time converged in layered viewpoints and voices and compressed images splinters the narrative and frustrates expectations of sequential or logical order.

A capsule of old Uncle Ike's life that Faulkner composed to open the novel permeates all of *Go Down, Moses*. A later "moment," such as young Ike's blood baptism or its recurrence, shifts the work's center of gravity and rearranges the parts in another intermodulant design. The destabilized work becomes aggressively metonymic, recapitulating itself in multiple reversals and transformations and bypassing a simple resolution for suspended polarities. As time/sense compressions and their mutations intertwine and resonate in one another, the narrative constantly inflects itself. Faulkner advises the reader of his centered/decentered narratives to apprehend simultaneously "thirteen different ways of looking at the blackbird" so as to obtain "his own fourteenth image of that blackbird," which is "the truth" (*FU* 274). Evoked by antithetic strategies of fragmentation and integration, of centering and divergence, the fourteenth "image produced by words occurs in silence" (*LG* 248).

The same germ-unfoldings "design" imprints the "sum" of Faulkner's lifework. The "little postage stamp of native soil" (*LG* 255), a "cosmos in miniature" like that of Balzac and Dickens (*FU* 232), reproduces a number of works. "One country" and its fictive people engender "a great deal of writing" (*LG* 133). *Sartoris* (1929), the first published Yoknapatawpha novel, contains the "germ of my apocrypha in it," and a "lot of the characters are postulated in that book," Faulkner states (*FU* 285). But the true matrix of the canon lies in the original novel, *Flags in the Dust* written in 1927 (1974), where "the shady visions of the host . . . stretched half-formed," with "that verisimilitude which is to bind into a whole" his "teeming world." Such an inexhaustible source reproduces "infinite mutations of man's capacity" for good or ill (*UV* T-145). An abstract of Flem Snopes's life in *Flags in the Dust* (181) generates diverse but affiliated configurations through three decades. Martin Kreiswirth traces through subsequent works the development of seeds of character and motifs of heredity, lovelessness, and self-destruction embedded in *Flags in the Dust*.[11] Faulkner charts the same capsulizing-generating pattern when he talks about *A Fable*, "perhaps the last book I'll write and I am putting all the rest of it into it"; but, as usual he predicates, "it may contain the germs of several more books" (*SL* 254–55). A fractal design of source and mutations that contain and are contained in one another imprints the canon and its components.

Art transforms fact to a fabulous "lie," but the substance and theme of fiction reflect the author's concept of a polar world and of human beings who are responsible for making choices and for the consequences of their deeds. An overview of Faulkner's poetics and metaphysics in the context of the critical tradition may further clarify his place in the history of the theory of language and of narrative.

IV. METAPHYSICS AND POETICS

Faulkner's paradoxical poetics and art lies grounded in his view of an antipodal universe, and his faith in bisected man who is "capable of almost anything," "folly and savagery and inhumanity," but also "courage, honor, pride, compassion, pity," and above all, of improving the human condition "by his own efforts" (*LG* 32, *SL* 382, *FU* 133, *FN* 157–59). The "free will to choose" and "the courage, the fortitude to die for his choice" distinguish the "free" but "responsible, terribly responsible" (*LG* 70) human being. In Faulkner's cosmos, volition "functions against a Greek background of fate" (*FU* 38); neither exists without the other. Some characters simply submit to fate, but others cope as best they can, like Lena in *Light in August,* who becomes the "captain of her soul" (*LG* 253). An amalgam of free will and determinism, deed and responsibility throws light on the metaphysical status of characters like Joe Christmas, Ike McCaslin, and young Bayard Sartoris.

Though striving to do right, the human being is "not just subject to failure but doomed to it" (*ESPL* 214). Failure, intrinsic to all endeavor, regulates Faulkner's philosophy. But no inadequacy may deflect human efforts to communicate with the treacherous word, to achieve a great dream, or to act on the "moral sense" (*LG* 71). The "impossibility" or "tremendous difficulty" of "communication" is a "tragedy," but man, though he lives in "isolation, aloneness" (*LG* 70, *SL* 297), tries "endlessly to express himself and to make contact with other human beings." Two years after receiving the Nobel Prize, Faulkner confesses he finds it "impossible to communicate with the outside world," and fears he "will end up in some kind of self-communion—a silence—faced with the certainty that I can no longer be understood." Driven to "create his own language," he risks becoming unreadable, but he is resigned to his insatiable "demon": "I will certainly keep on writing as long as I live" (*FU* 160, *LG* 70–71).

Like other human beings, artists are also "doomed to fail," for what they create never quite matches "the dream of perfection." But a dream "splendid" and "valuable enough" measures the quality of writing and other undertakings (*ESPL* 143, 145). Thomas Wolfe is the "most glorious failure" for trying "to do the greatest of the impossible," to "reduce all human experience to literature" (*LG* 225, 81). *Moby Dick* is an "attempt that didn't quite come off, . . . bigger than one human being can do" (*FU* 15). Sutpen's "design" miscarries on faulty vision and means, but the "gallantry" of the "effort" registers his courage and endurance. Sutpen, like John Sartoris and other flawed dreamers, "had the force and strength to have failed so grandly" (*FCF* 15).

Though prone to wrongdoing and failure, human beings possess an innate capacity for good: "Man comes from God," and has a "soul in conflict with his evil nature or his environment" (*LG* 71). Proofs of his "immortality" lie in his conception of God, his creativity, his "will to freedom," his desire to combat "terror" and "injustice," and to aspire "toward a better human condition" (*LG* 103, 241, 124; *FN* 157–59). His "moral conscience," a "curse" he accepts from the gods for the "right to dream," impels him to choose between good and evil and to do what he knows is right so he could "live with himself" (*LG* 253). There is a "quality in man that prevails," that "will never stop trying to cope with Snopes," a force eroding the foundations of human comity. "It doesn't mean that they will get rid of Snopes or the impulse which produces Snopes, but always there's something in man that don't like Snopes and objects to Snopes and if necessary will step in to keep Snopes from doing irreparable harm" (*FU* 34). Ratliff and Stevens fail to circumvent Flem's machinations or to save Eula, but they persist in their campaign against Snopesism. Proprietorship will remain, but Isaac McCaslin acts to meliorate inherited "wrong and shame." Other people like Bayard Sartoris, Dilsey, Colonel Sartoris Snopes, WallStreet Panic Snopes and his wife withstand invincible forces. "That they go down doesn't matter. It's *how* they go under," trying "to defy defeat even if it's inevitable." These deficient strugglers, like the great writers, celebrate the human "ability to always prevail and endure over circumstances and over [their] own destiny." The heroic are those who make a stand, not while sure of success, but though certain of defeat: "To fail is better. To try to do more than you can do." "To try it and fail, then try it again" is the measure of "success" (*LG* 221, 88–89). The doctrine of repeated trials materializes in the reiterative form of fiction, as in *The Sound and the Fury*, and in the enduring struggle to do right, as in *Go Down, Moses* or the Snopes trilogy. Literary creativity and moral endeavor are for Faulkner parables of the eternal play of attempt-failure-possibility.

Faulkner's poetics, founded on the duality of human beings and of language, combines tenets from classical and modern theories of art as imitation, illumination, expression, and invention. The theory excludes Plato's reduction of art to a copy of the shadow of the Idea, or the postclassical view of art as a mirror of reality. It transcribes instead the Aristotelian doctrine of imitation, not of a completed product, but of the process of becoming, an uncoiling from "germ" or "seed" to its diverse but analogous mutations in achieved form. The writer's verbal "means" (Aristotle's term) may not appropriate its object, hence reality lies outside the scope of fiction; but the simulation of organic evolution in art form embodies "truth" in "make-believe." Faulkner echoes Aristotle's organicism when he affiliates substance with form, although he consistently valorizes form over substance.

Like Aristotle and his Renaissance disciples, Faulkner locates the realm of poesy not in what is, but what could or should be. For Faulkner, however, the could or should assumes the form of a language construct recasting reality to fable, and conversely, the unreal to a truth/lie. "You make Lion a little braver than he was, and you make the bear a little more of a bear than he actually was. I am sure that Lion could have done that and would have done it, and it may be at times when I wasn't there to record the action, he did do things like that" (*FU* 59–60). Advancing only what conforms to the probable could or inevitable should, Faulkner's storylines tend to be stark. A whole novel's action may be rendered in brief. What gives the fiction its non-Greek quality are the echoic recurrences, the intermeshed contradictions, and the countermotions from compression to dispersal and back that, unlike Aristotle's standard of the single plot with a single outcome, discloses "thirteen different ways of looking at the blackbird," and intimates in silence the reader's fourteenth way.

Faulkner's idea of structure digresses from the supreme Aristotelean doctrine of the "structural union" of beginning, middle, and end according to the "law of probability and necessity" (*The Poetics [P]*, chapters 7–10).[12] For Aristotle, the "necessary or probable result of the preceding action" frames the "internal structure of plot" (*P* chapter 10). Faulkner, who claims he observes neither "order" nor "plot," instead disperses beginnings and middles and ends, then entwines them "contrapuntally" backward and forward. But he also heeds Quentin Compson's notion that story should hold "some regard for cause and effect even if none for logical sequence and continuity" (*AA* 247/199). Whether causality differs from "logical sequence and continuity" may be argued; but in a narrative like *Absalom, Absalom!* fragmentation and discontinuity supplant Aristotle's prescribed "orderly arrangement of parts" conforming to the "rule of probability and necessity" (*P* chapters 7, 11, 15, 18,

25). At the same time, segments of the line tracing Sutpen's progress from deed to consequence surface intermittently through the
splintered narrative.[13] An intermodulant design among discrete
parts replaces the classical concept of a "proper structure" matching the organic or logical unity of a "living organism" (*P* chapter
6–7, see also chapter 23).

Faulkner deviates from Aristotle's concept of form, but he adheres to the Greek view that the ground of happiness or misery lies
in freedom of choice and action. The Aristotelean principle of
moral responsibility operates in his world, even for characters often
regarded as "determined." Faulkner holds people responsible "to
make choices between good and evil" and for their consequences
(*LG* 253). Joe Christmas's conception, birth, and childhood confine
him within a circular street that runs over thirty years. Hightower,
unable to escape his grandfather's past, betrays marriage and calling. Joanna Burden's grandfather sets her on a path that ends with
her head twisted backward. Some choices are narrow, others open
to alternatives. Joanna's choice is limited to free or kill Joe. But the
reticent Byron finds with love the courage to defy society and become Lena's protector. Hightower, a reluctant midwife, rejoins the
human community, damaged but regenerated. Joe Christmas escapes the circle when he chooses to walk the straight line to his
elected end.

Like Aristotle, Faulkner admits the mutual operation of determinism and contingency in nature's organic unfolding and in human
life and art. Dawson Fairchild doubly analogizes the idea in *Mosquitoes* when he says an acorn yields only an oak, but the "happy
conjunction" of seed and elements creates a unique tree, just as the
"proper conjunction" of words produces a unique tale (*M* 210). The
interplay of fate and free will in human life is reified in the structural pattern of a "germ" that contains, and thus predetermines, the
direction of story, but its variant unfoldings open the narrative to
diverse possibilities.

Faulkner's theory owes in part to the classical tradition, but his
views on the subversive nature of language and literature may have
been influenced by early modern thinkers like Henri Bergson, and
classic British, American, French and other European writers.[14] His
practice exemplifies an antithetic form that, shot through with
ironic countertones, intimates sense beyond the intractable word
and thus transcends its medium.

Assembled here for the first time, a coherent poetics whose main articles address the problem of subduing the killer word should open a fresh approach to language and form in Faulkner's fiction. Shifting the focus from patterns of action or theme in most studies on structure, this study examines the way the writer contrives variant simulations of synchronic time and a contrapuntal design of intermodifying segments that tell in silence beyond the word.

The parallel theories of Bergson and Faulkner should clarify the scope and significance of the language of "true duration" and its formative effects on the form and theme of the fiction. Each of the six novels applies various theoretical tenets, but all exemplify Faulkner's concept of the language of synchronic time and a modulant structure for disjunct narratives. *Light in August* (1932, chapter 2) deploys the Bergsonian "indivisible" duration against successive time, but threads through the segmented form the motival line of causation, a combination that sheds light on the meaning of Joe Christmas's life and on the themes of other works. In *Absalom, Absalom!* (1936, chapter 3), "elapsed and yet-elapsing time" that Quentin Compson prescribes for narrative stratifies voices and intimates an unworded tale that obtains some plausibility for the improbable, worded story. The four composite novels that follow exemplify Faulkner's dual solution for discontinuity, a "germ" or "source" generating variant but correlated unfoldings, and a vortex-like "moment" that coalesces the fragments around it. *The Sound and the Fury* (1929, chapter 4) entwines two complementary sources whose modulations reinforce one another. The Benjy section encodes germs of character and action developed throughout, but it is Caddy's inflections that highlight by contrast and interweave the other voices. *The Sound and the Fury* exemplifies the doctrine that the word turned to voice, or in particular for this work, to *tone* of voice, discloses the hidden being. In *As I Lay Dying* (1930, chapter 5), the splintered-conjoined components of form empower the word to signify more than it designates. Addie Bundren's censure of language and solution, a concentric "moment" later in the work, sets the segments leading "up to" and "away from it" modulating inside one another. Rival moments, like the Darl sections, realign the parts in another pattern of congruence, and thus decenter the narrative.

Faulkner's changes in the printed stories he gathered for *The Unvanquished* (1938, chapter 6) and *Go Down, Moses* (1942, chapter

7) alter markedly each novel's structure and sense. In the first work, the juvenile style converted into the language of synchronic time and the single voice to a bitonal voice and point of view fashion a polyphonic narrative that turns the maligned romantic nostalgia for a lost age to a hard appraisal of moribund values. The expanded opening scene encodes germs unfolded through the six stories and brought to a climax in the last story the writer composed for the novel. At the head of the seven stories gathered for *Go Down, Moses,* Faulkner implants a germ of character and action from which the stories unfold and to which they return. A powerful "moment," like Ike's blood baptism or its repeat, rivals the initial source but, at the same time, reinforces the entwining segments.

The conclusion records an encounter with William Faulkner that prompted this study.

2

Light in August: Bergson and Faulkner on the Language of Time and Narrative Form

> *Real duration* is what we have always called *time,* but time per-
> ceived as indivisible. . . . [It] would thus include in an undivided
> present the entire past history of the conscious person—not as
> an instantaneity, not like a cluster of simultaneous parts, but as
> something continually present which would also be something
> continually moving . . . in the direction of the future. Real dura-
> tion is made up of moments inside one another.
>
> —Henri Bergson, *An Introduction to Metaphysics:*
> *The Creative Mind; Time and Free Will*

> There isn't any time. . . . In fact I agree pretty much with Berg-
> son's theory of the fluidity of time. There is only the present
> moment, in which I include both the past and the future, and that
> is eternity.

> The aim of every artist is to arrest motion, which is life, by arti-
> ficial means and hold it fixed so that 100 years later when a
> stranger looks at it, it moves again since it is life . . . , immortal
> since it will always move.
>
> —Faulkner, *Lion in the Garden*

FAULKNER IDENTIFIES HENRI BERGSON AMONG HIS PRECEPTORS:
"I was influenced by Flaubert and by Balzac, whose way of writing
everything bluntly with the stub of his pen I admire very much. And
by Bergson, obviously. And I feel very close to Proust. After I had
read *A la Recherche du Temps Perdu* I said, 'This is it!'—and I
wished I had written it myself" (*LG* 72). Formulas like foreshadow,
montage, and flashback in the fiction are generally attributed to the
French philosopher.[1] Those devices, in fact, abound in the works of
writers noted above, and others Faulkner knew, including Herman
Melville, Joseph Conrad, James Joyce, T. S. Eliot, and Henry
James, whom he dismisses as a "prig" (*FU* 16), but whose explora-

52

tion of time in human consciousness prefigures his concept of narrative time. These sources have received less credit than Bergson.[2]

The credit to Bergson, nonetheless, seldom goes beyond his distinction between apparent and real duration at the superficial and
deeper levels of consciousness.[3] Overlooked are his extensive speculations on mind and time, and on language and literature, punctu-
ated with analogues from the creative process and art (see I). The
philosopher's primary doctrines of mind, time, and language reecho
in the novelist's theory of fictive language, form, and structure, and
the underlying psychology of art and metaphysics. Both men decry
their treacherous medium, but Bergson relies on the novelist's
tropes and images to render a "shadow" of the inner mind, while
Faulkner contrives a language of "true duration" that assaults temporality in *Light in August* (1932) and other works. Their combined
precepts illuminate the technique of converged time whose unfoldings resonate inside one another. Faulkner's revisions, most significantly on Joe Christmas, signal the writer's increasing
compulsion to condense time and meaning. A capsule encasing the
man's history and character early in the work uncoils backward and
forward, tracing the roots of Christmas's being in childhood and
prefiguring his actions to the end of his life (see II). Matching Quentin
Compson's idea of narrative that foregoes "logical sequence and
continuity" but observes "cause and effect," Christmas lives in the
fragmented interplay of diachrony and synchrony, but simultaneously pursues the undeviating line of responsibility for action—
counterpatterns of form and sense that clarify his metaphysical
status. This thematic line of causation, like an intermittent undertone beneath the broken surfaces of alternating-converging temporal patterns in narrative, secures deed to consequence (see III).

I

Bergson associates the two primary components of the human
psyche with two distinct beings, each with its own mode of time
and language. The intellect governs the "practical life" of the
"phantom self," while the "living self" lies rooted in the intuition
and imagination. The "ego" with its "superficial psychic life" apprehends time "spatialized" in disjunct "befores" and "afters"
(*INP* 79, *TFW* 165, 236, 125; *CM* 149). The functions of the intel-

lect "are separated from one another and easily expressed in words," and thus meet "the requirements of social life." "Refracted, and thereby broken to pieces," the external self "gradually loses sight of the fundamental self," whose states "permeate one another" and whose time of "true duration" is made up of "moments inside one another" (*TFW* 138–39, 128, 232; *CM* 149).

"That time implies succession I do not deny," says Bergson; but in deeper states of mind "*succeeding each other* means *melting into one another* and forming an organic whole" (*CM* 149, *TFW* 128). Intuition perceives time as "the uninterrupted prolongation of the past into a present which is already blending into the future." "Anterior perceptions . . . remain bound up with present perceptions, and the immediate future itself" becomes "partly outlined in the present" (*CM* 32, 157). Time and being are homologous functions of consciousness, and mental and temporal states are synonymous in Bergson's lexicon.

Unlike the "shadow of the self," whose disjoined "lifeless states" may "be translated into words" (*TFW* 128, 133), the deeper self's interpermeant states, "each of which points to what follows and contains what preceded" (*INP* 14–15), "cannot be expressed in the fixed terms of language" without "arresting" their "mobility" (*TFW* 237, 129). The "utilitarian" language of the intellect with its "sharply defined words" may not represent the "indivisible" flow of time in the imagination or intuition (*CM* 80, 32; *TFW* 171), where mental states, without "a beginning or an end . . . , all prolong themselves into each other" (*INP* 15). There is "no common measure between mind and language," which is "not meant to convey all the delicate shades of inner states" (*TFW* 164–65, 160). In less philosophical terms, Faulkner considers the killer word the enemy he must defeat.

But "whether it be intellection or intuition, thought . . . always utilizes language" (*CM* 35). The intuition, however, eludes the taxonomic language of the intellect, and "must find a method of expression" for the "indivisible" inner mind *(INP* 85), the source of "the radically new and absolutely simple idea, which catches as it were an intuition" (*CM* 35). Bergson finds the answer in the dual nature of language, "an external thing" that is also "an immaterial thing" with the "mobility" to "be extended from things to ideas." "By nature transferable and free," language can "be extended, not only from one perceived thing to another, but even from a perceived thing to a recollection of that thing, from the precise recollection to a more fleeting image, and finally from an image fleeting, though still pictured, to the picturing of the act by which the image is pictured, that is to say, to the idea. Thus is revealed to the intelligence, hitherto always turned outwards, a whole internal world—the spectacle of its own workings" *(CE* 174–75). The capacity of language to render at once outer and inner worlds offers the writer the means to transcend it. In Bergson's system, two distinct modalities of language match the two kinds of self, the "deep-seated" being and the "superficial ego," the "two aspects of conscious life," and the "two very different ways of regarding duration"*(TFW* 125, 128).

Bergson finds paradigms of "immaterial" language in the work of the "bold novelist," whose tropes and images, "extraordinary and illogical" like the imagination, cast "an enormous mass" in a "fusion" and "suggest what cannot be expressed" *(TFW* 133–34; *INP* 106, *CM* 42). Tropes function like "dreams, in which two images overlie one another" and two different persons "make only one" *(TFW* 136). Encompassing matter and mind, the "mediating *image*" embodies the "original complexity" of a "thousand sensations, feelings or ideas" *(TFW* 18, *CM* 118) and, like "the primordial function of consciousness," comprehends "lengthy changes we witness within us and in the external world" in "a single identical time" *(CM* 89, 150). The artist "imitates with mere images" the "tension, concentration" in the deeper mind where past and future converge in "a present which endures" *(TFW* 136–37; *CM* 89, 152). Bergson's "undivided present" *(CM* 152) encasing past and future and Faulkner's "moment" comprising "the sum" of a person's past and future too *(FU* 84) alter the accepted notion of Benjy Compson's time, an "is" generally equated with the absence of time. For both Bergson and Faulkner, "is" denotes a confluence of "all time."

Anticipating the "objective correlative" of T. S. Eliot, the "image" of Ezra Pound, and the imagism of James Joyce and Faulkner, and of contemporary novelists like Gabriel García Márquez and Toni Morrison, Bergson says the writer chooses "among the outward signs of his emotions" that which can "transport us all at once into the indefinable psychological state which called them forth." "Feelings develop into images," and images "into words." "Seeing these images pass before our eyes we in our turn experience the feeling," which is "their emotional equivalent" *(TFW* 18,

15). Imagistic correlatives of the interpermeant mind are metonymic, "in the simplest of them the whole soul can be reflected"
(*TFW* 98). The metonymic image, like the "skeleton of a dessicated
leaf" which, Faulkner says, may evoke the "lost forest,"[4] "dis-
penses with the imitation of nature" for the "more efficacious
means" of intimation: "The faint suggestion of an idea will then be
enough to make the idea fill the whole of our mind." The novelist,
Bergson goes on, could "sum up a more or less considerable part"
of a person's history in a single object or represent his "whole personality" with a single mental state or a "free act" (*TFW* 16–17,
165). "Condensation" or "epitome," which for Faulkner always
entails suspended contraries, discloses past the word the inner
world of a Benjy or a Joe Christmas or the import of a gesture
evolving through time.

"Inner experience" will "nowhere find a strictly appropriate language," Bergson admits, but the synchronic image and Faulkner's
other devices, like the stratified voices, viewpoints, and styles, embody "that contradiction, that interpenetration which is the very essence" of deeper mind (*CM* 45, *TFW* 134). At the bottom of
consciousness, "the thesis and antithesis of the antinomies" operate
"synchronously" (*INP* 102). "Opposite feelings" or contrary ideas
"once dissociated, seem to exclude one another as logically contradictory terms" (*TFW* 136). There is, however, "scarcely one concrete reality about which one could not assume two contrary points
of view at the same time" that are irreducible to "two antagonistic
concepts" (*INP* 47). Interpenetrating contrary elements function
congruently.

Paradox governs both writers' thought. "Antithesis" and "counterpoint" convey the "fundamental absurdity" and "illogical nature" of the imagination and of language itself. Empowered by
form beyond its literal sense, the totality-enclosing word may embody its referent, as Hightower's "mute chair" becomes "somehow
the *symbol* and the *being* too of the man himself" (*LIA* 342/362,
italics added). When "symbol" equates "being," language evolves
beyond representation to incarnation. The word then signifies a gesture of life, an "avatar" of its meaning.

Both writers recognize the fragmenting effect of time/sense compressions. Bergson bypasses traditional patterns of sequence or
logic or causality and prescribes for disjunct narratives the "mutual
penetration, an interconnection and organization of elements, each

one of which represents the whole" (*TFW* 101). In Faulkner, counterpoint effects the "mutual penetration" of discrete components, each one of which encloses the others. A character's "psychic state," says Bergson, gains "importance in relation" to "what goes before and what follows." The "interplay" among the "final act" and "all the antecedents" establishes "a conflict or a composition of forces" (*TFW* 185, 190). In Faulkner's fiction, counterpointed parts penetrate one another in a "conflict" that is also a "composition" of reciprocal "forces" constituting the whole. Bergson believes the interaction of "structure and rhythm" in literature intimates the poet's "thought and feeling" and causes "faint emotions" to "play upon" the "fixity" or "immobility" of the plastic arts (*CM* 86–87; *TFW* 15). Faulkner likewise trusts the polar rhythms of converging-expanding time to "arrest" life's motion and hold it "fixed" so "it will always move" (*LG* 253). In the Bergsonian system, the pattern of interpenetrating antinomies in consciousness inscribes as well a structural design for literature. Faulkner relies on "contrapuntal . . . integration" to conjoin the splintered elements of form and sense.

Bergson closely affiliates metaphysics with psychology and poetics. "Real duration" is "impregnated with spirituality" (*CM* 33), and the source of human freedom and volition lies in the deeper mind where "our whole personality concentrate[s] itself in a point, or rather a sharp edge, pressed against the future and cutting into it unceasingly. It is in this that life and action are free." In "pure duration," the "different parts of our being enter into each other" (*CE* 220), and mental states "permeate and strengthen one another" and lead "by a natural evolution to a free act." Past the intellect and its segmented time and language, the struggle for freedom lies within the "whole soul, . . . which gives rise to the free decision" (*TFW* 171, 167). One willed act attests to Joe Christmas's free self, and throws light on the debate over his "fate."

Faulkner's language of "real duration" discloses Christmas's true identity, divided yet whole, reprobate yet responsible, determined yet free. Like the inner consciousness where the "parts, although distinct, permeate one another" and form a "totality" (*TFW* 100), suspended binaries stipulate the meaning of Christmas's life and of the whole novel. The other five novels in this study, *Absalom, Absalom!*, *The Sound and the Fury*, *As I Lay Dying*, *The Unvanquished*, and *Go Down, Moses*, exemplify in form and theme the parallel prescriptions of Bergson and Faulkner on the language of time in fiction. Close correspondences between the philosopher's doctrines and the novelist's theory and practice suggest the influence over Faulkner may be more comprehensive than previously thought. For Faulkner and his master, Joseph Conrad, and other writers he read like Henry James and James Joyce, events are less than their reverberations in mind and time. Faulkner's linguistic formulations of "indivisible" time in *Light in August*, among the most powerful in the canon, include divided/layered mental stages, voices and points of view, flashforths, and the "mediating *image*" (*CM* 118) or the metonymic trope, which casts an "enormous mass" in a "fusion" (*INP* 106) and the past/present/future in "a single identical time." Synchronic condensations break up diachronic succession, but counterpointed fragments intimate past discourse the cause and effect latent in a deed. "Contradiction" and "interpenetration," which mark the "very essence" of technique and structure, and theme counterpoising fate and freedom, tell beyond the discursive planes of language. An irreducible constituent of the Faulkner story lies in the gaps between what words state and what form signifies. Language thus empowered to "triumph over time"[5] surpasses itself.

The author's extensive revisions and additions, traced from an early Holograph manuscript to the Typescript manuscript that resembles the printed text,[6] reveal an increasing drive to crystallize time and meaning. The metonymic images and tropes added to Christmas's first appearance encode a germ of character whose separate but filiated evolvements contribute largely to structural design. Temporal concordances delineate a divided but whole self in a society split by hatred between black and white. Shifting points of view heighten the ironic contrast between the people's erroneous conjectures about the stranger and the revelation of Christmas's inner being where, in Bergson's view, lies the origin of the "free decision" and the "free act." The subjective segments on Christmas in the central chapters of the book (5–12) disclose the roots of character in the orphan child, who learns early to wield his instinct of self-preservation against an inimical world and to pursue requital for wrongdoing. The line of causality is driven neither by the "mechanical" succession of events in life nor the fusion of "all time" in the deeper regions of mind, but by the child's instinctive sense of justice that leads the youth through a bifurcated life and the man to his chosen end (see II). The "tension, concentration" (*CM* 89) of synchronous antinomies in form and substance offsets the common view of Christmas as victim of circumstance and projects past the word the "composite picture" (UV T-112) of a being both determined and free (see III).

II

Two modes of time operate concurrently in the Reverend Hightower's mind. Life unreels sequentially, but its meaning precipitates in durational moments:

> [Hightower] lives dissociated from mechanical time. Yet for that reason he has never lost it. It is as though out of his subconscious he produces without volition the few *crystallizations of stated instances* by which his dead life in the actual world had been governed and ordered once. Without recourse to clock he could know immediately upon the thought just where, in his old life, he would be and what doing between the two fixed moments.[7] (*LIA* 346/366, italics added)

Hightower's consciousness (Bergson's "intellect") progresses in diachronic succession, but the synchronic "crystallizations" of time ("true duration") in his "subconscious" ("intuition") govern his "dead life in the actual world" of "mechanical time." One such "fixed" moment, his grandfather's mad raid, capsulizes "the sum of his life" in a "suspended instant out of which the *soon* will presently begin," a moment that he realizes has destroyed it: "My life died there" (460/486, 452/478). An "entire past history," compressed in an "undivided present" that also moves "in the direction of the future" (Bergson, *CM* 152–53), promises repetition, as well as the possibility of change or reversal. The interplay of succession and convergence in Hightower's mind typifies the pattern of time in narrative described by Bergson and Faulkner, and recent writers like Frank Kermode and Paul Ricoeur.

Hightower's paradigm frames the story of Joe Christmas. Time layers as Byron Bunch's initial impression of the stranger fuses with knowledge gained over the years: "Byron Bunch *knows* this: It *was* one Friday morning three years ago" (27/31, italics added). The shift from the present "knows" to the past tense "was" compresses in a moment the length of time it has taken Byron and the townspeople to find out about the stranger who suddenly appeared among them. Faulkner's extensive additions to the Christmas episodes, from his initial appearance in chapter 2 to his death in chapter 19, multiply the durational devices that disclose the man's "fundamental self." All additions to the printed text, which are missing in the Holograph manuscript, are double-bracketed in the passage below and in other passages thereafter:

> He looked like a tramp, [[yet not like a tramp either.]] . . . He wore a tie and a stiffbrim straw hat that was quite new, cocked at an angle arrogant and baleful above his still face. He did not look like a professional hobo in his professional rags, [[but there was something definitely rootless about him, as though no town nor city was his, no street, no walls, no square of earth his home. And that he carried his knowledge with him always as though it were a banner, with a quality ruthless, lonely, and almost proud.]] (27/31)

The metonymic images added to this embryonic capsule distill an "entire past history" in the present that is "continually moving" in "the direction of the future." "Arrogant and baleful" like his angled hat, the thirty-three-year old Christmas deliberately chooses to distance his divided yet whole being, [["rootless"]] and [["ruthless,"]] from human society and nature, and flaunts this [["knowledge with him always"]] against every threat to being. The defiance inscribed on that "still face" fortifies the boy against indifference or injustice, the youth against McEachern's cold religion and Bobbie's betrayal of love, and the man against the white community's stereotype of black people. He forfends every assault on his "lonely" yet "proud" isolation, until death fulfills his separateness, "of itself alone serene, of itself alone triumphant" (440/465). In addition, the "air of cold and quiet contempt" abstracts Christmas's abiding distrust of people, as the men's "baffled outrage" (28/32) signals the irrational hate and terror he inspires. This character germ in the second chapter joins episodes from the past thirty-three years to the man's final destiny. Bound to one another by their common source and by contrapuntal reciprocity, the pieces leading to and issuing from this condensed moment become essential components of one another.[8]

Other kinds of temporal compressions appear in the opening Christmas episode. Unlike prolepsis or foreshadow, which previews the future, the flashforth or flashforward embeds the future in the present and past: " 'As if,' as the men said *later*, 'he was just down on his luck for a time, and that he didn't intend to stay down on it and didn't give a damn much how he rose up' " (27/32, italics added). The import of the moment resounds through the future and the past. Time spirals forward and backward when Byron thinks on that first day they should have sensed in Christmas's name "an augur of what he will do," for the "sound of it" carried an "inescapable warning, like a flower its scent or a rattlesnake its rattle. Only none of them had sense enough to recognize it" (29/33). The oxymoronic flower/rattlesnake image epitomizes sensibility and violence coexisting in this fractured man and his way with the world. The next sentences abridge Byron's progress from ignorance, through hearsay and surmise, to actual knowing: "This is not what Byron knows now. This is just what he knew then, what he heard and watched as it came to his knowledge" (31/36). The mental stages layered in this passage and throughout Christmas's history fuse time and signal the men's bafflement over this inscrutable stranger.

In the first section of the novel (chapters 1–4), Christmas appears through the townspeople's objective view. During a late revision,[9] Faulkner inserts the subjective Christmas chapters (5–12) between the first section and the third section (chapters 13–21), where the external viewpoint interlaces with segments exploring Christmas's consciousness during the last days to his death (chapters 14, 19), and also the inner mind of Byron (chapters 17–18), and of Hightower (chapters 16, 17, 20). The envelope arrangement sets the three insular sections modulating inside one another, and sharpens the ironic contrast between the people's external view of Christmas and his "true self." Where in the first section Byron and the townsmen detect a proud separateness in the stranger, Christmas discloses in the central section the "loneliness" haunting him down an "always empty" street, "driven by the courage of flagged and spurred despair" toward no hope. Broken into "numberless avatars" (213/226), the "refracted" Christmas (Bergson's term) is reduced to a "shadow" (216/230), "more lonely than a lone telephone pole in the middle of a desert," a "phantom, a spirit, strayed out of its own world, and lost" (106/114). The people see only a "phantom" or "shadow," disjoined from its "fundamental self" (Bergson's terms); but in the latter days when they misread

Christmas's motives, they ironically confirm the man's lifelong struggle to preserve his true self and volition against their stereotypes. Synchronous antinomies in form and sense tell of a bisected but whole being caught in a fractured world.

The "germ" of the thirty-three-year-old Christmas's character and history in chapter 2 unfolds mainly in the subjective chapters where episodes in the present and in childhood and youth shift back and forth in time. The central section opens hours before Joanna's murder (chapter 5), an act deferred through several chapters and completed toward the end of the section (chapter 12). In between, concordant time constantly interrupts succession as the story recycles back to the child, the youth, and the man's life with Joanna. The five year old's limited comprehension and the man's interpretive knowledge overlap, as at the beginning of chapter 6: "Memory believes before knowing remembers. Believes longer than recollects, longer than knowing even wonders. Knows remembers believes" (111/119), the last three stages ranked according to Bergson's and Faulkner's taxonomy of mind.[10] Flashforths fuse the stages marking the mature mind from the immature when little Joe at the orphanage wonders about the man who watches his every move: "If the child had been older he would perhaps have thought *He hates me and fears me. . . .* With more vocabulary but no more age he might have thought *That is why I am different from the others*: *because he is watching me all the time*" (129/138). The time planes, "although distinct, permeate one another" like inner mental states (Bergson, *TFW* 100): "But not yet. That was to come later, when life had begun to go so fast that accepting would take the place of knowing and believing" (167/177). A flashforth brings the future to bear on past and present, and also casts past and present into the future: "It was years later that memory knew what he was remembering" (145/155); while recollective phrasing gathers up the past in the present which is its future: "He could see now what he discovered that he had known all the time" (186/199).

The roots of the man's obsessive drive to shield the identity he has claimed for himself and to pursue an act to its logical end go back to the earliest years (chapters 6–11). When the three year old is abandoned by his mother-figure, the kind Alice, who "was not and never would be his enemy" (127/136), the child and later the man will thereafter hold suspect any kindness and other menaces to his separate being. Alice, the child soon realizes, "had not been the first and would not be the last" of the unreliable females (128/137). Little Joe learns early to protect himself from betrayal and loss by contemning such gestures of care and love. The five year old signals a firmly defined sense of self when he rebuffs his adopted father McEachern's proposal to change his sacrilegious name: "He didn't even bother to say to himself *My name aint McEachern. My name is Christmas* There was no need to bother about that yet. There was plenty of time" (136/145).

Caught eating the dietitian's toothpaste, the five-year-old Joe, "with complete and passive surrender" admits to himself his wrongdoing, "Well, here I am." Having been "taken in sin," the boy seeks the "punishment" that would "strike the balance and write it off." When instead she gives him a shining dollar and promises more, the boy is utterly shocked and outraged, even revolted (114–17/122–25). The seed of responsibility for error, embedded in the child, fructifies in the man who seeks just "punishment" for the sin of murder. Unlike the "mechanical" succession of events in time or the artistic contrivance of temporal concord, an instinctive moral imperative drives the causal line from deed to retribution.

The eight year old, resisting McEachern's demand to memorize his Bible verse, takes the whipping "with pride perhaps and despair," or "the stupid vanity of a man" (140/149). To the mature Joe, the child's prideful acquiescence to chastisement marks his entrance to manhood: "And memory knows this; twenty years later memory is still to believe *On this day I became a man*" (137/146). That childhood scene, synoptic and prophetic like other notable events, augurs future incidences of responsibility for transgression. It also cycles back to Joe's initial appearance a hundred pages earlier, undergirding the man's defiance of all threats to his being. From eight to fifteen, young Joe welcomes with a kind of vainglory every penalty for breaking McEachern's rules. When he and his friends stay out late with a Negro girl, he takes the strapping "like a hermit, contemplative and remote with ecstasy and selfcrucifixion" (150/160). He hated worse than the "hard and ruthless justice" of the man the "soft kindness" of Mrs. McEachern, who "lies" to protect him from "the punishment which, deserved or not, just or unjust, was impersonal, both the man and the boy accepting it as a natural and inescapable fact" (157–58/167–69).

At fifteen Joe tries to escape from the man and wife who threaten that self, feeling "like an eagle: hard, sufficient, potent, remorse-less, strong"; but a flashforth qualifies his present illusion of freedom with future reality: "He did not then know that, like the eagle, his own flesh as well as all space was still a cage" (150–51/160). Still, no cage impedes his defense of the being secured from childhood. He temporarily escapes the "cage" when he falls in love, but Bobbie's betrayal hardens his distrust to cynicism. It rises to murderous fury with Joanna Burden, who, to her misfortune, combines all the emblems of female "soft kindness" that Christmas suspects, food and sexuality, as well as generosity grounded on religion, and a patronizing fascination with Negro. The youth's prideful contempt, which the man wields against circumstance, illuminates the question of Christmas's true "identity." To the end, he resists society's stereotypes and reclaims his "living self," confirmed when the people rage at a "nigger" who refuses to behave like one.

The evidence against readings of a "passive" victim, who is unable to choose his own identity, begins with Christmas's first appearance, proudly wielding [["his knowledge"]] of alienation from his ruptured society like a [["banner"]] of victory. "Black" in that community, Christmas knows from experience, signifies evil, death, hell, and "white," the opposite values of good, life, redemption. Gavin Stevens, pitting Christmas's black blood against his white blood, identifies the "black jungle" as a place "where life has already ceased before the heart stops and death is desire and fulfillment" (424–25). Though without certain proof, the people proscribe the stranger to the inferior side. Christmas defies these preconceptions, an act quickened by the conjunction of circumstance and volition, and exercises the "free decision" to be *neither* black nor white, but rather, inextricably *both* white and black. He deliberately exploits his "refracted" self to confront both camps. Revolted by the woman's secret dishes and the man's cold-blooded righteousness, young Joe plans to shock the McEacherns, who think they adopted a white child, with the disclosure that they had "nursed a nigger" (157/168). The years telescoped from eighteen to thirty-three chronicle his compulsion to challenge one or the other group. Entering "the street which was to run for fifteen years" (210/223), he taunts white women with his Negro strain, then assaults one who refuses to be outraged. He tricks men into calling him Negro so he could beat them, or be beaten up; but then he attacks the black woman who calls him white. Among Negroes, he tries "to expel from himself the white blood and the white thinking and being," but "all the while" his "whole being [would] writhe and strain with physical outrage and spiritual denial" (212/226). He lays claim on duality when he says to the white Bobbie, "I think I got some nigger blood in me. . . . I don't know. I believe I have" (184/196–97). When Joanna asks if he knows his father is "part nigger," he replies, "I don't know it. . . . If I'm not, damned if I haven't wasted a lot of time" (240–41/254). "If *I'm* not," rather than the syntactically logical, "If *he* isn't," underscores Christmas's sense that he is *his own*, not his father's, doing. Neither black nor white, the being depicted in these segments is suspended between, precisely the *identity* Christmas takes for his own. But he recognizes the corrosive effects of bigotry: "Just when do men that have different blood in them stop hating one another?" (236/249). To be neither, but to embrace black *and* white is to choose not only the world's hatred but self-hatred as well.

Gavin Stevens and concurring readers think the mixed blood that Christmas claims without proof signifies his lack of identity, reducing him to a pawn of circumstance. Bobbie's friend sees the same lack in the youth: "*She still dont know any more about what he is than he does*" (205/219). But such one-sided readings, including the author's statement, "He didn't know what he was, and so he was nothing" (*FU* 72), are offset in form entwining "contradiction" and "counterpoint," and in content melding acquiescence and choice, fate and free will.[11]

Faulkner's revisions of many salient passages emphasize the protagonist's resistance to forces obstructing his chosen way. The person acted upon in the Holograph manuscript, "Maybe *it has already happened to me*" (46, italics added) becomes an agent in the printed text: [["Maybe *I have already done it*"]] (104/111, italics added). Just before Christmas enters the "Dark House" (Faulkner's original title for the novel) to murder Joanna, the passive acquiescence reappears: "*Something is going to happen to me*" (110/118). The phrase recurs in the next chapter (6) where the child at the orphanage waits to be discovered among the dietitian's clothes "with astonished fatalism for what was about to happen to him" and with "complete and passive surrender" (114/122). These few instances of seeming "fatalism" in fact attest to the child's intuition and the man's recognition of the inexorable force of causality, which, however, does not negate the exercise of free will.

Thinking of leaving Joanna, Christmas sees "perhaps with fore-boding and premonition, the savage and lonely street [[which *he had chosen of his own will*, waiting for him"]] (243–44/258, italics added). The clause appended to the printed text confirms volition. In the Holograph and Typescript manuscripts, as well as the printed text, Christmas resists the temptation to marry Joanna for "*ease, security.*" The Holograph manuscript continues: "But then he saw the street again: freedom. He thought that was it. He did not realize that it was pride. A threat against that which he had spent 30 years in building: the . . . well-made . . . edifice" (102). In the text, Faulkner adds a single line that distills the intransigent will ingrained in the child and youth, and pictured in the man's initial appearance: [["No. If I give in now, I will deny all the thirty years that I have lived *to make me what I chose to be*"]] (250–51/265, italics added). To protect his self-chosen entity, the man resolves, "I have got to do something. There is *something that I am going to do*" (256/271, italics added). The child's resistance to all threats to his being now explodes in a violent act defending the man's "well-made . . . edi-fice."

"The volitionless servant of the fatality," a phrase often adduced to prove "the quintessential victim,"[12] is refuted explicitly in the rest of the sentence: "He believed with *calm paradox* that he was the volitionless servant of the fatality *in which* [[*he believed that*]] *he did not believe*" (264/280, italics added). The passage, like oth-ers taken to prove determinism, provides its own denial. The brack-eted clause Faulkner adds to the Typescript manuscript and the printed text underlines the "calm paradox" of one who admits, as well as denies, his fated condition. Referring to the murder not yet committed in "the past tense: *I had to do it,*" as though it were already done, suggests a sense of compulsion (264/280); neverthe-less, he does "*not believe*" he is "volitionless," a conviction veri-fied when he pursues the causal line traversing the mutually engaged polarities of free will and necessity.

Hours before the murder, dense images of incomprehensible voices, an ironic turn on Faulkner's trusted resource against lan-guage, and the false written or printed word emblematize the man's attempt to make sense of his life and destiny. "He was hearing a myriad sounds of . . . voices, murmurs, whispers: . . . his own voice; other voices evocative of names and times and places—which he had been conscious of all his life without knowing it, which were his life, thinking *God perhaps and me not knowing that too"* (97–98/105). A God who knows nothing of the man's "life" of echoic voices negates the notion of an All-Knowing the McEacherns instilled in the child.

Voices, though often mystifying, imply a subtext. The printed word, on the other hand, flaunts a bold message that negates itself, satirizing the falsity of God's love: "He could see it like a printed sentence, fullborn and already dead *God loves me too* like the faded and weathered letters on a last year's billboard *God loves me too*" (98/105). The young Hightower at divinity school soon discovers "how false the most profound book turns out to be when applied to life" (454–55/479–81), while Byron deprecates the word itself when he seeks to distance *"other folks,"* who *"were just a lot of words that never even stood for anything"* from Lena and himself, *"what was us . . . going on and going on without even missing the lack of words"* (380/402).

Equivocal like language, the printed word may be false but telling. McEachern's voice, "not human, . . . just cold, implacable, like written or printed words" (139/149), rules the family. The truth about Joanna comes to Christmas "complete, like a printed sentence" (255/270). Gavin Stevens thinks the man's fate "had already been written and worded" the night Mrs. Hines bore his mother Milly. Mrs. Hines herself "learned it beyond all forgetting and then forgot the words" (423–24/448), and therefore knows beyond words. The written word may even render the essential being, as Lucas Burch's "labored and hurried pencilling" to the sheriff "succeeded for an instant in snaring his whole soul and life too" (413/436).

The printed words of a magazine Christmas reads through the day before he kills Joanna gauge his diminishing time and life. He counts the "remaining pages" of the story, then paces with words the sun's dying motion and his last free hours. "He read now like a man walking along a street might count the cracks in the pavement, to the last and final page, the last and final word. Then he rose" (104/112).

That scene in chapter 5 concludes in the last chapter (12) of the middle section, but images of coalescent time now displace the printed word, a signal of the writer's reliance on synchronicity to render the import of the critical moment. Convergent time sums up

Christmas's life, but finally he must re-enter the "time" of causality:

[[The dark was filled with the voices, myriad, out of all time that he had known, as though all the past was a flat pattern. And going on: tomorrow night, all the tomorrows, to be a part of the flat pattern, going on. He thought of that with quiet astonishment: going on, myriad, familiar, since all that had ever been was the same as all that was to be, since tomorrow to-be and had-been would be the same. Then it was time.]] (266/281)

The "flat pattern" contracts a "long history," not in a timeless moment, but one enclosing "all time" when "to-be" and "had-been" fuse. But "then it was time" for Christmas to commit the deed that leads to retribution, a moral course that cuts through any temporal pattern. He emerges from the disorderly alternations of diachronic and synchronic time in the circle to tread the unswerving line of justice.

Most readers, searching for motive, agree with Christmas's reason for murdering Joanna, her praying over him ("She ought not to started praying over me" [104/112]). Olga W. Vickery uncovers a greater threat to the man's self-chosen ambiguity when Joanna proposes to rescue him from "his uncertainty" and make him the unequivocal Negro.[13] Christmas, to whom division is certainty, refuses, and she shoots first, confirming his ingrained suspicion of woman-kindness. Images of "true duration" inscribe the shifting tides of Christmas inner mind as he defends the self he has known since childhood against the external forces of circumstance and defies the community's rules to pursue his own way to retribution. The interplay of contrary elements delineates the true condition of Christmas's "living self."

III

In the last days and hours, images of concordant time probe Christmas's deeper consciousness, where Bergson locates the seat of moral cognition and the source of the "free act." After thirty years "inside an orderly parade of named and numbered days like fence pickets," he emerges "outside of them" (314/331–32). From "mechanical time" he enters the freedom of an "instant" of pure duration from which issues a "radically new and absolutely simple idea," as Bergson describes it (*CM* 35). "A strange thing came into his mind" for which "he could discover neither derivation nor motivation nor explanation. . . . Now and at last he had an actual and urgent need to strike off the accomplished days *toward some purpose, some definite day or act,* without either falling short or overshooting." The "strange thing" becomes "so crystallized that the need did not seem strange anymore" (317/335, italics added). The crystallization of "need" and "purpose" releases the man from the thirty-year circle of alternating time. Instead, he now [["follows a *straight line*"]] (318/336, italics added) to a definite "act," the "natural and inescapable fact" of "punishment" (157/167) he had accepted as a child. His "direction is straight as a surveyor's line, disregarding hill and valley and bog. Yet he is not hurrying. He is like a man *who knows where he is* and *where he wants to go* and how much time to the exact minute he has to get there in." The next sentence in the Holograph manuscript (not in the printed text), "It is as though he had a purpose, in the course which he took: or like a man condemned" (129), underlines the exercise of judgment behind the willed intent. Ceasing to run, "he walks steadily on" to his chosen end (320/338, italics added).

Reclaiming his "living self" also reverses Chrismas's alienation not only from the human community but from nature as well: "It is as though he desires to see [inserted here in the Holograph manuscript: "with his new eyes" (129)] his native earth in all its phases for the first or the last time," a reverse echo of "no square of earth his home" at his first appearance (27/31). His "physical shape and his thought had been molded by its compulsions" yet "he remained a foreigner to the very immutable laws which earth must obey," "immutable laws" of cause and effect the child did know and obeyed, instinctively, and now the man discerns, cognitively. He partakes of nature's "actual shape and feel," and, while "looking and seeing," attains what has eluded him in the human community, "peace and unhaste and quiet, until suddenly the true answer comes to him" (320/338).[14] Freed from "time and distance" (321/339) Christmas perceives volition and causality intertwined in his life: "The street which ran for thirty years . . . had made a circle and he is still inside of it. Though during the last seven days he has had no paved street, yet he has travelled further than in all the thirty years before. And yet he is still inside the circle. [['And yet I have been further in these seven days than in all the thirty years,']] he thinks. 'But I have never got outside that circle. I have never broken out of the ring of what I have already done [[and cannot ever undo' "]] (321/339). Christmas's last recorded thoughts, framed in counterbalances underscored by the echoic, "and yet," acknowledge the constraints of freedom, but, the additions stress, the choice to take a new course, [["And yet I have been further in these seven days than in all the thirty years,"]] and to assume accountability for action, [["and cannot ever undo,"]] remains open. Both options release him from the ring. The circle-line image charts Christmas's transition from the purposeless "shadow" seen by the community, to the inner-directed self, made whole when he reconnects with "his native earth" and returns to human society.[15] The youthful rebel believes he is beyond "honor and law" (194)/207), but the man recaptures his childhood loyalty to the law linking deed to consequence. With honor and dignity, Christmas proceeds to fulfill the law.

Christmas finally realizes that whatever he [["chose to be"]] (251/265), the community has sentenced him, a Negro, to be hunted by white men into "the black abyss which had been waiting, trying, for thirty years to drown him and into which now and at last he had actually entered." The "black shoes smelling of negro" he exchanges for his own, mark "the gauge definite and ineradicable of the black tide creeping up his legs, moving from his feet upward as death moves" (313/331, 321/339). Acceding to the "definite and ineradicable" rise of the "black tide" of death signals his acceptance of the penalty for murder; but, still a rebel, he repudiates the people's formula of violence, hunting the "nigger" down like an animal. He instead elects his own way to end the "accomplished days."

The inner being unveiled by Faulkner's changes, viewed against the people's misreadings, generates ironic overtones. In the third and final section of the novel (chapters 13–21), where the objective and subjective perspectives collide, the community's stereotypical views substantiate indirectly the man's affirmation of his own "true self." Defiant to the end, he infuriates the people when, instead of running away as a "nigger" would, Christmas deliberately returns to the town, "like he had set out to get himself caught like a man might set out to get married" (330/349). He admits his identity and quietly takes the blows: *He never acted like either a nigger or a white man.*" That "was what made the folks so mad," his flouting their set codes. "For him to be a murderer and all dressed up and walking the town like he dared them to touch him, when he ought to have been skulking and hiding in the woods, muddy and dirty and running. It was like he never even knew he was a murderer, let alone a nigger too" (331/350, italics added). The people, threatened by the man's aberrant behavior, unwittingly corroborate Christmas's refusal to be cast in either mold, and ironically certify the moral certainty of one who accepts his guilt: "He neither surrendered nor resisted. It was as though he had set out and made his plans to passively commit suicide" (419/443). He challenges to the end the town's simplistic categorical imperatives. Synchronous antinomies divulging Christmas's true being also herald the import of his death. Two other pieces of evidence throw light on that final scene.

About thirty pages after Christmas enters the "straight line" to the "selfcrucifixion" he has deliberately pursued throughout his life (150/160), the narrative cycles back to the childhood years at the orphanage where a Negro man pronounces on the boy Joey: "You are worse than [a nigger]. You dont know what you are. And more than that, you wont never know. You'll live and you'll die and you wont never know . . . because dont nobody but God know what you is" (363/384). Christmas, as noted earlier, does not think God knows either. This curse late in the book offers many readers decisive proof of an unformed identity, vulnerable to determinant forces. In addition, Doc Hines's epithet for his newborn grandson, the "devil's walking seed" (362/383), has been taken to prescribe the child's fate. Counterevidence massed before and after the passage, however, verifies the identity the grown man has elected, a bifurcated self against his bisected world. That proud unbelonging displayed from the start (27/31–32) directs his actions toward both camps. His self-chosen being, not one nor the other but both "*nigger*" and "*white man,*" both evil and conscientious, that the reader perceives but not the people around him, belies the old man's prophecy.

Gavin Stevens, more sensible than the townspeople, nonetheless mirrors their prejudices. He confirms Christmas's responsibility for his destruction, not by "pursuers: but himself: years, acts, deeds omitted and committed" by an equivocal being who would "*not be either one or the other*" of his sundered blood. But unable to see the man whole, Stevens mouths the jargon about Christmas's inferior black blood that, as "in crises all his life, . . . failed him again," until, as he has tried for thirty years, he defies the black blood "for the last time" and lets "them shoot him to death" (424–25/448–49, italics added). Echoing the social bias, Stevens attributes the courage to accept guilt and punishment to the man's superior white blood. Christmas's whole moral history, capped with the durational images and panoramic perspective of the death scene, decisively refutes the idea.

That scene, where Faulkner's rhetoric rises to unmatched heights, crowns the cumulative evidence that neither life nor death is simply inflicted on Christmas. Having attained the "definite . . . act" to which he has set his "purpose," the "so cold, so baleful" eyes at the start (chapter 2) now turn "peaceful and unfathomable and unbearable." From his loins "the pent *black blood* seemed to rush like a released breath," like "the rush of sparks from a rising rocket; upon that *black blast* the man seemed to rise soaring into their memories forever and ever. They are not to lose it, in whatever peaceful valleys, beside whatever placid and reassuring streams of old age, in the mirroring faces of whatever children they will contemplate old disasters and newer hopes. It will be there, musing, quiet, steadfast, not fading and not particularly threatful, but of itself alone serene, of itself alone triumphant" (439–40/464–65, italics added). A violent death, "the rush of sparks" and "that black blast," counterpointed with "peaceful valleys" and "placid . . . streams," and a "musing, quiet" but unfading memory, encapsulate Christmas's past, present, and future, and, spiraling in reverse, the lives as well of Percy Grimm and the other townsmen.

The soaring "black blood," transformed into an emblem of the life-death cycle made whole and dignified by accepted retribution, passes judgment on their "shameless savageness" (438/463). The solitary fulfillment of that blood will haunt the men, to whom such elevation will forever be unattainable. Something about this life that has struggled through perverse gropings to moral lucidity leaves its mark on the people. Paradoxical like the end of tragedy, "black" now precipitates all negative attributes in one "serene" and "triumphant" affirmation. Christmas, partly a victim, in the end becomes the victor.

The unconventional tense shifts from past to present to future in the last three sentences on Christmas render this life's abiding significance: "Upon that black blast the man seemed to rise soaring into their memories forever and ever. They are not to lose it. . . . It will be there" (440/465). By such "artificial means" Faulkner's art "holds it fixed" in perpetual resurrection.[16]

Each part, Bergson maintains, is important "according as the final act is explained by it"; and, in turn, the "completed" final act sets in "mutual penetration" (*TFW* 186, 190, 101) the beginning and end and parts in between, as well as the counterforces of freedom and necessity. Faulkner's language of the durational mind and time offers the "bold novelist" the means to overcome the word so "the thunder and the music of the prose take place in silence" (*LG* 248). Storytelling and reading a story may then evoke a "shadow" of the elusive "living self." Like Mrs. Hines, perhaps it is only when we "tell it" that we "then for the first time, actually [see] it whole and real at the same time" (422/447).

3

Absalom, Absalom! Story as Self-Deception

there is that might-have-been which is the single rock we cling
to above the maelstrom of unbearable reality
—Faulkner, *Absalom, Absalom!*

I

FAULKNER OVERCOMES THE DUPLICITOUS WORD WITH DUPLICITY. HE violates the canons of form and verisimilitude, yet claims for "fiction" a credible "lie." In *Absalom, Absalom!* (1936) Miss Rosa reprises his distrust of language, while Quentin Compson reformulates two of his main strategies against the false word: assault diachronic progression with synchronic "true duration" and frame with antithetic elements a discontinuous form; then weave through the fractured tale the line of causality and gain belief for a falsehood. The word turned to voice or, in this work, to intermingled voices and points of view and other configurations of temporal concord constitute form that designates one thing but signifies another. As paradoxical as its deceitful yet compelling medium, the novel enacts a central precept of Faulkner's theory: convey through disjunct and incredible form a credible silent story of human action and consequence. But there always remains a residue of disbelief or, perhaps with a writer bold enough, of wonder.

Miss Rosa stipulates the intractable nature of the word: "*There are some things for which three words are three too many, and three thousand words that many words too less.*" Even "*three thousand sentences*" leave only unanswered whys (166–67/134–35).[1] "*Even less inferential of thought or intention than the sounds which a beast and a bird might make to each other*" (154/124), words render only a semblance of reality. Yet, Grandfather Compson points out, only the "meager and fragile thread" of language may

74

join for "an instant" the "corners and edges of men's secret and solitary lives" before they sink "back into the darkness where the spirit cried for the first time and was not heard and will cry for the last time and will not be heard then either" (251/202). The "instant" occurs only "now and then," but the unreliable word shaped into deceptive form may sound the spirit's cry.

Unlike Miss Rosa and Hightower, who distrust words or books, Thomas Sutpen puts his trust in words and learns "only from books" the "scope of man's abilities" to perform "deeds, good and bad both." His teacher's tales equip him for what he "should later design to do" (241–42/195). For Sutpen, signifier matches signified, story equals a life plan, and, blinded by the iron logic of his design, he detects no web of consequences entangling each deed. If his first wife is not "adjunctive or incremental to the design," there is no reason not to "put her aside," along with his son (240/194). Cursed by moral "innocence," as the Compsons put it, Sutpen draws from tales heard in childhood a powerful text that consumes him and his people. He discovers too late what Quentin Compson and his author know, that words are deadly. One word is all Charles Bon asks of his father. Failing to get it, *"No word to me, no word at all?"* (356/285), he drags down the Sutpen house of words and perishes with it.

Quentin Compson, on the other hand, believes human action and the words about it are endlessly reverberative: *"Maybe nothing ever happens once and is finished. Maybe happen is never once but like ripples maybe on water after the pebble sinks, the ripples moving on, spreading, . . . to the next pool which the first pool feeds . . . to the old ineradicable rhythm"* (261/210). "Deeds, good and bad both," *"spreading"* to the *"old ineradicable rhythm"* of cause and effect, leave nothing simple or "innocent." The storyteller Quentin, like his author, knows a *"happen"* in story is *"never once"* for the word, like a sinking pebble, sends *"ripples"* out among other words and tellers and dimensions of time. Sutpen presumes control over the word and its equivalent sense and action, but Quentin sees both event and word *"moving on"* beyond the speaker's intent. The Sutpen story spreads from generation to generation, from storyteller to storyteller, each one refracting the tale in his or her own image and thus telling a falsehood. To gain belief for the spurious *"happen,"* told with the "meager and fragile thread" of language, Quentin re-echoes his author's two main principles of narrative form and content: surmount the word with converged time and thread the incongruent fragments of story with the line of causality. The "telling" may have "that logic- and reason-flouting quality of a dream," Quentin postulates, but it gains "credulity . . . upon a formal recognition of and acceptance of *elapsed and yet-elapsing time* as music or a printed tale" (22/15, italics added). Like a past *"happen"* that continues *"spreading"* from pool to pool, the paradoxical pattern of "elapsed and yet-elapsing time" emblematizes the interplay of diachronic and synchronic time in "a printed tale," the counter-process of an "elapsed" past precipitated at a point that, *"moving on,"* continues to elapse in variant configurations.[2]

"Crystallizations" of time, like those in Hightower's life (*LIA*), generate *"ripples"* through time. The meaning of Sutpen's life appears in "a very condensation of time" (249/201) that portends his future. "An explosion—a bright glare" at the moment a "nigger" drives him from the front door of the landowner's mansion (237–38/192) directs Sutpen toward his destiny. His son Charles Bon looks for the epiphanic moment when the "integers" would fall in a "pattern" and, "like a flash of light, the meaning of his whole life, past" would be revealed (313/250) and his long future directed. Miss Rosa discerns the true import of events in *"some globed concentrate"* (144/116), or in *"a forever crystallized instant"* that, like the shot that kills Bon, ripples through *"imponderable time"* (158/127). Sutpen's proposal of marriage casts *"a sudden over-burst of light, illumination"* on her past and future. His vain struggle against time congeals in *"a prolonged and unbroken instant of tremendous effort"* within *"the accelerating circle's fatal curving course of his ruthless pride,"* confronting *"invincible and unafraid, what he must have known would be the final defeat"* (162–63/131–32). Synchronic time fuses motive-action-result, and while "yet-elapsing," partakes of both the real and the imaginary. Storytelling may forego logic or reason, be unreal and incredible, but it must resurrect the past *"happen"* to life in the present which is its ongoing future. Each retelling, however, is a lie, for "shadowy inscrutable . . . words" or "symbols" bring from the past to the present nothing but "synthetic and spurious shadows and shapes" (101/80, 73/57). The challenge for the writer is to win belief for a lie with an ever-resurging past, or, conversely, with a present that revivifies the past. Faulkner contrives with "elapsed and yet-elapsing time" a dual story, an implausible worded one and an un-worded one that completes the other in silence beyond the word.

The word turned to voice, the chief technical device in the work, fuses past/present/future time. Voices "speaking the speech" inside one another evoke rather than simply communicate, like Father's speech, which does *"not tell you anything so much as it struck, word by word, the resonant strings of remembering,"* as Quentin explains (213/172). What is remembered is re-created, and a *"happen"* that is "fixed" in the past will "always move" to new life in the present and future (*LG* 253). The invoked "ghost" then gains a semblance of lifelike "solidity, permanence" (13/8). But, typical of Faulkner's deception, the individual voice identified in the text disguises a conflux of voices and time, a fusion of the long past in the present that casts it into the future. Miss Rosa's voice blends her decades-long "impotent yet indomitable frustration" (7/3) over the "evil's source" of pollution for her family (18/12) with numerous versions of hearsay and surmise. That overlay of voices from different temporal periods empowers her "talking" voice to resurrect the "long-dead object" and transports the "listening" Quentin to where he watches the ghost "possess sentience" and "abrupt" upon a "peaceful and decorous" pre–Civil War South (8/4, 13/8), a violent metamorphosis that sunders the young man into "two separate Quentins." The listener who is enthralled with the "old ghost-times" and the storyteller who looks ahead to Harvard and beyond communicate to one another past the word in the potent "long silence of notpeople, in notlanguage" (9/4–5). That "long silence" of the "twenty years' heritage" from his father and grandfather and the town's "eighty years' heritage" (11/7) resounds in the present that harbors the two Quentins' destiny, to become one with his "baffled ghosts" (9/4). Miss Rosa's speaking voice, though factitious, converts an "elapsed" into a "yet-elapsing" *"happen"* that overwhelms the young man's future.

Incongruities proliferate as the individual voices, each a conglomerate of voices and time, displace one another and merge in Faulkner's narrative. The story opens with the singularly pure voice of an objective narrator, henceforth, the Omniscient.[3] Without any sign of transition, that objective voice metamorphoses into Quentin's voice summarizing the whole Sutpen history, then twice more to its "violent . . . end." At the same time, Quentin laces his synopsis with the old lady's thoughts and feelings and repeatedly cites her (*"Miss Rosa Coldfield says"*) as his source of information (9–11/5–7). Those germinal encapsulations of the saga produce enlarging *"ripples"* through the work and recast the temporal and narrational status of succeeding chapters. What the printed text represents as the forthcoming and "yet-elapsing" tales of Miss Rosa and of Father have actually "elapsed" at some indefinite past time when the young man heard those tellers narrate their refractions of the legend. That Quentin "had grown up" with the legend, "breathing the same air and hearing his father talk about the man Sutpen," so he *"knew it all already, had learned, absorbed it already without the medium of speech"* (11–12/7), explains in part the incongruity. But his foreknowledge of events specific to each narrator's angle suggests untold occasions when Miss Rosa and Father (assisted by the Omniscient) recounted their tales. Those hidden episodes allow Quentin's voice to supplant the actual speakers, as well as the ghosts echoing through their voices. In the second half of the novel, Shreve in turn commands information beyond Quentin's resources in the printed text, and even displaces voices he has never heard.

The author himself assumes the existence of those virtual occasions in the fall when Quentin, approximating the words and voices of narrators heard and unheard, transmits to Shreve the mass of tales both recorded and unrecorded in his sources.[4] Faulkner declares, "The story was told by Quentin to Shreve" (*FU* 75), but then he omits those decisive events from his narrative. He instead deliberately contrives an incredible second half that further alters the seemingly ongoing tales of Miss Rosa and Father in the first half. Modulating into something other than their textual guise, they now appear to be parts of Quentin's earlier recountings to his roommate. Faulkner's metamorphic text belies itself as voices merge or displace one another, and as events occurring or yet to occur have already occurred. Adding to the duplicity, untold components of story precipitate the unfolding action. Sounding "a dialogue without words" (111/88), the "implied story" and the worded tale together celebrate the power of the false word to render at once revelation and mystery, and to obtain congruence for the work's "inchoate fragments" and belief for its truth/lie. A narrative shaped along the lines of Quentin's (and his author's) premises on time weaves a tissue of incredible/credible deceptions.

Sutpen, "too big," like truth (*FU* 273–74), for anyone to see entire, materializes in a work of "inchoate fragments" the writer fears "wouldn't coalesce" (*FU* 76). But as the spreading *ripples* of a "*happen*" conjoin in "mutual penetration," the novel reveals itself fully in "the long silence of . . . notlanguage" (9/5).[5]

Quentin prescribes not only for a modulant form, but also for the content of an implausible tale. Narrative should hold "at least some regard for *cause and effect* even if none for logical sequence and continuity" (247/199, italics added). Foregoing "logical sequence and continuity" in form and substance, the disjunct novel records the intermittent progress of causation traversing the formal design of counterpointed segments, uncoiling from Quentin's germinal summation of the violent founding of the dynasty to its violent end. Balancing the exercise of free will and choice are the recurrent signals of responsibility for action: a "Creditor" who demands payment for "*hereditary evil and harm*" (178–82/145–48); "nature" that "held a balance and kept a book," exacting vengeance for the "old unsleeping blood" (251/202); the "current of retribution and fatality" that a "minor tactical mistake" of moral "innocence" initiates (269/216, 265/213); and "a fate, a doom" that hounds the man until he has "*Paid*" enough "to balance the books" (325/260). Sutpen himself recognizes the force of causality: "Perhaps a man builds for his future in more ways than one, . . . toward actions and the subsequent irrevocable courses of resultant action which his weak senses and intellect cannot foresee but which ten or twenty or thirty years from now he will take, will have to take in order to survive the act" (243/196). The "old impotent logic and morality" (279/224), as the older Compsons mistakenly label the force of deed and consequence, prove to be an inexorable agency in human affairs. The sporadic but infallible course of causation regenerates the past in the present and future, and gains for fabrication a degree of credulity.

Miss Rosa's refraction of the old legend, the paradigm for other narrators, including the author who records their tales, may flout logic and reason, but, her true purpose, Quentin surmises, is to retrace the line from action to reprisal. She wants her people to "*know at last why God let us lose the War: that only through the blood of our men and the tears of our women could He stay this demon and efface his name and lineage from the earth*" (11/6). Ironically, ravaging a whole nation to obliterate one man does not "*efface*" Sutpen; it immortalizes him. The hyperbole underlines the work's moral base: the sacrifice of life requites evildoing and opens the possibility of amending the "allotted course" (11/7) of a person or a people. Woven in the tapestry of Southern history and the divine plan, fabulation obtains a semblance of "reality."

Absalom, Absalom! bears the "hallmark of the true self-conscious novel," which is a "keen perception of paradox in the relationship between fiction and reality."[6] Illusory evocations are *"incorrect and false and worthy only of the name of dream"*; yet *"true wisdom"* does *"comprehend that there is a might-have-been which is more true than truth"* (143/115). Quentin, who, like Miss Rosa, discredits fact, insists, *"If I had been there I could not have seen it this plain"* (190/155). His hearing and "seeing" and remembering engender the *"might-have-been,"* fables of the imagination that, free from the temporal or "logical sequence and continuity" of real happenings, assume a quality neither true nor false, but a truth/lie. As Shreve and Quentin discover, "the creating of this shade" involves "sifting and discarding the false and conserving *what seemed true*" so as "to overpass to love" or some other truth; in the telling then, "there might be paradox and inconsistency but nothing fault nor false" (316/253, italics added). Faulkner celebrates in theory and fiction the paradoxical enterprise of suspending "truth" in falsehood and thus reanimating the past in the present. As deceitful as the word, Faulkner's tale is not what it appears to be.

II

Like Quentin, who foreknows the information he has yet to receive and supplants Father and many tellers before his time, the alien Shreve relates facts unrecorded in Quentin's sources and, more incredibly, usurps recounting a legend unknown to him. Like the first half, untold "elapsed" events underlie and gain for the "logic- and reason-flouting" (22/15) second half (chapters 6–9) an aura of believability. Father's letter about the death of Miss Rosa initiates the present action when, on a cold January evening, the Harvard roommates recall to new life the "dead" past. The southerner would logically be the primary teller; but, like Quentin's inexplicable knowledge of as yet untold facts in the first half, the Canadian dominates the antiphonal exchange with his comprehensive knowledge of a remote Southern tale. More improbably,

Shreve overhears Quentin's unspoken reflections and addresses the specific point, or retells the episode, or replaces Father who recounts to his son what his father General Compson heard from Sutpen himself.

Only Quentin could have provided Shreve the details of Southern history and the Sutpen story. Nowhere does the narrative record that covert action, though it does certify its existence. Quentin reports Shreve's queries about the South through the fall: "and that not Shreve's first time, nobody's first time in Cambridge since September: *Tell about the South. What's it like there. What do they do there. Why do they live there. Why do they live at all"* (174/142). Like Quentin, who at the beginning had already heard the tales that the text falsely represents as yet to come, Shreve has obtained before the present action a wide range of information that now enables him to anticipate and preempt the retelling of many episodes. Implausibilities nonetheless flout credibility. Shreve hears and interrupts Quentin's silent recollection of Miss Rosa's trip to Sutpen's Hundred and rehearses the history of the old woman and Sutpen. Listening to Shreve, Quentin thinks, *"He sounds just like father"* (175–81/143–47), the main source of information he transmitted to Shreve, who now supplants Father, the narrator identified in the text. The displacements of voice and time and space become increasingly complex through the evening. Quentin thinks Shreve sounds like Father, but in fact both Father and Shreve sound like Quentin.

Other improbable situations confirm indirectly the hidden exchanges in the fall. The text depicts Father at the site recounting to his son the history of the Sutpen tombstone, while Quentin silently protests at having to listen to a lengthy tale he already knows (193/157). In the midst of Father's narration, and without any signal of a change of speakers, Quentin unaccountably directs his protest at Shreve, who last spoke twenty pages back: *"I have heard too much, I have been told too much; I have had to listen to too much, too long . . . Yes, Shreve sounds almost exactly like father."* Father then ostensibly resumes his tale, but again Shreve takes over as Quentin muses, *"and now I am having to hear it all over again because he sounds just like father"* (207–11/168–71). Shreve's implausible presence in Mississippi with Father and Quentin translates the episode to another time and place, some occasion in the fall when Quentin rehearsed Father's tale to Shreve, who now recounts for

Father. Decidedly absent from the graveyard scene, the Canadian may displace Father, whose words, filtered earlier through Quentin's voice, have become part of his lexicon. The temporal pattern of this unlikely episode is of a past long elapsed, but still elapsing in the present that is its future.

As Miss Rosa's potent voice conjures to life a "long-dead object" (7/3), Quentin's voice in turn empowers Shreve to instill with living blood "shadows" that "perhaps had never existed at all anywhere" (303/243). Shreve surmises motives and actions that elude Quentin: the rejected wife's scheme to avenge herself on Sutpen (chapter 8); why Sutpen insults Rosa (180/146–47) and prohibits Judith's marriage to Bon (295–96/237); why Bon would rather die than give up Judith (chapters 7 and 8, in particular, 340–45/272–75), yet replaces Judith's picture with the octoroon and her son (358–59/286–87). He also solves the riddle of the wounded son's identity (344–45/275). Miss Rosa's voice takes Quentin eight decades back; now Shreve's voice transports the two of them to forty-six years earlier where they become one with the "shades" and enact Henry's encounter with his father Sutpen, whose repudiation leads to the older son Bon's despair (*"No word to me? No word at all?"*), and eventually, to his murder, Henry's exile, and the destruction of the Sutpen dynasty (303/243, 351–58/280–86). Shreve alludes to the scythe's "symbolic shape" and Sutpen's death (177–78/145) before Quentin recalls the incident *in his mind* (185–87/152). Quentin's voice alone would be "unreal," but Shreve's voice entwined with his imparts to the tale "something of reality, . . . believable, creditable," Faulkner claims (*FU* 75). Shreve's voice in fact augments the incredible, but its contrapuntal role, a mocking echo of Quentin's fatal obsession with the past that would not die, moves the *"ripples"* on, "yet-elapsing."

Shreve's model for the specious storyteller is, of course, Quentin, who apprehends Miss Rosa's thoughts before she relates her story, and anticipates Father's reconstruction of what Sutpen told General Compson about his early years and his family, what the General told his son Mr. Compson—events Quentin himself had not witnessed (see chapter 7, for example). In the middle of Quentin's long account, Shreve, who like Quentin, "already knows" the story from repeated listening in the fall, takes over the telling. Quentin's silent response distills the work's strategy of diffusion and confluence that recasts the verbal surfaces of narrative: *"Maybe we are both*

*Father. Maybe nothing ever happens once and is finished. Maybe
happen is never once but like ripples maybe on water after the pebble sinks, the ripples moving on, spreading . . . to the next pool
which the first pool feeds . . . Yes, we are both Father. Or maybe
Father and I are both Shreve, maybe it took Father and me both to
make Shreve or Shreve and me both to make Father or maybe
Thomas Sutpen to make all of us*" (261–62/210). (Italics, the standard type for the inner voice, represent Quentin's thoughts here, but
more often misrepresent the spoken words of Miss Rosa [chapter 5]
and other speakers.) From a single source, Sutpen's story spreads
through converging voices. The single voice, another textual mis-
representation, is now openly belied: "Shreve speaking, though
save for the slight . . . [(]differences not in tone or pitch but of turns
of phrase and usage of words[)], it might have been either of them
and was in a sense both: both thinking as one, the voice which happened to be speaking the thought only the thinking become audible,
vocal" (303/243). This "happy marriage of speaking and hearing"
(316/253) may account for the uniform style, often singled out for
criticism. Quentin, through whose supervening voice the eighty-
year cumulation of voices overlaid with many tones and angles
reaches Shreve, delivers the burden of many decades in a stylized
manner that Shreve in turn reechoes. The language of oral narration
that revivifies "elapsed" time is notable even for Faulkner for its
fabulous, expansive gestures.

Incredible narrators like Quentin or Shreve, the dumb Benjy in
The Sound and the Fury, or the clairvoyant Darl in *As I Lay Dying*
underscore the fictionality of fiction. But the aim of the process of
speaking–hearing–re-creating is to render, despite "paradox and inconsistency," what "seemed true" ("love" for Quentin and Shreve)
and, transcending falsity, to claim belief for its lie (316/253). Faulkner's fabrication deceives to reveal the hidden, lies to tell a "truth."
The transmutations of that lie may be close to indecipherable, like
Father's letter, which, even without the "added distortion" of lying
half-raised at the crease, Quentin finds almost impossible to read.
Increasing the distortion is the mismatch between an antithetic,
modulant form and a "distinct, uncomplex" story of "simple passion and simple violence" and its consequences (89/71, 101/80).
Storytelling, however, is not about simple human gestures, but
about the different ways of refracting those "inexplicable" gestures
(101/80) or, as the author puts it, "thirteen ways of looking at a

blackbird" that evoke the reader's fourteenth way. What the printed word veils, untold yet *there*, tantalizes and induces the reader to join the numberless voices resurrecting the legend.

The paradox of the potent word's credible truth/lie that inspires Sutpen's "design" and frames Faulkner's tale of the man's rise and fall materializes in a "scrap of paper" that Judith Sutpen claims, may not "mean anything in itself," but like "*spreading . . . ripples*," would "be remembered even if only from passing from one hand to another, one mind to another, and it would be at least a scratch" (127/101). "That scratch, that undying mark on the blank face of the oblivion to which we are all doomed" (129/102) rejuvenates itself in a cycle of hearing and retelling "that is immortal since it will always move" (*LG* 253). Faulkner's "scratch" recounts an elapsed "*happen*" resurging to new life in an ever-elapsing present and future.

A playful element characteristic of reflexive fiction assumes the reader remains unenlightened about the South and its legends, like Shreve, who was not born there, or even like Quentin, who was born there. Yet the high stakes in this serious play leave open the possibility that if, with luck or hard work, we discern through these "shadows" and "shades" the "presence of volatile and sentient forces" (101/80), then we will gain something forever. We glimpse through "*obscurity's myriad components*" the "complete picture . . . scarce-seen yet ineradicable" and, like an old letter, "almost indecipherable, yet meaningful" (143/115, lll/88, 10l/80). We also risk, as do Sutpen and Quentin, contriving our own unreal but compelling refraction. To Shreve's question about the South, "*Why do they live at all?*," Quentin offers no affirming defense, only his own terrible sense of desolation: "Nevermore of peace. Nevermore Nevermore Nevermore" (373/299). Evoking "harmless" yet "deadly" ghosts, Sutpen's story warns us, is perilous. Shreve envisions a dark world overrun with idiotic Jim Bonds (378/302).

The second half of Mr. Compson's letter (204 pages after the first half) counterpoints the young men's despair with conjectures about Miss Rosa's peculiar but partially fulfilling heaven ("*perhaps there is*"), the possibility of hope reified in a frozen yet renascent redworm, and the power of the "*written*" word, a "scratch" that, typical of Faulkner's antithetic form and creed, now overpasses the treacherous word: "*It will do no harm to hope—You see I have written hope, not think. So let it be hope*" (377/302). For though life declines inexorably to doom and death, there remains the counter-struggle to renew life perpetually. If a book is an author's one more completed step toward oblivion, it offers nonetheless, like Miss Rosa's *"dream"* of *"freedom,"* a fabrication that *"mirrors and repeats (repeats? creates, reduces to a fragile evanescent iridescent sphere) all of space and time and massy earth."* The mind may be a dangerous tool of human illusion and delusion, Sutpen and his true heir, Quentin, discover; but the writer who subdues the false/potent word to inscribe his incredible/credible *"dream,"* proclaims the *"freedom"* of the imagination to enclose *"all of space and time and massy earth"* in a *"fragile evanescent"* yet prismatic totality in whose magical circle life regenerates itself, like *"ripples moving on, spreading."* Those who dare enter it must seek *"no boon of death but only how to re-create, renew."* For, as Miss Rosa claims, *"There is a might-have-been which is more true than truth, . . . the single rock we cling to above the maelstrom of unbearable reality"* (143/114–15, 149–50/120).

4

The Sound and the Fury: Voice and Structure

I

AMONG FAULKNER'S MANY COMMENTS ON HIS NOVEL *THE SOUND and the Fury* (1929), he reiterates through the decades two claims. The first refers to the Benjy section he set at the beginning during a late stage of revision: "The story, the book is all there in that first section" (UV TS of "The Introduction to *The Sound and the Fury*," p. 5).[1] What "that idiot child saw" establishes "the groundwork of that story" (*FU* 63–64). The seeds of character and action encoded in the opening section and amplified through the succeeding chapters confirm its genetic position. More importantly, the first section establishes the implausible voice of a dumb idiot ("deef and dumb," according to Luster [60/49]) that renders the essence of each person, including himself, and the Compson world of orphan-like children, irrevocable loss, and decay. Faulkner admits Benjy "probably hasn't" either the "qualities" or the voice of a story-teller, "which is the fact, but maybe he should, which is the truth" (*FWP* 116). A truth/lie, the work then becomes as duplicitous as the voiced word.

The second statement, repeated many more times, specifies the purpose for writing the book. The "beautiful one, . . . my heart's darling" was *what I wrote the book about*," using "what seemed to me the proper tools to try to tell, try to draw the picture of Caddy" (*FU* 6, italics added). Faulkner's reformulations of the germ or source of his "most gallant failure" all center on the coura-geous but "doomed little girl" whose muddy drawers he labels the story's "symbolical" image (*LG* 180, 245; *FWP* 111).[2] But in this story that would not get told (four tries, with the fifth in an Appen-dix seventeen years later), the image fails to find itself the right tale, and the girl's drawers merge with other images of degeneration ("a story of blood gone bad" [*LG* 222]). Caddy herself remains in shadow after the opening section, and eventually disappears. But her voice, sounded through the Benjy section, then stilled, resonates through the empty years in Benjy's hopeless cry, Quentin's haunted consciousness, Jason's hostility, and her daughter's misery. Faulkner's major strategy against his treacherous medium, the word transformed to voice, may provide a clue to the degree he achieves his intent, "to tell a story of Caddy" (*FU* 17).

Voice, just below silence in Faulkner's hierarchy of language, weaves a fabric of "image" and "sound" that amplifies sense beyond the word in silence. The formative effect of the voiced word on technique and structure and on the meaning of the whole work clarifies as well the question of its true source. Typical of his contrapuntal maneuver, Faulkner sets alongside Benjy's germinal voice a rival but requisite source, Caddy's singular inflections. Benjy's implausible yet reliable voice and chronicle initiate the counterprocess of confluence and diffusion from germ to variant expansions that designs the partitioned narrative. Caddy's compassionate tone, on the other hand, initiates modulations of being that concurrently reinforce the formal pattern of germ and evolvements, and also advances the theme of the work.

Quentin Compson, who in *Absalom, Absalom!* experiences the storytelling voice evoke "shadows" to life, witnesses in *The Sound and the Fury* a similar display of the power of the voiced word. He hears three fisherboys, though without hope of winning the $25 prize for an elusive old trout, argue over their plans for the money: "They all talked at once, their voices insistent and contradictory and impatient, making of unreality a possibility, then a probability, then an incontrovertible fact, as people will when their desires become words" (145/117).[3] "Voices insistent and contradictory," analogues of Faulkner's principles of repetition and contradiction, transmute "unreality" to "possibility," then to "probability," and finally to "incontrovertible fact." The process of conversion is deceptive, for the presence the boys iterate as their "desires become words" is an absence, a "lie."

The speaking voice creates of "dream" a falsehood, but the *tone* underlying voice transforms the voiced word to an ideogram of being and mind. Diction, sound, rhythm, and other components of style determine the quality of voice, but the motive driving the word sets the pitch.[4] Whether it is the "utilitarian" language of everyday life or the "immaterial" language of the imagination or intuition (Bergson's terms, *CM* 80, *CE* 175; see Abbreviations for the list of Bergson's works), tone of voice heightens the power of the word. The two modes of utterance combined serve the egocentric ends of Quentin and Jason, or the more elevated "desires" of Caddy, Dilsey, and the Reverend Shegog. When Quentin's "desires become words," his voice seeks an end opposite to that of the fisherboys, to dismantle fact and feed delusion or self-deception. Jason wields his vicious monotone to obtain reprisal for an illusory injustice. Counterpointing them and the factitious-toned mother and her feckless brother, the despair-ridden Father, the unkind Luster, and the uncaring Miss Quentin are Caddy's cadences, unheard elsewhere among her kin, and Dilsey's steady voice that tends to the decaying family and also comprehends the larger pattern of days beyond the Compsons' sad ones. The Reverend Shegog's transformative voice, not for self-destruction like Quentin's, traverses the limits of Caddy's voice and transports his people past the word and the world to the "incontrovertible fact" of renascent life beyond death.

Tzvetan Todorov thus declares: "One does not speak about the meaning of the words but about the voice which utters them." The word converted to *tone* of voice renders the quality of being, stratifies time and sense, and sets disjunct parts resonating inside each other. Literature then becomes language empowered in form that surpasses the word and infuses its silence.[5]

Benjy, a category by himself, is the author's supreme deception, a mute idiot who utters the voice of revelation. Without distortion or bias, this spurious/credible narrator records the sounds and beings of people around him and detects the truth behind the false word or deed. But true to his contrapuntal mode, Faulkner enlaces Benjy's distinct tone with multiple voices from different periods of Compson history and instantly consolidates time: the boy Quentin's sensitive inflections, the harsh voice of Jason the child and the man, Dilsey's caring pitch, and the varied intonations of other people around him. Caddy's gentle modulations weave in and out of those voices, from the present action in 1928, back to the 1910s, and further to 1898, the year of Damuddy's death. The entwined tones delineate the unvoiced inner life of the child-man, who through the decades hears among a cacophony of voices the one missing voice (see II).

Readers have ascribed a specific time frame to each main speaker. Benjy in the present, Quentin in the past, Jason in the future, and Dilsey in the "timeless."[6] The simple classification may serve some purpose, but as voices and time planes permeate and inflect one another, the frame modulates. Through the present and extended future swirling about him, Benjy perpetually returns to a past plenitude of his sister's kindly presence and voice. The many voices feeding into Quentin's shame and self-disgust at his failure to save his sister or the family from dishonor impel him toward the future cessation of time. Jason's bitter pitch funnels other voices toward a present that perpetually promises restitution for a fancied injustice (see III). An objective narrator chronicles events in succession, and locates Dilsey, not in the "timeless" generally attributed to her, but within earthly time of beginnings that lead to endings: "I seed de beginnin, en now I sees de endin' (371/297). The Omniscient also records the power of the false word to transcend temporality and release the black people from the prison of language and materiality to spiritual revelation (see IV).

II

An implausible narrative signifying the contrary accomplishes the writer's intent, to surpass the word. Though "he himself didn't know what he was seeing" (*FU* 64), Benjy "smells" the true import of events, the fact of "funeral" in a subterfuge like "party" (43/ 36), and makes plain with his wordless cry what everyone would conceal, that his sister's wedding occasions not joy but lamentation. Quentin confirms his brother's unerring sense: "He took one look at her and knew. Out of the mouths of babes" (124/100). The synecdoche rings darkly ironic, for though a babe with no speaking tongue, his cry manifests what speech veils. Benjy's words deny what they designate, but in Todorov's terms, the word then begins to signify. In the "quest for meaning," he says, one searches "not for what the word designates, but for what it signifies."[7]

The Benjy section initiates the technique of mixed voices and converged time, and frames a structure from germs of character and action that, like the motifs in musical counterpoint, undergo "continuous expansion" through the work. Benjy's unreal yet true voice inscribes the exact pitch of his people and their true being. The sensible Dilsey sounds the note of reason and order among the Compson disarray. Jason is a grown man in the present action (1928) with "his hands in his pocket" (12/11), a gesture reenacted backward in time when the five-year-old (1898) appears with "his hands in his pocket and he fell down," then threatens to "tell" on everyone because the bow and arrow Quentin had made for him is "broke now" (27/23, 23/20) The recurrent images and distinct tone prefigure the treacherous, self-serving man in the third chapter. The nine-year-old Quentin, who could not eat his supper because he heard "Mother . . . crying" and knew it was over the dying Damuddy (30–31/25–27), shows a sensibility that ultimately overwhelms the young man. The self-pitying mother's "I'll be gone soon" (12/12), and hollow, "my poor baby," counterpoints the seven-year-old Caddy's transparent tone: "You're not a poor baby. Are you. You've got your Caddy. Haven't you got your Caddy" (8/8–9). Benjy alone registers his sister's unique inflections of sympathy for the lesser ones, damaged humans and nonhumans. Once sounded, Caddy's voice sets off countertones against the self-engrossed voices around her. Its failure, on the other hand, highlights the steady though unavailing voice of the faithful Dilsey and the black preacher's resonant timbre that, surmounting human limitations, attains a higher reality. Quentin unravels fact with dissembling speech, and Jason fabricates with word and deed his distorted world, but the idiot's specious yet reliable words disclose unwarped the truth and in silence pass judgment on them all.

Germinal events in the Benjy section and their modulations in the next chapters reecho in one another and sound overtones past the word. Damuddy's wake (1898) that Caddy espies from a pear tree, entwines with Caddy's wedding (1910) that the bellowing Benjy glimpses through a window (47–48/39–40). Quentin's recollection of the event at Harvard in the second section is interrupted by Shreve, who mocks his dressed-up roommate, "Is it a wedding or a wake?" (100/82). The ironic polarity encompasses the Compsons' "long history." The original happy/sad wedding that boded devastation and death for the family portends Quentin's suicide, for which he has put on a formal attire, and Jason's vain search for his loss in the third and fourth chapters. A minor incident like Luster's search for a lost quarter that Faulkner added to the first pages during a late revision,[8] characterizes without explicit gloss other people's pursuits. Quentin's search for *"the clean flame"* to exorcise time's desecrations (144)/116) and for water "running swift and peaceful" to end his life (167/135) turns Luster's hunt to parody. On the other hand, Jason's protracted but fruitless chase for revenge and for the money he filched from his niece appears as trivial as Luster's search. Ironic counterechoes conjoin the "series of pieces" evolving from the beginning through the following chapters.

Benjy's time "is," says the author, and most readers agree; but Henri Bergson's concept of "true duration" reconfigures that "is" to an "undivided present" in which the past, filled with the beloved's voice and being, perpetually haunts the long future bereft of her presence. The singular inflections of the true "Caddy," weaving in and out of voices echoing through the past/present/future, signify the years lying in wait for her brother, empty but for the false "caddie." His forlorn cry at the opening scene in 1928, when a golfer calls for his "caddie," emblematizes that long privation after the true Caddy leaves in 1910. The derisive Luster's attempts to quiet the idiot disclose indirectly the ever "yet-elapsing" past in Benjy's protracted present and future: "Listen at you, now. . . . Aint you something, thirty-three years old, going on that way. . . . Hush up that moaning" (1–2/3). The ten-year-old Caddy's gentle tone addressing her six-year-old brother in 1901 cuts into Luster's harsh voice, an intrusion that establishes a pattern of "complete antithesis" among the alternating voices and temporal junctures. She guides him through a maze of words, like keeping his hands in his pockets so they won't *"get froze."* Having *"uncaught"* Benjy from the fence nail, Caddy tells him to *"stoop over,"* then gestures to help him understand, *"Like this, see."* Benjy can then report, *"We stooped over and crossed the garden."* Going by the pig pen, Caddy muses about the pigs, *"I expect they're sorry because one of them got killed today"* (3/4–5). Such cadences resonate through the long silences of her absence, for no other voice strikes that note of intuitive empathy for less fortunate beings.

Only Caddy seeks to penetrate the idiot's speechlessness, "What is it. What are you trying to tell Caddy." The solicitous gesture and voice evoke Benjy's formula of comfort: "Caddy smelled like trees and like when she says we were asleep." Luster's bark in 1928 shatters the moment: *"What are you moaning about"* (5/6). The next 1901 shift prompts the same mantra of security, "Caddy knelt and put her arms around me and her cold bright face against mine. She smelled like trees. 'You're not a poor baby. Are you. You've got your Caddy.' " Luster again blasts that assurance, *"Can't you shut up that moaning and slobbering . . . Aint you shamed of yourself, making all this racket"* (8/9). The juxtaposition of the two voices is illusory, for Caddy has disappeared years before Luster comes on the scene. (Caddy, born in 1891, leaves home after her wedding in 1910; Luster is born in 1914.) But their violent collocation enfolds present and future in the past, inscribing in the fullness of Caddy's presence the long years resonating with his cries for the "loss of her" (Appendix 423/the Corrected Text omits the Appendix), who "loved him and would defend him, and . . . was the whole world to him," the author explains (*FU* 64). (Benjy may have lived until 1935, two years after Jason commits him to the insane asylum.)

His sister's voice incessantly permeates Benjy's consciousness. In a segment from about 1912, after Caddy has left home and Quentin and Father have died, Benjy recollects the "shapes" flowing "bright and fast and smooth, like when Caddy says we are going to sleep." Luster's sudden taunt dispels the comforting evocation: *"Cry baby . . . Aint you shamed . . . You aint got no spotted pony to ride now"* (13/12). The fallen barn roof pictures the obliteration of everything that Caddy signifies for Benjy. Accenting that loss, a 1901 episode resurfaces (missing in the Holograph manuscript) when Caddy again holds Benjy's frozen hands and comforts him. She then takes him on a secret mission for Uncle Maury past the intact barn where they hear the cows and horses stomping inside. The smoke by the branch reminds her of the Christmas pig, "That's where they are killing the pig." With that innate compassion, she breaks a piece of ice and holds it against Benjy's face, saying, "Ice. That means how cold it is" (13-14/12–13). The addition underlines Caddy's unique role, to touch and give voice to a being locked in wordlessness, and thus to open a world closed to the idiot.

A longer 1928 segment follows the scene above, and the next event cycles back to 1898 (19/17) when Damuddy is dying and the children are playing in the stream. From this point on until the end of the section, scenes from the present action in 1928 continue to intrude among past episodes chronicling the deaths in the family, Caddy's first encounters with boys, and, finally, her wedding. At the end of the ceremony, Caddy comforts the wailing Benjy as she has always done, but with reverse effect: "Caddy put her arms around me, and her shining veil, and I couldn't smell trees anymore and I began to cry" (48/40). The end of Benjy's formula of perfection signals the frustration of Caddy's compassionate nature and Benjy's deprivation of "the tenderness, the help, to shield him in his innocence" (*FN* 104).

The Caddy germinal "moment" stands by itself, unmatched among the Compsons (Dilsey is not a Compson). Contrapuntal form valorizes without explicit assertion this true-toned voice rising above the harsh sounds of the false-toned Mother, the indifferent Quentin, the savage Jason, and the self-absorbed Miss Quentin who calls the idiot "pig." Father's cynical strain, neither deliberately mean nor false but incapable of affection or wisdom, fails to enlighten his children about death or family loyalty. It is Caddy, her voice turning fierce, who chastises Jason for cutting up Benjy's paper dolls. Jason acts on "meanness" (79/65), but Father colors everything meaningless. Father's words on human beings, nothing but "dolls stuffed with sawdust swept up from the trash heaps where all previous dolls had been thrown away" (218/175) attend Quentin at his death. Quentin in *Absalom, Absalom!* is an "empty hall" echoing with ghost voices, but *The Sound and the Fury* attests, it is finally by Father's voice that Quentin lives and dies.

In the concluding fourth section, the thirty-three-year old Benjy continues "wailing in his hoarse, hopeless voice" as the golfers call, "Here caddie." Luster, knowing the cause of Benjy's cry, takes pleasure in torturing him: " 'You want somethin to beller about?' . . . then he whispered: 'Caddy! Beller now. Caddy! Caddy! Caddy!' " Even the faithful Dilsey could not put things right for Benjy, or for anyone else (394–96/315–17). Benjy's ongoing present and future, turning upon a vanished past filled with the pure voice and touch of the true Caddy, yield nothing but the mock "caddie," an icon of the false/potent word.

Benjy renders Caddy's intonations that, unrefracted by delusory language or intent, rise above the unloving Compsons' frequencies. Caddy in turn hears and responds to the "voiceless misery" in Benjy's voice. That absent figure's inflections of love, sounded in the first section and silenced in succeeding sections (the woman who reappears briefly in the Jason section speaks an altered tone), silently appraises every strain of Benjy's dehumanization and plumbs his people's indifference, hypocrisy, malice, or despair. Together

Benjy's fallacious voice of truth and Caddy's empathic tones set the touchstones of veracity and humanity for the other voices.[9]

The "mutual penetration" of heterogeneous parts of form and substance "redoubles everything" (Fredric Jameson's phrase); "everything has already been foretold," and "foretells what will follow," Tzvetan Todorov adds.[10] The first half of *The Sound and the Fury* seems like a "resonant . . . remembering," the storytelling mode in *Absalom, Absalom!*, and even the current action in the second half appears to replicate past events or promises fulfilled. The discrete parts played "against each other . . . contrapuntally" *(LG 36)* precondition story to paradox and irony, and send echoes spiraling beyond the word.

III

With the false word Quentin converts not the unreal to "incontrovertible fact," as the fisherboys do, but fact to "unreality." Time then becomes his enemy. Father persuades his son to "forget" time "now and then for a moment and not spend all your breath trying to conquer it" (93/76). But an unbearable past overwhelms the young man's present and impels both into the future when time would cease: "It's not even time until it was," when "I am" becomes "I was not. . . . And then I'll not be. The peacefullest words" (222/178, 216/174).

But as "desires become words" for Quentin, who longs to end the "long diminishing parade of time" (94/76) and of being, the word fails him. He registers present events with the sensitivity he showed as a child, but the sharp details disintegrate in a confused melding of the past and the future. The morning of his suicide, he pictures vividly the sparrow on his window ledge: "His eye was round and bright. First he'd watch me with one eye then flick! and it would be the other one, his throat pumping faster than any pulse. The hour began to strike. The sparrow quit swapping eyes and watched me steadily with the same one until the chimes ceased, as if he were listening too. Then he flicked off the ledge and was gone." That graphic present action instantly decomposes in a chaos of past chimes, "still ringing in the long dying light-rays and Jesus and Saint Francis talking about his sister," and finally in a future "hell" where time is "finished," and there would be nobody else "but her and me." But still in life for a few more hours, Quentin recalls his attempts to obliterate with the voiced word the horror of fact. The "sound" of the spurious "incest" would erase the fact of Caddy's promiscuity "as though it had never been." When Father asks if he tried to make Caddy do it, he replies: "i was afraid she might and then it wouldnt have done any good but if i could tell you we did it would have been so and then the others wouldnt be so and then the world would roar away" (219–20/177). But no words or sounds may undo past or present, and time, the "mausoleum of all hope and desire," as Father puts it, must be annihilated (93/76).

A clear-sighted Caddy offsets Quentin's logocentric view. When Quentin asks, *"Why must you marry somebody Caddy,"* she points up her brother's delusion, *"Do you want me to say it do you think that if I say it it wont be"* (151/122). Caddy confronts a reality no words may expunge, and the grown woman in the third section acknowledges she has lost her child forever (260/209–10). Quentin, on the other hand, unpacks his fevered brain with words, although he does recognize the value of the unspoken: "I suppose that people, using themselves and each other so much by words, are at least consistent in attributing wisdom to a still tongue" (146/118). But drowning in words and voices, he fails to catch the "wisdom" the Easter congregation discerns in silence beyond words.

Quentin's efforts to undo a past reality with the spoken word fail as Caddy and Benjy relentlessly haunt him, and dominate, as Caddy does Benjy's consciousness, the overlay of people and events in his memory and through the extended present action of his last day. The two at first materialize in tag-ends of thought, or eruptions of oblique references to Caddy ("that never had a sister," "Did you ever have a sister?" [94/76, 96/78]), or fragments of Benjy's reactions to his fallen sister, as though they touched a nerve Quentin could not bear. A quarter of the way into the chapter, however, extended scenes from their childhood, Caddy's sexual adventures, and finally her marriage breach the present. Recollecting the time he learns of her pregnancy evokes a memory of the broken bone that had to be broken again (140/113). No subterfuge may efface fact, Quentin eventually realizes, as the past resurges to life with the immediacy of ongoing events. His despair precipitates in a cascade of words picturing Benjy's reaction to the "incontrovertible fact" of Caddy's fall, the signal of the end of her loving touch for the idiot and the beginning of Quentin's search for annihilation: *"one minute she was standing in the door the next minute he was pulling at her dress and bellowing his voice hammered back and forth between the walls in waves and she shrinking against the wall getting smaller and smaller with her white face her eyes like thumbs dug into it until he pushed her out of the room his voice hammering back and forth as though its own momentum would not let it stop as though there were no place for it in silence bellowing*" (154/ 124). Agonizing images of the past overwhelms a present only the future could still.

Thirty pages later the scene with Benjy recurs. While the smell of honeysuckle mingles with "*the horror the clean flame,*" Quentin asks, "*did you love them Caddy,*" and she replies, "*When they touched me I died*" (185/149). That opens a dam of memories recorded in the longest continuous passage on Caddy, when Quentin tries to commit suicide with her, but loses his knife in the water. As futile is his attempt to threaten Dalton Ames away from his sister. The three juxtaposed incidents, interlaced with Father's fatalism, underline Quentin's guilt at his failure to avert Caddy's fall and his desperation over the implacable movement of time, when the family disgrace would ripple on, undeterred by water or fire.

Quentin's "talking" voice in the second chapter, the longest in the novel, amplifies the germ of character recorded in the Benjy section. Each uncoiling from those initial seeds spirals back to the germinal source and adumbrates what follows. The feckless older brother who admonishes the wet Caddy, then falls into the branch with her (20–21/18), and the studious child (76/62, 88/72) who lags behind the other children and has to be fetched after, prefigure the "half-baked Galahad" (136/110), an ineffectual defender of maids and family honor (82–83/67–68, 197–203/159–64). The time- and word-ridden Quentin finds telling easier than acting. Father's dark voice casts a shadow over the son's spirit, but Quentin's dependence on the delusive word finally obliterates meaning: "All stable things had become shadowy paradoxical all I had done shadows all I had felt suffered taking visible form antic and perverse mocking without relevance inherent themselves with the denial of the significance they should have affirmed thinking I was I was not who was not was not who" (211/170). Life, "inherent" like the word "with the denial of the significance" it should have affirmed, leaves Quentin nothing but the end of time and being.

Quentin circumvents fact with guileful words; but when Jason's "desires become words," they erupt in his "impatient," bitter monotone: "Once a bitch always a bitch, what I say" (223/180). He wields the voiced word like a whip (or like the belt he would lay on Miss Quentin) against a world that has frustrated his hope to become a banker. Whether it is Caddy, or her surrogate daughter, or his mother and uncle, or Luster or Dilsey, or Earl, his boss, or the sheriff, or that "damn redneck" customer at the store (242/195), those "damn trifling niggers" or "damn eastern jews" (237/191), "these college professors" (311/249), or those "damn good women" (307/246)—everyone seems to obstruct the way to his desire, to redress that past injustice. Neither his niece nor the money Caddy sends for her, which he appropriates and the girl finally retrieves, means anything but "the job in the bank of which he had been deprived before he ever got it" (382/306). Waging his battle against the past in the present, he recounts action in the past tense but narrates all dialogue, direct and indirect, in the present tense with "I says," or "she says." Voiced words, whether spoken in the distant past or in present action, converge in a perpetual present when every betrayal or injustice becomes vulnerable to Jason's own perfidious word or deed.

Speech and action betray Jason's treacherous nature in the scene when Caddy returns for Father's funeral and offers him fifty dollars to see her daughter Quentin for "a minute": " 'Give me the money,' I says. 'I'll give it to you afterward,' she says. 'Don't you trust me?' I says. 'No,' she says. 'I know you. I grew up with you.' " But she lets her guard down and gives him the money. Waiting until dark, Jason holds up the baby for an instant while the buggy speeds past the unseeing mother. The rabid pitch, colloquial diction, and mixed tenses register Jason's outrage at an injury that the present, which is its future, must requite: "I says I reckon that'll show you. I reckon you'll know now that you cant beat me out of a job and get away with it"; and again, "I says I reckon you'll think twice before you deprive me of a job that was promised me" (253–56/204–6). The tone registers a being warped venomous by empty promise.

Jason's story concludes in the fourth section where an objective narrator, the Omniscient, chronicles successive events entirely in the preterite. The lengthened perspective traces the man's past and present to its culmination in just retribution. The Omniscient echoes Jason's frenzied inflections to record his defiance not only of earthly beings like the sheriff, but divine forces like the "Circum-stance" and the "You" who obstruct his pursuit of his niece and the stolen hoard that belonged to her in the first place: " 'And damn You, too,' he said, 'See if You can stop me,' thinking of himself, his file of soldiers with the manacled sheriff in the rear, dragging Omnipotence down from His throne, if necessary; of the embattled legions of both hell and heaven through which he tore his way and put his hands at last on his fleeing niece" (382/306). The hyperbolic pitch echoes Jason's tone in earlier sections, but the Omniscient's mock-heroic diction that displaces the colloquial speech elevates and, at the same time, derides the man's enterprises. The counter-tones silently appraise the moral quality of action. Jason himself finally discerns "clear and unshadowed the disaster toward which he rushed" (386/310), and watches "his invisible life ravelled out about him like a wornout sock" (391/362).

Benjy's picture of the whining tattler and cheating kite entrepre-neur previews the heartless man who repudiates "the sort of con-science" he has "to nurse like a sick puppy all the time" (284/228) and cheats everyone around him for the loss he blames on the guilty mother and innocent daughter. For meanness the child cuts up Ben-jy's paperdolls; the man now defrauds his kin, taunts Luster with the show tickets before he burns them, and holds in contempt alike the "damn loony," Dilsey, and other black and white people. Dilsey, whose life-nurturing activities censure by contrast Jason's reprehensible course, sums him up, "You's a cold man, Jason, if man you is. . . . I thank de Lawd I got mo heart dan dat, even ef hit is black" (258/207–8). The grown Caddy's appraisal caps Jason's condemnation, "You never had a drop of warm blood in you" (259/209). Some readers admire Jason's hard-headed practicality, but there is no denying the mean spirit of the child now fulfilled in the man. The Quentin and Jason chapters amplify the germs of charac-ter and action in the Benjy section, and reenforce the contrapuntal interplay of disjunct parts.

IV

The Omniscient, the objective voice of the so-called Dilsey sec-tion, shifts from the subjective tones and perspectives of Benjy, Quentin, and Jason to an external view of people and events. But his ornate style and tone modulate and reflect the quality and "desires" of each person. He mimics Jason's frenetic tone and degrades the man; conversely, he dignifies Dilsey's daily ministry and elevates the lowly. He shocks the reader with Benjy's repulsive appearance (342/274) but then endows Benjy's *"moaning and slobbering"* (8/9), as Luster puts it, with universal significance. That "hopeless and prolonged" cry "was nothing. Just sound. It might have been all time and injustice and sorrow become vocal for an instant by a conjunction of planets" (359/288). Its repetition underlines the paradox of a self-immolating novel (originally titled "Twilight") built on "sound" that is "nothing": "But he bellowed slowly, abjectly without tears; the grave hopeless sound of all voiceless misery under the sun" (395/316). Now endued with cosmic dimension, the "nothing" exceeds words in the telling. Benjy's apocalyptic cry lies at the opposite pole of the Easter sermon's hope, but both exemplify the word surpassing itself.

Shifting from the frantic pace of the Jason scenes, the Omniscient adopts a tone of quiet grace and dignity to portray Dilsey's baking ritual and spirit (336/270, 341/274) and of heightened intensity to match the rapture at Easter (366–71/293–97). Dilsey, early in the Benjy section, remains in the background. It is Luster who remarks she bought Benjy's birthday cake with her own money because, she later discloses, Jason would not spare one egg for her to bake it (1–2/3–4, 69/57, 73/60). The tender gesture, derided by the mother, epitomizes Dilsey, the counterforce to selfishness and cruelty. When after Father's death she appears in person, her sensible voice balances the manic voices around her. Though beset by a false-toned clock, Dilsey lives in a present enfolding the past, where she gains the "courage and fortitude" to continue singing her "repetitive" wordless song into the future (331/266, 336/270). That voice of faithful nurturing through several generations silently censures lives devoted to self-interest and ruin.

But, like the other narrators, the Omniscient's voiced word is equivocal. The same high strain that exalts Dilsey's life-nurturing activities also punctuates her failed life mission. She saves no one; yet Dilsey alone offsets the puerile Mother and nihilist Father for whom "no battle is ever won," since "they are not even fought" (93/76). Dilsey gains no abiding victories, but she wages battles, defending the Compsons against themselves. She may not comfort Benjy as Caddy could, but she remains faithful to those who trust

her, as Caddy could not, and holds steadfast against the foolish bul-
let-headed Luster, the heartless Jason, the parasitic Mother, and the
desolate orphan, Miss Quentin. Idealizing her role, however, misses
the counterpoise intrinsic to antithetic form. The irony of her trying
to bring up baby Quentin as she did the other children draws a sneer
from Jason. Her song sounds faint beside Benjy's "hopeless
sound," with which the novel opens and closes (1–2/3–4, 400–401/
320–21). Still, Dilsey remains indomitable: "I does de bes I kin"
(396/317). She endures, Faulkner testifies, because she goes under
"trying to do more than you know how to do. It's trying to defy
defeat even if it's inevitable" (LG 221). After Caddy, Dilsey stands
alone against people who diminish rather than nurture life, and retains virtue and grace in the midst of Compson disarray. Her true
measure lies between her faithful but unavailing ministry. The novel's moral center, as it is in works like The Unvanquished and Go
Down, Moses, upholds neither defeat nor victory, but the enduring
struggle.[11]

Dilsey's time, rather than "timeless," in fact, encompasses "de
first en de last" (371/297, 375/301), the diachronic progression of
the Compsons' unwisdom through past, present, and future. Her vision is apocalyptic, and her song, "without particular tune or
words, . . . mournful and plaintive," laments a dying world, but
being "repetitive" (336/270), suggests the possibility of life re-
newal that she and the other Easter worshippers celebrate.

The Omniscient explores through the Reverend Shegog's intonations the transmutative force of the voiced word. Caddy's tone
counters the voices around Benjy, but her vision and deeds fall
short of her "desires." When the black people's "desires become
words" in the magical tones of their preacher, they reach the ultimate end of word and being, self-transcendence. The Reverend
Shegog's "insistent and contradictory," though never "impatient"
voice beguiles like the fisherboys' voices, but, unlike them, it surmounts the illusory word. He begins "like a white man" with a
"level and cold" voice "too big" for him. The congregation listens
"at first through curiosity, as they would have to a monkey talking," an audience detached from the performer. But witnessing the
"virtuosity" with which he plays "upon the cold inflectionless wire
of his voice," the people forget his "insignificant appearance," and
when he comes to rest with a "swooping glide," they awake as
from a "collective dream" (366/293–94). An artful performance

transports them from reality to an enchantment unlike Quentin's delusions.

The "sad, timbrous quality" of the preacher's other voice, "different as day and dark from his former tone," begins "sinking into their hearts and speaking there again when it had ceased in fading and cumulate echoes." More effectual than the performative one, this transfigurative voice redeems preacher and hearers from their limited selves and from language. "Succubus like" the "voice consumed him, until he was nothing and they were nothing and there was not even a voice but instead their hearts were speaking to one another in chanting measures beyond the need for words" (367/294). Images of "fading" but "cumulate echoes" and hearts speaking in "chanting measures beyond . . . words" reify the silence that holds a higher truth "beyond the need for words."

Shifting from the impersonal, "I tells you," the preacher's incantatory "I sees . . . de arisen dead whut got de blood en de ricklickshun of de Lamb!" resurrects an absent past event in the people's emptied state, a "nothing," now filled with renascence that alters external reality. The preacher's "monkey body" and "monkey face" assume the form of "a serene, tortured crucifix that transcended its shabbiness and insignificance and made it of no moment" (368–70/295–97). Time, too, is "of no moment" as the "dead" past perpetually resurges to new life. The congregation responds on two levels, with words at first, "I sees, O Jesus!" and then "without words, like bubbles rising in water" (370/296).[12] When, unlike the distancing first voice, this "voice took them into itself" (368/295), together the people speak the spirit's wordless tongue.

The sermon, drawing on the reiterative rhythms, present tense verbs, parallelisms, and concentric images of Southern black rhetoric, analogizes language and fiction that, in the hands of Bergson's hero, the "bold novelist," overpasses the shabby insignificance of people and the inadequate word. While the voices of the fisherboys and of Quentin subserve the ends of delusion, the black preacher's voice transforms a seeming "unreality" to the "incontrovertible fact" of life beyond death.

The mystical transfiguration of Dilsey and her people seems to parallel rather than to engage the novel's main course. But the interplay of "elapsed and yet-elapsing time" binds the Easter story with Compson history as a resurgent synchronic event counters a diachronic span bordered with death. Roskus's pronouncement in the first section, *"Taint no luck on this place"* (34–37/29–31), comprehends a panorama of unnatural deaths. Quentin is a suicide and Father virtually so. Mother and the parasitic Uncle Maury, whose actions belie their words, barely exist. Little Maury is sacrificed for Mother's spurious pride in her worthless name, and Caddy, whose "name aint never spoke" is considered dead (37/31) because, in an ironic twist, she "died" for Dalton Ames every time. Miss Quentin, doomed in more ways than her name, regrets being born and wishes they were all dead (234/188, 324/260). Like her mother, she disappears as though she had died. Jason alone survives, but without a heart, continues the Compson death-in-life state. Dilsey sees death within life's spectrum: "Show me the man what aint goin to die"; but Roskus's reply, "Dying aint all" (35/29), passes judgment on the Compsons' life, and conversely, magnifies the death that conquers death itself. The resurrection story obtains full significance counterpointed against the living-dead Compsons.[13] Caddy's voice fostering love in human relations and the preacher's voice attuned to eternity are unduplicated constituents that bear significantly on the structure and theme. But where one voice falters and abandons its people, the other regenerates in the hearts of the congregation a Presence, "elapsed and yet-elapsing." As equivocal as the synchronous antinomies in form, the theme embraces the coexistence of despair and hope, annihilation and resurgence.

Like *Light in August* and *Absalom, Absalom!*, *The Sound and the Fury* poses the same challenge, to give substance to dream with the false word that renders being and mind in silence past the word. "Insistent and contradictory" voices embody the author's repeated efforts to tell with his recalcitrant medium a truth/lie. Structured neither by continuity nor logic, but by interpermeant components, each of which, like Bergson's deeper mental states, "points to what follows and contains what preceded" (*INP* 14–15), the modular narrative perpetually gathers up its horizontal progress in vertical overlays of converged time and meaning. Faulkner's work may have fallen short of his conception, but language turned to interactive voice and silence lifts the word past itself to a mode of knowing.

5

As I Lay Dying: The Voiced and Voiceless/ The Seen and Unseen

. . . if he had said he knew with the words I would not have believed . . .
—Faulkner, *As I Lay Dying*

I

"THE WORDS KILL . . . EXPERIENCE," BUT PEOPLE HAVE NO OTHER means to overcome the "impossibility—or at least the tremendous difficulty—of communication" (*ESPL* 187, *LG* 70).[1] Addie Bundren in *As I Lay Dying* echoes her creator's distrust of the killer/ potent word. But, like him, she has only language to sound her difficulties with the "no good" and seemingly "harmless" word that sunders people from themselves and from one another and, ultimately, perverts life itself. From her deathbed, she reviews her attempts to reach with the word the "secret and selfish life" of her people and, failing that, to escape in God's "dark land" where she hears a "*dark voicelessness* in which the words are the deeds" (162–63/170–71, 165–66/173–74, italics added).[2]

Language offers Addie no recourse, but her author contrives with the voiced words a "dark voicelessness" that tells more than words say. Faulkner explores in *As I Lay Dying* a wide range of linguistic modes, from the transparent utterances of Addie, to the confused involutions of the child Vardaman, to Anse's evident duplicity, and, most significantly, to Darl's explorations in the delusive and revelatory power of the word. Addie articulates without distortion or falsity her disillusionment with language: "Sin and love and fear are just sounds that people who never sinned nor loved nor feared have for what they never had and cannot have until they forget the words" (165–66/174). "People to whom sin is just a matter of words, to them salvation is just words too" (168/176). She condemns the use of the double-sided word to veil true intent, but she herself fails to attain the "dark voicelessness" past the word. It is her rejected son, Darl, who commands the opposite functions of language, the voiced word to deceive or inflict hurt and the voiceless to penetrate the hidden. "He knew *without the words*," Dewey Dell says of her brother, whom she hates for knowing past the word, spoken or unspoken (26/27, italics added). The duplicitous word emblematizes the Bundrens, who, by word or deed, enact a deception or betrayal. Behind the pretense of attending to the dead mother, they pursue their secret "desires." What Henri Bergson labels the "external" language of "social life" that often "turn[s] against the sensation" it seeks to express, corrupts the Bundrens (*CE* 175, *TFW* 130, 132; see Abbreviations for the list of Bergson's works).

Faulkner laments his own inability to match word and "dream," but counterpointed heterogeneous elements in form transmit "not the message," but "a signified which you receive *in addition*, marginally," as Roland Barthes describes the language of "the literature of suspended meaning."[3] Faulkner intensifies that marginal addition with splintered/stratified dissonant parts, that, enhanced with concentric tropes, inflect one another and project sense past the denotative limits of the word. Darl's divided voice and style, entwining the "utilitarian" language of daily life and the "immaterial" language of reflection, manifests his unvoiced self:

> "If you see a good-sized can, you might bring it," I say. Dewey Dell gets down from the wagon, carrying the package. "You had more trouble than you expected, selling those cakes in Mottson," I say. How do our lives ravel out into the no-wind, no-sound, the weary gestures wearily recapitulant: echoes of old compulsions with no-hand on no-strings: in sunset we fall into furious attitudes, dead gestures of dolls. Cash broke his leg and now the sawdust is running out. He is bleeding to death is Cash.
> "I wouldn't be beholden," pa says. "God knows."
> "Then make some water yourself," I say. "We can use Cash's hat." (196–97/206–7)

The second son of a hill-country farmer, Darl speaks a version of his people's dialect, which matches narrator with fictive figure; but he thinks in an elaborately ornate style unbefitting his background, which makes Darl implausible.[4] The disparity reveals past discourse a being emptied of direction or meaning, reified in Mr. Compson's doll image "stuffed with sawdust" (*SF* 218/175). High rhetoric on an unschooled tongue belies credibility but, Faulkner contends, it is a person's way to "justify himself or what he believes himself to be" (*ESPL* 186). As plausible/implausible as the mixture of styles are Darl's alternating points of view, traversing the seen and unseen, or the distant and immediate. Like Benjy Compson, Darl as narrator is both "reliable" and "incredible."

The wide range of viewpoints in *As I Lay Dying* creates "ironic effects" and "broadens the sense of social reality," observes Michael Millgate.[5] The mixture functions conversely to obscure reality in the Bundren world, where an event splinters in variant angles, and truth inheres in suspended polarities. In the gap between Darl's feigned concern for the family and his detachment from them lies his true motive. Sustained antinomies in fictive language also expand the boundaries of communication between the novel and the reader, who must hear past the unstable word and form a voiceless tale.

Andre Bleikasten thinks the recurring negatives in style signal the writer's "obstinate efforts to overcome the inadequacy of language."[6] Faulkner's efforts go beyond diction. He overturns the canons of fictive form to make words "designate the contrary of what they seem to designate."[7] Verisimilitude manifests itself in its violations, like mismatching country-folk with metaphoric style or printing a wordless exchange as dialogue. In *Absalom, Absalom!* layered voices and points of view, and concentric images and tropes tell an unvoiced story that recasts the indeterminate "printed tale." Some of the same linguistic formulations of synchronic time appear in *As I Lay Dying,* but the blend of incongruous styles and perspectives, common devices in Faulkner but unique in scope in this work, obliterates intervals of space as well. In addition, encyclopedic images and unorthodox syntax and typography, like the fluctuating tenses or misrepresentations of actual happenings, traverse the literal boundaries of language. The novel discredits its medium and thereby undermines itself, but Faulkner's *equi-*vocal language tells past the "no good" word about human relating and relating fiction.

The sequential plot readers claim for the novel (since journeys proceed consecutively in time/space) highlights by its absence the discontinuity. While some segments progress chronologically, recurrent temporal concordances and spatial dislocations fracture the journey framework. Successive events in life, the "fable," exists outside the novel, a phantom counterpoint to Faulkner's "plot," in which events occur without regard "for logical sequence and continuity" (*AA* 247/199). The fifty-nine variations on events around Addie Bundren's death, told by fifteen narrators, strain the idea of structure in *As I Lay Dying*. One kind of structural pattern, a germinal source reproducing diverse but correlated expansions, organizes the segments in *Absalom, Absalom!* and *The Sound and the Fury*. The other kind of design in *As I Lay Dying* revolves around a "moment," Addie's chapter in the latter half of the book (161–68/169–76). Addie's strictures against language materialize in the words and actions of people in chapters before and after her own, setting the segments inside one another (see II). Darl's two large visionary chapters (46–51/47–52 and 71–76/75–81), from which germs of character and action expand in both directions, offer an alternative organizing "center" (see III). In yet another way, Cora Tull's erroneous observations early in the work (20–24/21–25) initiate corrective refractions of a mistake. Whether it is the dominant Addie section or the rival Darl sections, the "moment" interlaces the "pieces," backward and forward in shifting patterns of difference or contrast, and frames a metamorphic design.

II

Addie articulates most fully in the canon the perils of the ineffectual/potent word. Vivid images embody her misgivings at the damage the word effects on familial relations and on life itself, and her attempts to circumvent it. She imputes her "terrible" life to the separation of deeds from words that "dont ever fit even what they are trying to say at." Words go "straight up in a thin line, quick and harmless," while the "doing" creeps "terribly . . . along the earth." Words thus signify a double absence, "just the gaps in peoples' lacks." Conforming to her author's hierarchy of values, she sets "just sounds" below the "no good" word, doubly censuring the self-righteous Cora, in whose speech "the high dead words in time seemed to lose even the significance of their dead sound" (163–67/171–75).

Readers generally reduce Addie's charge to the separation of word from deed. Addie, in fact, decries the "formidable powers" of the word, which, though a "harmless vacuity," as Andre Bleikasten puts it, sunders human beings from themselves, from one another, and from the divine.[8] She sees her family "use one another by words like spiders dangling by their mouths from a beam, swinging and twisting and never touching," unable to relate except through hatred or deceit. "Hidden within a word like within a paper screen," her husband, Anse, strikes through and violates her "aloneness." His conception a trick of the word ("love"), his birth an outrage, her second son Darl embodies for the mother the word's duplicity. In "revenge" for Darl, she exacts Anse's word to bury her at Jefferson with her kin. Darl, condemned by language to a motherless state, in turn schemes to avenge his deprivation of love with the same false word Addie denounces. As love to Anse is "just a shape to fill a lack," his name to Addie is but a "word," a "significant shape profoundly without life like an empty door frame," a blank "   ." His word as vacuous as "dead sound," and nothing himself but "the shape and echo of his word," Anse is doubly "dead" (164–67)/172–75). The family suffers in varying degrees from the falsity of language and the consequent impairment of being. The title of the novel denotes Addie's physical decline, but it also signifies her people's word-blighted existence.

Addie seeks to reach the inner life of people and to do her "duty to the alive" (162/170, 166/174), but she fails, for she knows only perverse ways of physical or sexual violence to break through the wall separating persons from one another. She strives "to straddle" the "two lines . . . too far apart" of vertical word and horizontal deed with adulterous passion that could "shape and coerce the terrible blood to the forlorn echo of the dead word high in the air" (165/173, 167/175). But the doubly absent signifier, the "forlorn echo of the dead word," falls short of the signified "boiling" blood. Frustrated with her attempts to relate to people with word or deed, Addie retreats to "the dark land talking of God's love and His beauty and His sin" with a "dark voicelessness in which the words are the deeds." People who are unable to speak God's Word resort to "words that are not deeds." Addie's attempt, though vain, to escape into God's universe "talking the *voiceless speech,*" where signifier matches signified (The Word) further discredits the word; but it also points a way to surpass it (166–67/174–75, italics added). The writer must surmount the enemy with the "dark voicelessness" of word-subjugating form.

The duplicitous word charts the life of Addie and her family. Her oxymoronic image of Anse, "a significant shape profoundly without life," yet therefore not wholly insignificant, emblematizes as well her marriage and role as mother, her family's posturings of grief, and the journey ostensibly to honor her wish. The death pilgrimage rehearses the quest myth, a passage of heroic trials culminating in spiritual regeneration. To fulfill Anse's promise exacted by Addie's vengeful word, the Bundrens battle the elements and people blocking their way, and succeed in their efforts. From start to finish, however, their pilgrimage subverts the tenor of myth. The roots of myth lie in the spiritual, but the Bundren quest springs from an unholy cause, Addie's despair over the deceitful word and bitterness against her kinfolk. The self-serving ends of Anse and most of the family likewise parody the sacramental journey. Darl's laughter exposes their spurious loyalty and satirizes their exploits. They turn Addie's revenge against her and to their secret benefit, but they achieve no final victory over what Cleanth Brooks calls her "tremendous intensity," which, even after death, holds "vital power over her family."

The Bundrens' suffering and losses are real, their resilience admirable, and deserve Brooks's accolade, "heroic." Faulkner's antonymous method, however, celebrates but also debases their enterprise. Since "their motivation lies within her life,"[9] Addie's conviction that "the reason for living was to get ready to stay dead a long time" (161/169) reduces to absurdity her people's seeming solidarity and brave sacrifice. Addie initiates the "significant shape" of sacred ritual, but insidious like the word, she empties it of meaning. The form, substance, and theme of Faulkner's narrative reflect the ambiguity of language and of human beings.

The Addie chapter illuminates the whole work, Bleikasten concludes, but it has "no immediate logical connection with the current action."[10] That view might befit a traditional structure built on "logical sequence and continuity" (AA 247/199), but not a narrative organized on the "reciprocal friction" of discordant fragments. Addie's view of language, a powerful "moment" late in the work, silently calibrates deception in people's word and deed and casts an ironic light on adjacent and remote sections. It highlights the sham behind Cora's protestations of honesty and piety in the preceding section and, in the next, detects through Whitfield's pious cant his hypocrisy and arrogance. Farther out, backward and forward, that germinal "moment" exposes various forms of betrayal and deceit, effecting the "mutual penetration" of contradistinct parts.[11]

Like his mother, Darl discerns truth behind subterfuge, and like Benjy in *The Sound and the Fury*, he renders each essential being and appraises his people and their enterprises. Surpassing both Addie and Benjy, Darl wields the voiced word to obtain his "desires," but he also penetrates the unvoiced word. The main Darl sections, competing with the Addie section at the work's center, set the insular units modulating inside one another and enkindle the silences past the "cold" word.

III

In nineteen of the work's fifty-nine sections, Darl, the primary voice among the multiple voices, explores the counter-operations of language, its power to deceive and, conversely, to manifest the "secret and selfish life" of people inaccessible to Addie. For this plausible/implausible narrator, Faulkner deliberately distances word from sense to intimate the suppressed. He combines the congruous/incongruous low and high styles with a split point of view encompassing both the visible and the invisible. To the usual array of temporal convergences, he adds deviant syntax and typography to fuse time and intimate past the word a truer tale.

Darl's style, noted earlier, fluctuates from the vernacular for practical matters to the "mobile" language of images and tropes that embodies his despair: "How do our lives ravel out into the no-wind, no-sound, the weary gestures wearily recapitulant: echoes of old compulsions with no-hand on no-strings: in sunset we fall into furious attitudes, dead gestures of dolls" (196–97/207). Life unraveling in furious yet dead gestures echoes the mother's view of life, hollowed out by the word. For Darl, however, the cause of despair appears to be the deprivation of love. His speech, an improved version of the dialect, places him among hill-country people, but his musings set him apart. Where Cash says at the edge of the flooded river, "I ought to come down last week and taken a sight on it," Darl replies, "We couldn't have known. . . . There wasn't any way for us to know" (137/144). The war years abroad may account for the standard grammar and diction, but Darl's poetic evocations transgress the credible. A character speaking "better speech" than he is "capable of" vindicates his right to believe in what he thinks he is or could be, the writer contends (*ESPL* 186). The incongruity in this instance justifies what Darl's "queer eyes, . . . filled with distance beyond the land" (119/125, 26/27), discern through his people's dissembling. He knows the mother's beloved Jewel is not Anse's son, and, on the way to Jefferson, Anse will steal Cash's hard-earned money. The vernacular compounded with the tropical style, often explained away as intrusions of the author's voice,[12] mirrors in form the "illogical" interpermeation of mental states Bergson detects in the deepest regions where intuitive perception supersedes rational cognition (*TFW* 134).

Dewey Dell is certain Darl knows about her lover Lafe and her condition "*without the words* like he told me that ma is going to die without words, and I knew he knew because if he had said he knew with the words I would not have believed. . . . And that's why I can talk to him with knowing with hating because he knows" (26/27, italics added). Their unspoken communication materializes in an antiphonal dialogue, a form designating the spoken word but here signifying "voiceless speech":

> "What you want, Darl?" I say.
> "She is going to die," he says. . . .
> "When is she going to die?" I say.
> "Before we get back," he says.
> "Then why are you taking Jewel?" I say.
> "I want him to help me load," he says. (26–27/27–28)

The typographic disguise embodies Darl's capacity to see through pretext and also to delude as his words gainsay his deeds. He proposes to sell lumber for the journey to Jefferson (16–19/16–20), but that seeming concern for the family turns hollow when his true motive appears in the unspoken message of voiced words. Like the other members of the family, who take the occasion of Addie's death to pursue their true intent, Darl plots to deprive the dying mother of her favored son and so requite his own motherless state. On the way, he tortures the son he has separated from the mother: " 'Jewel,' I say. . . . 'Do you know she is going to die, Jewel?' " The repeat, " 'Jewel,' I say, 'do you know that Addie Bundren is going to die? Addie Bundren is going to die?' " (38–39/39–40), renders without explicit gloss his brutal intent, to inflict pain on the

expiring woman and her "jewel." Dewey Dell and Jewel, who welcome neither truth nor revelation, hate their seer-brother, who perceives the family's spurious ends and tries to halt their absurd
journey with water and fire. Darl is the touchstone of veracity
among his people, but unlike Benjy in *The Sound and the Fury*, he
is also the worst dissembler of them all.

While on the road away from home, Darl envisions the scene
around Addie's last moments. In these main clairvoyant sections
(46–51/47–52 and 71–76/75–81),[13] his point of view fluctuates between the spatial immediate/distant, the psychological objective/
subjective modes, and among the planes of the past/present/future.
That improbable perspective abstracts in a gesture each essential
being. Cash pantomimes for his mother the finished coffin, a gro-
tesque farewell typifying the defective judgment that mars his
mathematical exactness with bone-breaking falls and his good will
with erroneous deed as, Jewel reports earlier, when he fills his
mother's bread pan with dung to help her till the garden (14/14).
Soon after he announces, "She's gone," which Pa confirms, "She's
taken and left us." Cash looks "down at her peaceful, rigid face
fading into the dusk as though darkness were a precursor of the ultimate earth, until at last the face seems to float detached upon it,
lightly as the reflection of a dead leaf" (49/50). The shift to the
metaphoric style sounds possibly the only true note of veneration
for the dead from the sensitive, simple man. The "reflection of a
dead leaf" descending to "ultimate earth" hypostatizes Addie's
hard-earned repose that even death may not ensure, her unrestful
hands reveal (50/51). Accenting the folly of withholding that deserved peace, the passage indirectly reprehends the family's enterprise and their subterfuges. Dewey Dell shakes the "rotten bones"
in a paroxysm of grief but soon rises to her true preoccupation
(47–48/48–49, 50/51), which leaves no time for mourning (114/
120). Anse's hand, which, "awkward as a claw," disorders the quilt
over his dead wife, pictures his fecklessness, and his words betray
his feigned sorrow: "God's will be done. . . . Now I can get them
teeth" (51/52). Vardaman's "pale face fading into the dusk like a
piece of paper pasted on a failing wall" (48/49) pictures his unaided
confusion and also censures the adults who neglect the child. Darl
detects the gap between appearance and reality. But when the scene
shifts back to the brothers' immediate surroundings on the flooded

road, he resorts to the treacherous word to gain his insidious purpose.

The wagon has broken down and the dismayed Jewel attends to the broken wheel, but Darl, still held by his vision of Addie's decline, continues to torment his brother with repeated calls of ill tidings, "*Jewel, I say*" (48/49). The motive behind his dissembling words and actions finally surfaces when he harrows his brother with the bad news: "*Jewel I say, she is dead, Jewel. Addie Bundren is dead*" (51/52). Calling the mother by her full name as though she were no kin signals his alienation, but the chant-like iteration betrays Darl's satisfaction at his successful plot to deprive the dying mother of her favorite son. As "her failing life" drains "into her eyes, urgent, irremediable," the mother vainly looks for him: "It's Jewel she wants," Dewey Dell reports (46/47). The alternating perspectives and rhythmic cadences impart, without overt assertion, the bitter roots of Darl's vindictiveness and belie the maternal affection attributed to him by the deluded Cora, who fancies Darl the most devoted of sons (20–24/21–25).

The same equivocal word with which he unlocks people's faults or feigning betrays Darl's own secret, concealed behind disingenuous speech and action. Some critics ascribe Darl's obsession with Jewel to envy of his half-brother's masculine will and strength. Cleanth Brooks thinks Darl's "preternatural vision" has given way to "bitterness and pettiness as in his baiting of his brother Jewel."[14] The evidence is obscure for it lies not in what the word designates but in what word-liberating form signifies. Darl's preoccupation with the beloved son reflects his obsession with the loved/hated mother who avenges herself on him for her husband's guileful word.

Still, fulfilled revenge fails to lessen Darl's rage or dispossession, as the second large clairvoyant chapter discloses (71–76/75–81). He envisions Anse's face, streaming with rain, "a monstrous burlesque of all bereavement" (74/78), then, shifting his focus within himself, finds a nebulous being: "I dont know what I am. I dont know if I am or not." In contrast, Jewel, unaware of his conception, "knows he is, because he does not know that he does not know whether he is or not. . . . He is not what he is and he is what he is not." Sundered from the source of being, Darl appropriates his brother's selfhood, secured in the mother, to confirm his absent self: "And Jewel *is*, so Addie Bundren must be. And then I must

be, or I could not empty myself for sleep in a strange room. And so
if I am not emptied yet, I am *is*." But the concluding line negates
that affirmation. He recalls sad moments lying "beneath rain on a
strange roof, thinking of home," the home he never truly had (76/
80–81).

On their return the next day, Darl, who has suffered psychic loss
long before the "two flames" of his mother's eyes "go out" like
blown candles (47/47), continues to torture Jewel. Seeing the buz-
zards flying over their house, he punctuates his cruel words with,
"It's not your horse that's dead, Jewel. . . . See them?" (88/94).
Later Darl taunts his brother with the illegitimacy he has surmised:
" 'Jewel,' I say, 'whose son are you?' "; which he redoubles in vicious spite: "*Jewel, I say, Who was your father, Jewel?*" (202–3/
212–13). Darl fails to find redress for his lack, and the lost mother
continues to haunt him in Jewel's prized horse: "I cannot love my
mother because I have no mother. Jewel's mother is a horse" (89/95).

In an exchange with Vardaman, Darl's sense of the existential
void attending maternal deprivation materializes in syntactic desig-
nations of time:

> "Then what is your ma, Darl?"
> "I haven't got ere one," Darl said. "Because if I had one, it is
> *was*. And if it is was, it cant be *is*. Can it?"
> "No," I said.
> "Then I am not," Darl said. "Am I?"
> "No," I said.
> I am. Darl is my brother.
> "But you *are*, Darl," I said.
> "I know it," Darl said. "That's why I am not *is*. *Are* is too many for
> one woman to foal." (95/101)[15]

Vardaman suffers no uncertainty of being, "I am," or of relating,
"Darl is my brother." Unable to comprehend the man's desolation,
the boy tries to confirm his brother's entity, "But you *are*, Darl,"
and simply underscores the man's lack. To be "*are*," one among
"too many," denies Darl an individual self, "That's why I am not
is," a being connected by itself to the source. The delusive but potent word designating the always absent mother, "*was*," annulls his
selfhood, a "not *is*."

Vardaman's narration, fluctuating widely from childish incoherencies in the dialect to extremely complex introspection, reifies the child's bewilderment over his mother's altered state. Vardaman uses language not to deceive, but to make sense of the incomprehensible by setting it within the scope of his limited understanding. He collocates his mother with the fish that was, but is no more: "Hit was a-layin' right there on the ground. And now she's gittin ready to cook hit. . . . Cooked and et." The attempt fails, and his derangement materializes in Jewel's horse, resolving "out of his integrity, into an unrelated scattering of components." But the horse, ambiguous like other elements, also restores the boy's sense of a separate identity, a condition necessary to withstand the loss of the mother: "an illusion of a co-ordinated whole of splotched hide and strong bones within which, detached and secret and familiar, an *is* different from my *is*" (55/56). The high and low styles, resonating in one another, insinuate beyond words the child's unaided confusion.

When words could no longer voice their "secret" feelings, Darl discovers with his brother Cash the "dark voicelessness" their mother vainly sought. Darl contemplates the flooded river they must cross with the wagon carrying Addie's coffin: "Before us the thick dark current runs. It talks up to us in a murmur become ceaseless and myriad, the yellow surface dimpled monstrously into fading swirls travelling along the surface for an instant, silent, impermanent and profoundly significant, as though just beneath the surface something huge and alive waked for a moment of lazy alertness out of and into light slumber again." At this critical moment, the word appears sundered from thought or emotion, so some readers believe. But the ornate style infuses external objects with unspoken feelings. Elaborate metaphors render the brothers' "terror" and "foreboding" felt in "secret and without shame." Their "quiet, detached" voices talking about "old security and old trivial things" betray their unvoiced fear (134–36/141–43).

The men's shift to dialectal speech further widens the gap between what words designate and what they signify. But the mixture also accelerates the oscillation of time and space, strategies that embody the men's rising apprehension at imminent danger. Darl observes Jewel trying to force his trembling horse into the current and says to Cash, "If he'll just give the horse time, anyhow." *In his mind* he instantly flashes back to the mother and the newborn Jewel: "When he was born, he had a bad time of it. Ma would sit in the lamp-light, holding him on a pillow on her lap. We would wake and find her so. There would be no sound from them." The passage, distinctly marked off from speech, is an unvoiced monologue inaudible to Cash.[16] Yet, as though he heard his brother speak, Cash pursues the subject of Darl's musings: "That pillow was longer than him," then addresses their present plight, "I ought to come down last week and sighted. I ought to done it." As incredible as the mind-reading Shreve, Cash addresses simultaneously his brother's expressed concern over the threat around them and his unspoken recollection of a past event. Darl in turn mixes the heard and unheard when he answers Cash's reply to both his unspoken thoughts and their articulated concern: " 'That's right.' I say. 'Neither his feet nor his head would reach the end of it. You couldn't have known,' I say" (137/144). The incongruous fusions of the voiced and unvoiced and of "elapsed and yet-elapsing time," like those in the Quentin-Shreve exchanges in *Absalom, Absalom!*, transgress the codes of verisimilitude but inscribe in silence the men's unvoiced dread. Addie finds words insidious; but Darl apprehends past the word a revelation about himself and his people.

Abrogating the rules of syntax to delineate shades of feelings, Faulkner shifts in the hapless river crossing from the present tense to the past, and then back to the present tense:

> Cash takes the reins and lowers the team carefully and skillfully into the stream.
> *I felt the current take us and I knew we were on the ford by that reason. . . . What had once been a flat surface was now a succession of troughs and hillocks lifting and falling about us, shoving at us, teasing at us with light lazy touches in the vain instants of solidity underfoot. Cash looked back at me, and then I knew that we were gone. But I did not realise the reason for the rope until I saw the log. It surged up out of the water and stood for an instant upright upon that surging and heaving desolation like Christ. . . .*
> The log appears suddenly between two hills, as if it had rocketed suddenly from the bottom of the river. (140–41/147–48)

Italics lift the ominous moment above the flow of action, but transposing present to past tense at the height of danger usurps the traditional function of the present tense to render action with greater immediacy. Distinctions blur when the past tense appropriates the synchrony ascribed to present narration.[17] Alternating perspectives augment the effects of tense displacement. At the start and end of

the episode, Darl describes objectively in the present tense a panorama of turbulent action. The shift to past tense reverses the condi-
tions: the perspective foreshortens, the scene contracts, and the
focus turns inside Darl's mind, where observation modulates to
feeling. Outer and inner interfuse as the past tense translates external event to experience: "I felt," "I knew." Verbals embodying
Darl's dismay, *"lifting and falling about us, shoving at us, . . . that
surging and heaving desolation,"* intensify the threat with human
attributes. An ironic Christ-like log treading water crowns the
brothers' mute terror. Proceeding in the present tense, the conclusion sketches from a distance the spectacle of the log crashing
down on team, wagon, and men. Stephen M. Ross thinks the past
tense in the work distances character from event,[18] but the passage
above typifies the reverse function of the past tense, to transform an
external event into an intensely subjective experience. Rather than
distancing character from action, the deviant past tense sets Darl
inside the event, and the event inside his mind.

Fluctuating tenses and perspectives record the dissolution in
amorphous subjectivity of a world beyond control. Darl's fractured
being finally materializes in one Darl mocking the other (243–44/
253–54). The split threatens reason. He resorts to delusive verbal
constructs, but these collapse, leaving him with empty yesses (the
affirmative subverted) and bitter laughter (joy overthrown). Cash is
right about Darl; neither this world nor this life is his (250/261),
for Darl, like his mother, perceives a "significant shape profoundly
without life" in word or person. His author, however, disagrees
with the general view of an insane Darl. An unpublished segment
of tapes at the University of Virginia records Faulkner as saying,
"To me, Darl wasn't mad. I didn't set out to make a brother mad"
(UV T-144). A sane Darl, as his author apparently conceived him
to be, underlines the tragedy of man cursed with discernment
("eyes . . . filled with distance beyond the land" [25–26/27]) who,
seeing through and beyond his people and their doings, brings
about his own destruction.

Surpassing Darl's paradigms built on the voiced/voiceless word,
Faulkner shapes the written word into polyphonic form that both
denies and affirms. The reader "hears" written words "tell" of
life's ambiguities but also "overhears" unuttered verities. Anse
considers "writing" the touchstone of certainty in an equivocal
world, an ironic turn on his wife's view of the treacherous word. He

thinks Addie will construe Dr. Peabody's presence as a sign of her imminent death: "I knowed that when she see you she would know hit, same as writing. You wouldn't need to tell her" (44/45). But the statement intimates as well the word's duplicity (which Anse misses entirely). Dr. Peabody surmises his presence signifies, more than her impending death, Anse's vicious stinginess and, worse, his murderous intent to withhold help until it *is* clearly too late: "Why didn't you send for me sooner?" (43/44). Bringing home another woman as soon as his wife is buried divulges Anse's hidden motive and the insidious force of the word, voiced or unvoiced. Writing may not be so transparent after all, except to Anse. He remains unaware of the treachery Addie and Darl discern in the word, whose silence could deconstruct what it articulates.

Faulkner's implausible form signifies something other than what words designate and thus defers full appraisal of meaning in the voiceless tale. *As I Lay Dying* exemplifies the "new" novel, whose characters, unaided by the writer, communicate as best they can with equivocal words; and the reader must perceive in the gaps between synchronous antinomies a "shadow" of human experience. Addie and Darl, however, forewarn the reader that apprehending life through language may elicit despair. At the same time, the self-negating/potent word and novel may afford glimpses that delight, like Darl's magical water bucket, "a round orifice in nothingness" with "a star or two" glimmering in it (11/11).

6

The Unvanquished: The Doubling Voice

To have it told partly by a child, partly by a grown man, it's to hold the object up and look at it from both sides, from two points of view.

—Faulkner, *Faulkner in the University*

FAULKNER CONVERTS THE SINGLE-TONED VOICE IN THE SIX MAGAZINE tales he assembles for the novel *The Unvanquished* (1938) to a bitonal voice entwining the distinct styles and perspectives of the child and the grown Bayard Sartoris. In the first six stories, the boy, from twelve to fifteen through the Civil War, learns about his people and his heritage. In the seventh story the author composed for the novel, the twenty-four-year-old Bayard enacts the lessons of childhood and youth. During revision, Faulkner interweaves the man's mature view and interpretive voice with the juvenile voice in the earlier tales. Considerably apart in the first story, the two voices and viewpoints gradually close through the succeeding stories and finally merge in the final story as the protagonist progresses from ignorance to knowledge to self-determined action. The youthful voice speaks primarily the language of "practical life," while the older voice appraises events with the figurative language of the "deeper self" (Henri Bergson's terms, *INP* 79, *TFW* 125; see Abbreviations for the list of Bergson's works). Since each voice denotes a specific period of Bayard's history, the stratified perspectives and styles converge time and create an ironic redoubling in substance and theme.

Other modifications further change the tone, structure, and theme of the novel. Extensive additions in about twelve pages of the first story, "Ambuscade," transform the original univocal style to language shot through with countertones and knit the distinct parts as the man's reflective style intimates the future import of the bewil-

118

dered boy's war experiences (see I).[1] About nine pages of alterations in each of the next two stories, "Retreat" and "Raid,"
further develop the initial germs of action, character, and the heritage motif. The next three stories, which closely match the original
tales ("Riposte in Tertio," "Vendée," "Skirmish at Sartoris"),
chronicle Bayard's initiation into the manhood of killers. "An Odor
of Verbena," the longest story of fifty pages composed for the
novel, brings to a dramatic climax the moral question intimated in
the first alterations and amplified through the succeeding tales (see
II). All significant additions, including the entire final story, are
double bracketed in the following discussion, but brief or minor revisions and omissions have been disregarded.

The Unvanquished and the similarly modular *Go Down, Moses*
(1942) four years later both comprise seven self-contained tales
with no consistent protagonist. Studies have traced patterns of chronological action and recurring thematic motifs to certify the organization of these discontinuous works. Faulkner, however, conceives
of structure as the "contrapuntal . . . integration" of heterogeneous
elements of form, an operation that conjoins even the radically disjunct *Go Down, Moses.* Germs of action and character encoded in
the opening pages of *The Unvanquished* evolve variously through
the six tales to their fullest development in the final tale. Reinforcing that formal design is the motif of legacy—inherited values the
boy accepts, the youth questions, and the man repudiates.

What appears to be a "facile," "melodramatic," or "sentimental" treatment of a subject dear to the author's heart has inhibited
serious consideration of *The Unvanquished.*[2] Its genetic history,
tracing the transformation of language and form in the novel,
should cast a fresh light on these problems.[3] The bifurcated voice
and stratified styles and time planes in the revised stories, enhanced
with powerful metonymic images and tropes, sound a self-denying
tone that supplants the "facile" storytelling in the original tales.
Irony, touched at times with bitter sarcasm, dims youthful fantasy,
exposes the spurious, and scrutinizes with the merciless light of
truth the quality of Bayard's world and its legacy—lifting the novel
above a trivial exercise in nostalgia to a study of moral maturation.
The juvenile "pulp series" (*SL* 84) decried by the author himself,
becomes with the changes a noteworthy example of polyphonic art
that undermines what it elevates, censures what it praises.

I

The voice of an innocent child "that knew what he was seeing but had no particular judgment about it" (*FU* 116), permeated with the "judgment" of a mature person, implies past the discourse a somber counter tale. The gap that contracts and eventually closes between the two voices inscribes in form Bayard's psychological and moral growth. In the first story the boy and his "brother" Ringo find the initial events of the war scary but unintelligible and therefore not particularly dangerous. The original single-toned tale published in the *Saturday Evening Post* opens thus:

> Behind the smokehouse we had a kind of map. Vicksburg was a handful of chips from the woodpile and the river was a trench we had scraped in the packed ground with a hoe, that drank water almost faster than we could fetch it from the well. This afternoon it looked like we would never get it filled, because it hadn't rained in three weeks. But at last it was damp-colored enough at least, and we were just about to begin, when all of a sudden Loosh was standing there watching us. And then I saw Philadelphy over at the woodpile, watching Loosh. (*SEP*, 29 September 1934, 12)

In the novel the opening paragraph expands by a half more (double bracketed below and in later passages). The older narrator's multivalent images infuse the childish games and delusions with portents of disaster later fulfilled. Time converges as present action obtains meaning in the future, and the future manifests the true import of the present.

> Behind the smokehouse [[that summer, Ringo and I had a living map.]] Although Vicksburg was just a handful of chips from the woodpile and the River a trench scraped into the packed earth with the point of a hoe, [[it (river, city, and terrain) lived, possessing even in miniature that ponderable though passive recalcitrance of topography which outweighs artillery, against which the most brilliant of victories and the most tragic of defeats are but the loud noises of a moment. To Ringo and me it lived, if only because of the fact that the sunimpacted ground]] drank water faster than we could fetch it from the well, [[the very setting of the stage for conflict a prolonged and wellnigh hopeless ordeal in which we ran, panting and interminable, with the leaking bucket between wellhouse and battlefield, the two of us needing first to join forces and spend ourselves against a common enemy, time, before we could engender be-

tween us and hold intact the pattern of recapitulant mimic furious
victory like a cloth, a shield between ourselves and reality, between us
and fact and doom.]] (3–4/3–4)[4]

The man's elaborate tropes convert the children's game into an icon
of Southern history. The boys' "kind of map" becomes the "living
map" of events unfolding about them in this story and in succeeding stories. The wood chips and scraped earth "lived," for they signify "in miniature" the war "terrain" that reduces brilliant victories
or tragic defeats to nothing "but the loud noises of a moment," a
paradoxical view of human effort that underlies the theme. The
boys' "prolonged and wellnigh hopeless ordeal" with a leaky
bucket hypostasizes the South's protracted struggle to deny an impending collapse. "Time" is the "common enemy" for latent in it
lies defeat. The boys hold up like a "shield" a "pattern of recapitulant mimic furious victory" against "reality, . . . fact and doom."
The mature voice, however, intimates through this feigning the un-
deniable "fact" of loss. Faulkner's modifications establish the bifurcated voice with its layered styles and time planes, and the germs
of character and action whose unfoldings interpenetrate. The polyphonic narration infuses the original simple chronicle of events
with the expanding *"ripples"* of their true import in the present,
past, and future.

Bayard detects catastrophe in the air but fails to decipher the look
of "triumph" on Loosh's face or the black man's pronouncement:
"Hit's on the way!" (6/5). Ringo wonders if Loosh knows something they do not know, but Bayard denies it with a spate of words.
The older voice articulates what the boys sense but would not
admit, that no words may "shield" them against truth. With the additions, the narrative fluctuates between the child's unknowing and
the man's certainty of inexorable "fact and doom": " 'Do you
reckon that if there were Yankees at Corinth, Father [[and General
Van Dorn]] and General Pemberton [[all three]] wouldn't be there
[[too?' But I was just talking too, I knew that, because niggers
know, they know things; it would have to be something louder,
much louder, than words to do any good"]] (7/6). The last addition
forecasts Bayard's progress from dependence on illusory words to
understanding beyond words. The man will abandon what he has
been told for what he knows to be true and right.

But even as a child, Bayard possesses an intuitive knowing about human ties, shown in the next addition. [["That's how Ringo and I were,"]] he reports. Ringo was [["a little smarter, . . . but that didn't count with us, anymore than the difference in the color of our skins counted,"]] a kinship that undergirds the grown Bayard's belief in the human bond (91/81). Born the same month, suckled at the same breasts, they slept and ate together so long [["until maybe he wasn't a nigger anymore or maybe I wasn't a white boy anymore, the two of us neither, not even people any longer: the two supreme unde-feated like two moths, two feathers riding above a hurricane"]] (7–8/7). This brotherhood transcends cultural bias conditioned by words.[5] Bayard's view of a common humanity, impervious to race or politics, resurfaces at critical points in his life. The terrified boy, seeing his first Yankee soldier, discovers the enemy "looks just like a man" (28/25). After the war, his stepmother Drusilla justifies his Father's killing of the "new foe" (228/198), carpetbaggers who champion the Negro right to vote. Bayard refutes her with, [["They were men. Human beings"]] (257/223), an insert forecasting the mature Bayard's moral test. When he refuses to kill his own "foe," Father's murderer, he reenacts his childhood belief in human kin-ship and the evil of taking human life in war or peace.

Other revisions turn the boys' game portentous. Philadelphy's "queer" voice in the original becomes [["curious"]] in the novel, underlining what the boys detect but cannot comprehend in the [["urgent, perhaps frightened"]] note (5/5). They hide "invisible" within the dust they momentarily raise, but Louvinia's voice de-scends on them [["like an enormous hand, flattening the very dust which we had raised, leaving us now visible to one another."]] Nei-ther words nor dust nor yelling may screen them from "reality." Bayard, however, remains insensible to what the black people "know" without "words" (7/6), imaged in a great "tide" about to engulf them all. He continues to disclaim the signs of defeat and pictures Ringo and himself floating like "two moths, two feathers" above the "hurricane," but the transient fragility of moths and feathers presages their fall from feigning. Father's sudden return and the hasty secreting of stock from the advancing enemy shatter their "shield" against "doom." The older narrator's metonymic im-ages intimate in slight happenings far-reaching consequences be-yond the boys' grasp. As the portents materialize, they seem like echoes whose every redoubling amplifies the literal story past the word.

Bayard's increasing knowledge of his people and heritage is seldom articulated but rather implied in bitonal language and image, particularly those clustered around Father, who exercises the most influence on the boy and about whom Faulkner adds the largest number of words in the first story. Father inspires the son's most ardent fantasies about war, but the older speaker's equivocal phrasing punctures childish fancy and insinuates the wrong Bayard later discovers in his heritage. Father's physical appearance seems to elicit awe but, at the same time, casts doubt on his true stature: [["He was not big, yet somehow he looked even smaller on the horse than off of him, because Jupiter was big and when you thought of Father you thought of him as being big too and so when you thought of Father being on Jupiter it was as if you said. 'Together they will be too big; you won't believe it.' So you didn't believe it and so it wasn't"]] (10–11/9–10). What is affirmed is negated. Praise for Father [["doing bigger things than he was"]] is instantly qualified with [["the illusion of height and size which he wore for us at least"]] (11/10). Mature perception superimposed on the boy's ignorance offsets illusion with harsh truth.

The man's veracity, touched with cynicism, dissipates the boy's romantic construction of events. On Father's clothes and flesh the boy [["believed was the smell of powder and glory, the elected victorious but know better now: know now to have been only the will to endure, a sardonic and even humorous declining of self-delusion"]] (11/10). The mature voice identifies the true measure of heroism, not in the lad's delusion of chimeric victory, but the "will to endure" in defeat. The starry-eyed boy elevates Father to a knight charging the saplings for the stockpen and inspiring his troop of six children and black slaves with [["that passive yet dynamic affirmation which Napoleon's troops must have felt"]] (14/12). But the man's mock-heroic hyperbole accents the absurdity of this spurious chivalry and presages the lad's fall into disillusion. John Sartoris, who from war hero turns with his demotion to a brigand, to "a coward and a fool"(60/53), and finally to a killer, embodies Bayard's double-edged heritage.

Irony also punctures the melodramatic. The boys eagerly look forward to Father's tales of "the cannon and the flags and the [[anonymous]] yelling" (17/15) but instead are sent to bed so Father could bury the family silver. When they overhear Father tell Granny about Vicksburg, Ringo's reaction typifies their ignorance:

"Vicksburg *fell?* Do he mean hit fell off in the River? With Ginrul Pemberton in hit too?" (20/18). Faulkner favors youthful narrators who imply more than they understand. When the boys hear Loosh say General Sherman "gonter sweep the earth and the race gonter all be free!" Bayard runs to tell Granny, "It's General Sherman and he's going to make us all free!" (25–26/23). The humorous misstatement capsulizes a major motif: both enslaved and enslaver need liberating.

Certainty imaged in dream offsets the boys' confusion. Bayard and Granny dream that Loosh would know [["when it was getting ready to happen"]] (23/21) and divulge the buried silver to the Yankees. Both dreams come true. Bayard's nightmare of an apocalyptic darkness engulfing the house and cabins and a "frightened drove of little tiny figures" wandering about (27/24) epitomize their dying culture. "If you dremp hit," Ringo figures, "hit can't be a lie case ain't nobody there to tole hit to you" (23/21). The boys' "shield" of disbelief gives way to truth in dream. But that motif has its counterside as well, as the dream of freedom turns into a "delusion" for the slaves, pawns of political battles in war or peace (92/81, 228–29/198–99). Sartoris's "good dream" is "not a very safe thing" (257/223) for people.

The extensive changes in the first story initiate a self-inflecting form whose speaking silence appraises the quality of Bayard's divided world. Antinomies in language, form, and substance celebrate the valorous undefeated but register at the same time the boy's misgivings over inherited notions of right and wrong. In the end, the young man turns from mindless conformity to conscientious rebellion and disavows Father's "way" for his own. Faulkner's "method" of antithetic counterpointing converts juvenile melodrama to a moral appraisal of Southern history and legacy.

II

In the second story, "Retreat," Bayard's diction advances to match the extraordinary experiences that propel the thirteen year old to manhood. The older voice continues to puncture youthful delusions, but it also begins to identify the valuable components of the boy's heritage, like Uncles Buck and Buddy, who free their slaves years before the war (52–57/46–51), and the emblematic snuffbox of soil Bayard takes with him on their journey: [["(it was more than Sartoris earth; it was Vicksburg too: the yelling was in it, the embattled, the iron-worn, the supremely invincible)"]] (62/ 55). The illusion of invincibility fades when Bayard faces the reality of loss, but in defeat he sees his people prove their enduring spirit. Growing from thirteen to fifteen in the next five stories, he learns to distinguish society's standards from his own emerging values. In the concluding story, the lessons of the preceding twelve years compel the twenty-four-year-old man to repudiate a legacy of wrong.

The youth's increased awareness of ambiguity in people's words and deeds and his ability to detect through illusion the truth mark the stages of his growth. Where once, like Quentin Compson (*SF*), the boys used words to sustain self-deception, they begin to communicate without speech: " 'Which un you reckin she dremp about?' Ringo said. [['But I didn't answer that; I knew that Ringo knew I didn't need to' "]] (48/43). They hear Uncle Buck acclaim the heroic John Sartoris but also denounce the "selfish coward" and "damn fool" who "didn't fight; he just stole horses," a Confederate officer confirms (59–60/52–53). Hearsay becomes experience when Father approves the boys' horse stealing, and his men applaud, "Hooraw for Sartoris!" (70–71/62). Observing Father and his people, and later Granny and Drusilla, Bayard discerns through appearances the counterside of his heritage.

When Father tricks a Yankee company into surrendering, the lads marvel at his daring; but the older voice dilutes their pride when it insinuates the fault the boy soon apprehends behind the "incredible":

[[There is a limit to what a child can accept, assimilate; not to what it can believe because a child can believe anything, given time, but to what it can accept, a limit in time, in the very time which nourishes the believing of the incredible. And I was still a child at that moment when Father's and my horses came over the hill and seemed to cease galloping and to float, hang suspended rather in a dimension without time.]] (75–76/66)

Suspended time renders the child's wonder at Father's audacity; but the ignominy of plunder and his childish glee at the half-naked Yankees he denuded taints him and his exploit (76–79/67–70). The grown narrator's equivocal praise intimates the son's unrealized disapproval and prefigures the erosion of his loyalty to tradition.

Father earns Bayard's undiluted awe when he eludes the Yankees who cornered him: "He went up onto Jupiter's bare back like a bird. . . . [[Jupiter took the doors on his chest, only they seemed to burst before he even touched them, and I saw him and Father again like they were flying in the air, with broken planks whirling and spinning around them when they went out of sight"]] (82–83/72–73). But this univocal pitch rarely sounds in a work where irony qualifies what words designate and nullifies romance or delusion.

Bayard enters a critical stage in his development in the third story, "Raid." Through the fourteen year old's confusion the mature voice registers an old order breaking up. Abandoning traditional values, the people live by their wits rather than their principles. The defeated have been [["deprived of everything now save the will and the ability to deceive"]] (110/97). The youths witness Granny, their ethical mentor, dupe the enemy for gain. Bayard honors her absurd courage and genuine compassion for both the white and black poor, but he also detects her moral equivocation. Granny saves the boys from the Yankees, and, with the same straight-backed dignity, she cheats them of mules and horses, then sells back the animals over and over. She soaps the boys' mouths for cursing the Yankees, then joins them to curse "the bastuds" who burn the house (86/75). She orders them to pray for lying but considers herself forgiven for her considerable falsehood. A righteous end justifies the mule chicanery, and she tells God so. She confesses her sins before she dies, but the disparity between Granny's word and deed adds to the youth's moral uncertainty (167–68/146–47) Her valor nonetheless endures and resurfaces in the mature Bayard, who abjures the tradition of righteous murder.

The man's tropes anticipate the lad's progress from self-deception (he believes in a "supremely invincible" land) to the "fact and doom" of defeat, which occasions either ignominy or the valiant struggle for dignity and freedom. Ambiguous like most components of the work, freedom offers the black people both "hope" and "doom," while the defeated white people strive to stand unvanquished. The movement toward freedom (which the grown Bayard exercises against social constraints), converges in a cluster of images, the railroad–river–black tide, constellated with rain, clouds, creek, gully, precipice, and roadway. The "Jordan River" temporarily impedes the inexorable black "tide" when the Yankees dynamite the bridge before the black people could cross (94–97/83–85, 116–22/102–108), and the railroad, once the "straightest thing . . . full of sunlight like water in a river" Bayard had seen, is burned and twisted about the trees (99–100/87–88). The man, his understanding sharpened by a decade of accumulated knowledge, "now" articulates what neither youth could comprehend about the railroad: [["Only I know now it was more than that with Ringo."]] The railroad, about which Faulkner inserts almost eight pages (the longest continuous addition besides the final story), "symbolise[s]" the enslaved black people's "impulse" to freedom and the defeated white people's "motion" toward their liberation or, the sardonic older voice adds, both peoples' "delusion" and "dream" (91–92/81, 106–12/93–99).

Drusilla's telling, incantatory like Miss Rosa's voice in *Absalom, Absalom!,* transports the lads to the scene of the Confederate soldiers' final gesture of defiance, a race against the enemy on what is left of the shining rails, [["the path to glory"]]: [["We saw it, we were there."]] Years of courageous but vain battle, now [["congealed into an irrevocable instant,"]] epitomize for the youths an unbowed spirit: [["Because this, to us, was it"]] (106–12/93–99). The older narrator converts a pointless victory to an icon of Southern invincibility, but, at the same time, his cynical eye deflates what it elevates: [["It was like a meeting between two iron knights of the old time, not for material gain but for principle—honor denied with honor, courage denied with courage—the deed done not for the end but for the sake of the doing—put to the ultimate test and proving nothing save the finality of death and the vanity of all endeavor."]] The initial affirmation ends in negation, a reversal that places value at neither extreme of victory or defeat, but in between, where the humbled who strive to uphold honor achieve nobility of spirit. The moment of glory is soon [["gone, vanished. Only not gone or vanished either, so long as there should be defeated or the descendants of defeated to tell it or listen to the telling."]] Storytellers, like Drusilla, honor those who defy defeat, but it is Bayard and his author who immortalize those who dare to take [["the opportunity to endure"]] when they dispel romantic illusion with the true courage of the unvanquished (111–13/98–99).

[["They couldn't take that from us,"]] the youth says of his people's indomitable spirit, one side of his abiding heritage (112/99).

The other side will challenge the grown Bayard either to pass on what he knows is immoral, or, like Isaac McCaslin in *Go Down, Moses*, to defy tradition and take a stand against a legacy of wrong. A pattern of alternating protagonists hypostasizes Bayard's gradual liberation from his patrimony, "cursed" like Isaac's (*GDM* 298/ 284). The boy in the first three tales remains in the background, observing people lie, steal, and murder to survive. In the fourth story, "Riposte in Tertio," he and his "brother" Ringo, now fifteen, become joint protagonists, compelled by custom to champion family honor and avenge Granny's murder. The boys once saved Granny from their burning house, but at the height of their mule enterprise when they seemed invulnerable to friend or foe, they let her go to her death at Grumby's hands. Bayard takes responsibility for the mistake: "I could have stopped her, and I didn't" (174/153). In the fifth story, "Vendée," he and Ringo track and shoot Grumby, nail his body to a compress door, and his right hand on Granny's gravepost. After the ritual murder, the oblivion of sleep overcomes them, an emblem of the death of innocence and rebirth into a fallen state. But the tribal code elevates Bayard to a hero, as Uncle Buck declares: "Ain't I told you he is John Sartoris' boy?" (213/186). Irony redoubles here, for his father has proven a dubious model; and, some forty pages later, a critical addition underscoring the mature Bayard's compunction at having had to kill deflates Uncle Buck's proud exultation. They [["had to perform more than should be required of children because there should be some limit to the age, the youth at least below which one should not have to kill"]] (254/221). The older Bayard sees no glory in action constrained by social mores rather than elected by personal judgment.

   In the penultimate story, "Skirmish at Sartoris," the fifteen-year-old Bayard again retreats to the background, observing Father advocate injustice and murder for his "good" dream of white supremacy in the new South. The years of learning finally culminate in the last story, "An Odor of Verbena," when the twenty-four-year-old Bayard, now chief protagonist, rejects inherited for self-determined measures of right and wrong. The boy takes the forefront of action when he is initiated into the manhood of killers. Now the man reaffirms his childhood belief in humanity and disavows his people's way of "violence" (288/250) for his own moral code. The present action in the work actually proceeds through the last fifty pages, recasting the previous chapters into recollections of past events that lead to the climactic reversal of values at the end. The separate tales conjointly chronicle Bayard's moral development toward freedom from a legacy of injustice. The shifting viewpoints delineate that progression from the external perspective in the preceding stories to Bayard's inner mind, where experience precipitates to knowledge, knowledge to resolve. The voices and styles separating the youth from the older speaker now merge in the man's voice of comprehension laced with anguish. The grown Bayard admits his view of tradition has reversed and dreads the consequences of the choice he is about to make: [["what, despite myself, despite my raising and background (or maybe because of them) I had for some time known I was becoming and had feared the test of it"]] (247/215). Father's death occasions that test. He will now [[*find out if I am what I think I am or if I just hope; if I am going to do what I have taught myself is right.*]] *"Right"* for him crystallizes in the commandment, [[*"Thou shalt not kill,"*]] mankind's way to [["hope and peace."]] Neither social code nor religious dogma has taught him the lesson, for [["it went further than just having been learned."]] Its roots lie in the child's reverence for life and for human brotherhood transcending color. Bayard fears the stigma of [["cowardice"]] (248–50/215–17) and wants [["to be thought well of"]]; but to live with himself, he, like Isaac, must [["stick to principle in the face of blood and raising and background"]] (280/243, 276/240, 249/217). A conscientious choice exacts its price, but that deters neither Bayard nor Isaac, who does pay all his life. As in *Go Down, Moses,* conscience makes the past not "irremediable."[6] The concluding story Faulkner composed for the novel recasts the preceding chapters into a history of moral maturation and transforms the original adventure tales into a sober appraisal of Southern heritage.

Injustice and wrong in their family histories compel Bayard and Isaac to disclaim the old ways. In part 2 of "An Odor of Verbena," Bayard recollects Father's readiness to kill for his Sutpen-like dream (255–57/221–24) and his [["intolerant eyes"]] that [["acquired that transparent film which the eyes of carnivorous animals have . . . , eyes of men who have killed too much, who have killed so much that never again as long as they live will they ever be alone"]] (265–66/231). George Wyatt, a faithful follower, tells Bayard: [["I know what's wrong: he's had to kill too many folks, and that's bad for a man"]] (260/226). Two months before his death, John Sartoris confesses he [["acted as the land and the time demanded"]]; but [["tired of killing men,"]] he would now do [["a little moral housecleaning."]] Henceforth, he would go unarmed (266/231–32), although he clips a hidden weapon to his wrist. It is too late for housecleaning, but when his rival shoots him, Sartoris dies without firing the derringer whose efficiency Bayard has witnessed. Looking back, he detects guilt in the way Father killed, [["as if he were hiding from his own vision what he was doing"]] (268/233). With [["illimitable grief and regret,"]] the son now sees his father's life recorded in the eyes [["closed over the intolerance,"]] and the [["invisible stain"]] of [["needless blood"]] on hands that [["performed the fatal actions which forever afterward he must have waked and slept with,"]] hands that did [["so much more than they were intended to do or could be forgiven for doing"]] (272/236–37). John Sartoris, nonetheless, dies abstaining from further transgression, a gesture that, in parts 3 and 4 when the present action resumes, points his son toward a new direction.

His stepmother, Drusilla, the latest practitioner of the family's [["rapport for violence"]] (288/250), claims for Bayard an [["attribute only of God's . . . to be permitted to kill, to be permitted vengeance"]] (273–74/237–38), and tests to the limit the young man's convictions. Against the [["vulture-like formality"]] of the [["simple code"]] of killers she has adopted (267/232, 284/246), he must reclaim his childhood belief in human brotherhood and renounce murder even for an honorable cause. Earlier, Drusilla dismisses Bayard's scruples about killing [["human beings,"]] for such [["northerners, foreigners, . . . pirates"]] were [["not anything"]] weighed against Sartoris's [["good dream"]] (257/223–24). Now she would sacrifice Bayard to a custom that requires him to kill or be killed because, she contends, [["he believed what he could not help but believe and was what he could not (could not? would not) help but be"]] (261/227). The lonely steps the unarmed Bayard takes toward his father's murderer unchain him from mindless conformity (he *can* help *not* to believe nor to be) and from Drusilla's enveloping verbena and [["voracious,"]] [["passionate"]] desire for blood (269/234). The flower and the code associated with it are finally deflated in Bayard's image of Drusilla, pinching at once a half-dozen sprigs, all of a size and shape [["as if a machine had stamped them out."]] His break from machine-like behavior is complete when he demythicizes the fragrance that rises above [["the odor of courage,"]] Drusilla's sentimental phrase, to the [["smell of horses,"]] words that conclude the novel on an unromantic note (274/238, 293/254). Bayard's moral courage supersedes her creed of killers. In this work's pattern of ironic reversals, it is precisely the romantic Drusilla, [["priestess of a succinct and formal violence"]] (252/219), who dehumanizes. Faulkner's antithetic form counterpoints what appears to be a celebration of heroics in war and peace with reverence for life and human dignity.

Reflecting the writer's antonymous view of life, the novel pictures human endeavor of little consequence, nothing [["but the loud noises of a moment"]] (3/3); but the struggle against cowardice or wrong opens to possibility. Bayard's vision and deed, set within the span of Sartoris history, appear inconclusive. For old Bayard in *Sartoris* (1929) and *Flags in the Dust* (1973)—deaf, ineffectual, dreaming of his father's exploits (more imaginary than real, *The Unvanquished* tells us)—the youthful vision of the grail has faded. The "momentary flash and glare" of his valiant stand against a killer code does not save him or generations of death-bent Sartorises from self-destruction. A parallel reversal occurs in *Go Down, Moses*, where old Uncle Ike loses moral clarity and nerve. The young Bayard, nonetheless, is the true "unvanquished," who upholds the Faulkner creed of principled action, to redress "a little at least" a legacy of injustice, as does the young Ike McCaslin. For Faulkner, the exercise of moral conviction, despite limited results, signifies true value: [["the deed done not for the end but for the sake of doing, . . . not for material gain but for principle"]] (111/98). Against time, the spirit's moment is engraved forever.

Dilsey in *The Sound and the Fury* fails to keep the Compson family from disintegrating. But, though defeated, Dilsey and people like her "endure." The significance of the unvanquished vanquished lies neither in defeat nor victory, but in the struggle against despair or evil that regenerates humanity. Faulkner's magical changes transform the juvenile adventure tales to a noteworthy example of dissonant art that inscribes a people's progress from loss to "true human existence" in "the values of spirit."[7]

7

Structure and Meaning in *Go Down, Moses*

> Isaac McCaslin, "Uncle Ike," past seventy and nearer eighty
> than he ever corroborated any more, a widower now and uncle
> to half a county and father to no one
> this was not something participated in or even seen by him-
> self, but by his elder cousin, McCaslin Edmonds, grandson of
> Isaac's father's sister and so descended by the distaff, yet not-
> withstanding the inheritor, and in his time the bequestor, of that
> which some had thought then and some still thought should have
> been Isaac's. . . . But Isaac was not one of these:—a widower
> these twenty years, who in all his life had owned but one object
> more than he could wear and carry in his pockets and his hands
> at one time, . . . simply because he loved the woods; who owned
> no property and never desired to since the earth was no man's
> but all men's, as light and air and weather were.
>
> —Faulkner, *Go Down, Moses*

I

WHILE REVISING TEN PUBLISHED STORIES FOR THE SEVEN IN HIS
novel, *Go Down, Moses* (1942), Faulkner composed three paragraphs, including the passage above, and set them at the head of the
first story, "Was" (3–4/3–4).[1] Every story in the novel amplifies
that distillation of a life and its dual guiding principles. In turn, old
Uncle Ike's presence at the start looms over every tale.

Faulkner later says of the original "collection of short stories,"
"after reworking it became seven different facets of one field" (*LG*
54).[2] The fortuitous addition postulates the "one field," Uncle Ike's
two-sided creed, the first of which, "simply because he loved the
woods," entails the second, "owned no property and never desired
to since the earth was no man's but all men's." These precepts distinguish him from Sam's "grandfathers" who "owned the land
long before the white man ever saw it" (165/159), and from his own
forebears, who were owners, bequestors, and inheritors: "but Isaac

132

was not one of these" (3/4). "Different facets" of an embryonic source, the insular stories explore through several generations the roots and outcome of Isaac McCaslin's correlated principles.

Isaac, born in 1867, now "past seventy and nearer eighty," would put the present action in the 1940s, about 1945. "Was" goes back to 1859, "The Old People" to 1879, "The Bear" to 1877–88, and the other stories in the 1930s and 1940s. Old Uncle Ike's guiding precepts resonate through many decades and cast their light on events before and after his time. The dual creed sounds a counter-tone to young Cass's humorous tale of a pre–Civil War episode, which is filtered through the boy Ike's "hearing" and "listening" ("Was" 4/4).[3] His disavowal of ownership silently censures "the old time, the old days" when a system of acquiring and bequeathing reduced nature and black human beings to property. Turl, hunted like an animal, allows white men their illusion of sovereignty but appropriates their every move for his own ends. He wins his freedom to marry Tennie, while Uncle Buck loses his freedom to Miss Sophonsiba, an ironic reversal that derides the white masters and avenges the black man's violated humanity. Isaac's rejection of property highlights Lucas's absurd search for gold at the sacrifice of his dignity and marriage in the second story, "The Fire and the Hearth." The tone turns somber when Rider quests for love and, at its loss, for death ("Pantaloon in Black"), while Samuel "Butch" Beauchamp's hunt for gold on the streets of Chicago ends in his criminal death ("Go Down, Moses"). The right hunt in the central stories instills respect for the freedom of all beings and offsets the general "abhorrence and fear" of nature noted in "The Bear" (193/185). Isaac's fear, not of nature but of property, assesses all bad hunts, the "pursuit and lust" (255/244) for power and possession that desecrates the wilderness and dehumanizes the black people in "Was" and the other tales.

The reference to the land "some had thought then and some still thought should have been" his, contracts decades of censure for Isaac's defection from the family tradition of possessing land and people. Even his black kin, Lucas, who understands the white man's scruples, calls him an "apostate" (39/39); his cousin McCaslin throws at him with no small contempt a "loan" from the farm he disowns; while the uncertain Isaac himself, along with the author, has reservations about his refusal. Repeated incidences of indignity and loss, as when his wife proscribes the marriage bed, and the son he hopes to save from "wrong and shame" is never born, underscore the solitariness distilled in the first sentence: "a widower now and uncle to half a county and father to no one." Effects cited before cause compress a lifetime of blame for one conscientious gesture and also set the narrative spiraling backward to the source of his beliefs and forward to their results unfolding through time.

Some readers consider the work irreparably split between the motifs of the hunt and racial conflict, or the wilderness and society.[4] But joined inextricably in the initial germ, their diverse but complementary uncoilings entwine as well. When Faulkner composed and affixed at the start a capsule of life grounded on its dual creed, he probably foresaw the "novel" he could constitute with the separate stories. The two principles, "he loved the woods," and the correlative, "owned no property and never desired to," interlace in every segment, but the roots and effects of Ike's love for nature are recorded mainly in the central hunting tales, "The Old People," "The Bear," parts 1–3 and 5, and "Delta Autumn," while the effects of the lust for possession unfolds through the other four stories, "Was," "The Fire and the Hearth," "Pantaloon in Black," and "Go Down, Moses." To counterbalance the expanded development of the nature germ, Faulkner composed a few weeks before submitting the manuscript a section tracing the source and consequences of Ike's objection to property. The section grew large as the background to Isaac's deviant gesture against ownership took on cosmic dimensions, encompassing the history of the family, the South, all humankind, and God's plan for it. Typifying Faulkner's antithetic mode, however, the grandeur of that act diminishes at the conclusion, when the young Isaac's wife blackmails him with sex to obtain what she desires, the farm. The pivotal addition becomes part 4 of "The Bear," which Faulkner inserts among the hunt stories to "break the story of the bear" with a "counterpoint" or "discord" that would "suspend this theme for another" (*FWP* 102). But that displaced "moment" turns into a powerful vortex, intertwining the different motifs, including the hunt and racial conflict, clustered around nature's legacy of *"pity and love of justice and liberty"* (297/284) and society's opposite legacy of human rapacity[5] (see II).

Part 4 of "The Bear," which joins the two sides of Uncle Ike's guiding principles and their repercussions in human history, proves for many readers to be the true axis of the work. A few dissenters consider it (along with "Pantaloon in Black") an intrusion into the otherwise coherent segments. Two other dense moments offer possible alternative centers, the blood baptism in the first hunt story ("TOP") that encapsulates the import of the nature creed for Isaac's entire life, and the fullest articulation of its significance, deferred until the third hunt story, "Delta Autumn," when Isaac is past seventy. The germ initiates a framework of dispersal and reciprocity bonding the insular tales. Later moments decenter the work but, at the same time, reinforce the contrapuntal interpermeation of discrete parts. Faulkner's structural design allows the interplay of shifting nuclei and mutually inflecting expansions. As the narrative seeks the source of Isaac's beliefs before his time and advances forward to their influence on his life and beyond, each notable *"happen"* seems to have been foreseen, its effects, foreknown. The theme, evolving in fragments of the conflict between ownership that enslaves both possessor and possessed and freedom that preserves the integrity of the "wild" and the human, complements the formal design of an intermodulant network of "different pieces" (see II).

As widely debated as the work's structure is the significance of Isaac McCaslin's action and his life and the meaning of the novel as a whole. Isaac is generally regarded as a failure, for his break from tradition brings no cure for ills he deplores. In Faulkner's antonymous world, failure inheres in every human action; but such deficiency may not detract from the effort to acknowledge and then to take action, however limited, against "wrong and shame." Isaac's singular repudiation of the time-honored custom of owning and bequeathing land and people focuses the moral issue on the choice open to each person, to perpetuate or to take a stand against a legacy of evil. Synchronous antinomies in form and content render the meaning of Isaac McCaslin's action and life and of the novel as a whole (see III).

Though generally regarded as the greatest of the modular novels, the structure of *Go Down, Moses* remains a puzzle. The editor who affixed *"and Other Stories"* to the first edition of *Go Down, Moses* anticipated decades of perplexed readers. The author had the addition deleted, declaring, "Moses [sic] is indeed a novel" (*SL* 284). Studies trace patterns of action or theme linking the six McCaslin stories, but "Pantaloon in Black," dismissed by one reader as an "unintegrated and therefore non-essential part of the structure," leaves unresolved the original question of structural form.[6] Bypass-

ing the traditional frame of successive or logical order, Faulkner's
"new pattern," a joint formal and thematic design that set the segments inside one another, secures "the interplay" of "a conflict" of
elements that also resolves into "a composition of forces" (Henri
Bergson's terms, *TFW* 190; see Abbreviations for Bergson's
works). "Contrapuntal in integration," the "different pieces" constitute a "novel" (*SL* 278).

II

The blood baptism in "The Old People" retraces the genesis of
Ike's double legacy to Sam's forebears and portends as well the direction of his whole life. That synoptic-prophetic "moment" uncoils through the hunt stories and, chiefly by contrast, the other
stories as well. The twelve year old knows the blood of his first
buck "had merely formally consecrated him to that which, under
the man's tutelage, *he had already accepted,* humbly and joyfully,
with abnegation and with pride too" (165/159, italics added). Years
before the rite, Sam's vision of nature unpossessed and man a grateful recipient of its bounty instills in the child reverence for nature
(171/165), and the stories about his father arouse his misgivings
about rapacity (165–66/159–60). Sam's father Doom murders his
kin to seize land, people, and sovereignty, then sells his lover and
son Sam, crimes grandfather Carothers (the older Isaac discovers)
reenacts when he disposes of his black lover and daughter, whom
he later takes for his mistress, driving the mother to suicide. As
early as nine, the boy foreknows his childhood apprenticeship in
the wild tends toward "that for which Sam had been training him
all his life some day to dedicate himself" (173/167): his consecration at twelve to nature and humane values; and his repudiation at
twenty-one of a patrimony tainted with "injustice" to valuable animals and human beings (298/285)—the inevitable flowering of
Sam's stories of his lost people. When the ten-year-old Ike finally
enters the Big Woods in the second hunt story, "The Bear," he realizes he had "experienced it all before," and "had already dedicated
to the wilderness with patience and humility . . . *all the long life*"
before him (195–96/187, 199/191, italics added). Nature's lessons
on right hunting and living during the first two years in "The Bear"
(parts 1-3) anticipate and also return to the climactic blood rite in

the first hunt story ("TOP") and further back to the start of "Was."
Time spirals back and forth, interlinking the separate parts.

Matching the contrapuntal form, the substance of story balances
oppositions. The "hot smoking blood" bonds the boy to his old
mentor "forever" beyond death, and the two together with the wilderness (164–65/158–59); but the child at ten recognizes he is "a
little different because they were brute beasts and he was not" (200/
192), and "that thin clear quenchless lucidity which alone differed
him from this bear and all the other bears and bucks he would follow during almost seventy years" (207/198) ascribes to his humanity a grave responsibility for all exploited beings, natural and
human. Young Ike's deepening union with the natural world
(207–9/198–201) also initiates him to the spirit world where life
and death appear to be modulations of the same life force. From the
sacrificial buck and the old buck who walks out of "its death" and
receives Sam's homage: "Oleh, Chief, . . . Grandfather" (184/177),
the boy learns of immortality and with it, the code of the right hunt:
"Love and pity for all which lived and ran and then ceased to live
in a second" (182/175); and the rule of right living: "There is only
one thing worse than not being alive, and that's shame" (186/179).
Cass's words will resonate through Isaac's lifelong struggle against
the family legacy of "wrong and shame."

Bewildered by the interfusion of death and life, of flesh and spirit
(Old Ben himself appears to be both physical and incorporeal), the
boy learns from his cousin Cass about the "possibilities of living,"
which are not "invented and created just to be thrown away," but
are resurrected in the "unchanged" primal wilderness (186–87/
179). During the last hunt at Big Bottom ("The Bear" part 5), the
eighteen-year-old Ike declares at his tutors' graves "there was no
death," only a perpetual infusion of eternal spirit in flesh (327–28/
312–13). In the third hunt story ("Delta Autumn") old Uncle Ike
envisions a paradisiacal "dimension free of both time and space"
where "immortal game" and "immortal hounds" run forever,
"falling and rising phoenix-like" (354/337–38). The scene, often
read as the man's attempt to escape his failed life, caps the motif
of eternal return that offsets the lessons on killing and decay and,
reinforcing the counterthemes of decline and resurgence, clarifies
the meaning of Isaac McCaslin's life and the theme of the work.

After the sixteen-year-old Ike and Sam complete their divided
mission to save and also to end the "immortal" Old Ben's life (part

3), the long insertion of part 4 knits the wilderness lessons on man's unique humanity with his moral responsibility for the "wrong and shame" in human and family history, emblematized for Isaac in two images of violated freedom: Carothers's decaying "tremendous abortive" house and the farm, "that whole edifice . . . founded upon injustice and erected by ruthless rapacity and carried on even yet with at times downright savagery not only to the human beings but the valuable animals too" (262/251, 298/285); and the commissary ledger-pages the child mistook as "fading and harmless," but the grown Isaac comprehends as "one instantaneous field" of a long history of "condoned injustice" and the "specific tragedy" of Eunice's suicide, as well as "a little at least of its amelioration and restitution" (289/276, 298/284, 266/254, 261/250). Uncle Hubert's "legacy" of a gold cup and coins that degenerates to a tin pot of copper coins and a "rat's nest" of IOUs typifies progenitors who have overdrawn their moral credit (304–8/290–94). Isaac's ancestor's Sutpen-like dream of a legacy, "worthy of bequeathment for his descendants' ease and security and pride and to perpetuate his name and accomplishments," bestows instead a moral liability (256/245).

In the midst of the twenty one year old's discovery of his cursed heritage and "ravaged patrimony," an incident in the fourteenth-year hunt resurfaces. The lessons Ike learns from the little fyce, who, despite the odds, dares to be "brave" to be worthy of its name, McCaslin distills in one word, "truth," which, like John Keats's urn, *covers all things which touch the heart—honor and pride and pity and justice and courage and love . . . and love of justice and of liberty*" (296–97/283–84). The resurgence of an uncorrupted nature's legacy of virtues and the mortal/immortal bear's "fierce pride of liberty and freedom" (295/282) impels Isaac to add "a little" to the "amelioration and restitution" of injustice against black people and animals. His renunciation of property, however, goes against the very grain of time-honored custom and stands unique. The enlaced motifs of the hunt and racial injustice that culminate in this long section[7] constitute with other motifs the larger theme of responsibility for the twin legacies of nature and society (the latter is discussed in III). Together they underscore the grown Isaac's dilemma, the "shame" of owning land and the "shame" of repudiating the family tradition.

Part 4 may be omitted when "The Bear" is printed by itself,

Faulkner suggests, "but it's a part of the novel" (*FU* 273). Three months before his death, he recapitulates his lifelong view that part 4 is a "necessary portion of what to me was not a collection of short stories, but a novel" (*FWP* 102). The joint structural and thematic design bears out his claim. Synoptic and prophetic like the major segments, part 4 joins and caps the conflict between nature's values and human rapacity; it also prefigures the declining wilderness in part 5 of "The Bear," the ravaged woods in the third hunt story, "Delta Autumn," and the deleterious effects of greed that, initiated in the first story, "Was," climaxes in the final story, "Go Down, Moses."

The homologous uncoilings of the dual creed, oscillating time, suspended polarities, and the cohesive force of counterpoint integrate the segments, but the displaced blood rite and part 4 of "The Bear" nonetheless raise questions about structural coherence. The first four initiatory hunts in Ike's tenth and eleventh years in the second story, "The Bear," prepare him for the blood baptism at twelve, recorded in the previous story, "The Old People." In "The Bear," that momentous consecration to his life's creed is noted in a single sentence (209–10/201), a dislocation eluding studies on patterns of theme or action. If the baptism were placed in chronological order in "The Bear," Ike's union with the wild would accent the irony of his self-elected charge to bring about the death of the "immortal" Old Ben and the paradox of killing to nurture life. The dedication to nature and against ownership early in "The Bear" would lead logically to part 4, when nature's tutelage impels the man to take a stand against exploitation. Faulkner waives the rhetorical and thematic effects of sequential narration for a counterpattern of dispersal and the "mutual penetration" of discrete parts revolving around "one field." The resulting narrative inflects itself over and over.

In the third hunt story, "Delta Autumn," old Uncle Ike in "Was" reappears, but now like Old Ben he has become an "anachronism" (193/185) among remnants of the wild in "an outmoded time" (343/326). Faulkner, who favors a "discord" to "lift" the parts of story, counterpoises the diminished old hunter and woods and the panorama of greed and injustice with the fullest enunciation of the far-reaching *"ripples"* of the blood rite. What the "boy of twelve had been unable to phrase" is finally articulated at eighty: *"I slew you; my bearing must not shame your quitting life. My conduct for-*

ever onward must become your death; marking him for that and for more than that: that day and himself and McCaslin juxtaposed not against the wilderness but against the tamed land, the old wrong and shame itself, in repudiation and denial at least of the land and the wrong and shame even if he couldn't cure the wrong and eradicate the shame" (351/334). The right hunt requires for life taken life lived that would "shame" neither the sacrificial blood nor its recipient.

Two phrases recapitulate the components of the right *"conduct forever onward."* "For that" denotes the boy's dedication to the "wilderness," which "he had already accepted" from Sam. "For more than that" signifies the "tamed land," the "old wrong and shame itself," which at fourteen he thought he could cure and eradicate, but, wiser at twenty-one, "knew that he could do neither but at least he could repudiate the wrong and shame, at least in principle, and at least the land itself in fact, for his son at least" (351/334). Isaac reaches the same conclusion about his heritage as Bayard Sartoris in *The Unvanquished.* He knows that the wrong and shame from "the old time" in "Was" will go on, but "in principle" and "in fact" he must make some restitution ("I must do it" [288/275]) for life sacrificed in the hunt or in pursuit of power and property. That moment of consecration, resurfacing among the ravaged woods and lesser human beings, elevates nature's values over the "corruption" of ownership; but, equivocal like most events, it also underlines the failure of the dual creed to which the boy was dedicated by blood. Reverence for the wild and moral scruples against greed have waned, and the old man himself appears reduced. Injustice and dehumanization, lightened by humor in "Was," now darken the world and portend the coming at the end of a criminal Butch Beauchamp, modern man cut off from "our own sources" (167/161) in nature and familial "solidarity."

Faulkner's antinomic thought and art, however, would admit neither inadequacy nor failure to negate the worth of one person who recognizes "wrong and shame" and tries to effect "a little at least of its amelioration and restitution." Old Uncle Ike acknowledges that action taken "at least in principle" has fallen short of his purpose, "to set at least some of His lowly people free" (259/248) and to hold back the woods' "ultimate doom." But the reason for repudiation remains as valid and compelling in old age as in youth. "He had never wanted to own any of it" so he could "arrest at least that much of what people called progress, measure his longevity at least against that much of its ultimate fate" (354/337). The reiterative "at least" signals Isaac's rcognition of the limits of his modest endeavor. Readers who accuse him of such quixotic ends as saving the wilderness or curing "the wrong" and eradicating "the shame" (351/334) simply overlook the evidence in Faulkner's equilibrated language and form.

III

Isaac's human legacy offers him two models. Those who perpetuate evildoing, like Ikkemotubbe, Carothers, his namesake Roth, their descendant Butch, and lesser characters like the white deputy in "Pantaloon in Black." Then there are those, treated at greater length in the novel, who stand for love, justice, and liberty, and, above all, who, though limited, take a stand against wrong. Isaac's father and uncle, more humane than their father, disavow their corrupt legacy when they consign Carothers's "abortive edifice" (262/251) to the slaves they had freed; but they retain an inbred warp that reduces the black man to animal prey, divesting both hunter and hunted of integrity and freedom. Still, their repudiation of slavery initiates a line of resistance against hereditary wrongdoing.[8] Isaac, the latest in that continuing line, takes the more extreme step when he renounces the family tradition of owning and bequeathing, the McCaslin drive to subjugate natural and human beings encoded in "Was." In Faulkner's system of values, which ranks "failure . . . the best" (*FN* 3), that doomed effort against misdeed marks true nobility of spirit.

Surveying the "stereoptic whole" history of "impervious" evil, Isaac holds no illusions about his conscientious gesture. "And you are just one. How long then? How long?" McCaslin queries. "It will be long," Isaac replies; but every attempt promises its redoubling: "And more than me" (299–300/286). Though dissenting, McCaslin admits that Isaac's father and uncle were "not the first and not alone. A thousand other Bucks and Buddies in less than two generations . . . fumble-heed that truth" about inherited wrong, but there are "not even enough of them" (261/250, 282–83/269–70). Generations striving to free human beings "held in bondage" to those who have "power of life and death" effect some melioration of injustice (254/243).

The twins' half-brother, Lucas Beauchamp, joins the rebels when he repudiates his white ancestry (281/269) and transgresses society's rules to show his white kin, Zack, a measure of manhood other than property: "I'm going to be the man in this house" (12l/ 117). Lucas, however, falls victim to greed; but, unlike the twins who hunt for human game, he forsakes his obsession with buried gold to preserve the hearth fire commemorating his and Molly's wedding night. This deviation from the prevailing hunt pattern that seldom foregoes the pursuit reaffirms the values of love and family underlying the story of another black man, Rider. The Lucas-Zack-Roth story in "The Fire and the Hearth" uncovers beneath the hilarious surfaces of "Was" the seeds of a cursed heritage.

Unlike Lucas, who affronts tradition, Roth preserves the "old curse of his fathers, the old haughty ancestral pride based not on value but on an accident of geography, stemmed not from courage and honor but from wrong and shame," Isaac's formula of inherited evil. The boy Roth disdains the bed and table he has shared with his black brother (Roth's mother died at childbirth and Molly nursed the white baby with her own black baby); and so with "grief" and "shame" he "entered his heritage" and "ate its bitter fruit" (111–14/107–10). Roth's conclusion about Lucas, who "beat" his father, *Even a nigger McCaslin is a better man, better than all* " white men (115–16/112), belies his stereotypic view of the superior white over the inferior black. Isaac's defense of the black's enduring qualities in "The Bear" goes against conventional preconceptions.

The white deputy in "Pantaloon in Black" rehearses the formula when he labels "them damn niggers" a "damn herd of wild buffaloes" incapable of "normal human feelings and sentiments of human beings" (154/149–50).[9] Such notions are refuted, without explicit assertion, in the wordless message of shifting viewpoints and antithetic images in the story. The subjective narration of Rider's experiences with transforming love and, at its loss, with consuming grief, gives way after six condensed pages ("Those six months were now crammed and crowded into one instant of time" [137–41/133–37]) to the white community's exterior view of an inhuman animal. People admire Rider's unusual strength and reputed promiscuity, the conventional attributes of Negro "manhood," but deny him the capacity to feel love and desolation, the marks of his humanity. The reader, who witnesses in the early pages Rider's liberation from a social stereotype to a man who delights in his home life centered on Mannie and their hearth fire, shares his joy and comprehends what the people could not know, the reason for his suicidal despair. Rider's capacity for profound feelings delineated in the first section contravenes the deputy's conclusion that the Negro "aint human" (154/149). The loveless white couple, their food indifferently prepared and eaten, lie at the opposite pole of the black couple's joyous rituals of cooking and eating, bathing and loving. The contrast defines the import of Rider's life, which undergirds the meaning of the whole novel. His story interlinks Tomey's Turl's struggle for his freedom and integrity and Lucas's choice over an enticing treasure the fire in his hearth, symbol of "human coherence and solidarity" (380/361), for which Rider lives and dies.

Set alongside the intensely human Rider and other black people, the white folk, devoted to the "pursuit and lust" of property or power, appear incapable of affection and, thus, less human. Carothers disposes of his pregnant lover, copulates with his own daughter, destroys the mother, then acquits himself of his son-grandson with a thousand dollar bequest. His legacy of a loveless union and betrayal portends Uncle Buck's obligatory marriage to Miss Sophonsiba, their son Isaac's loss of his embittered wife and unborn son, and Roth's abandonment of his lover and child. Isaac himself undermines his life's premises when he who "loved the woods" denies human love transcending color lines. The mulatto woman's indictment of Uncle Ike in "Delta Autumn" resonates throughout, for rarer than the love of nature is human love: "Old man, . . . have you lived so long and forgotten so much that you don't remember anything you ever knew or felt or even heard about love?" (363/346). Embracing a common humanity and abjuring dehumanizing codes, the young Ike does what is right by his moral sense. When in old age he reverts to society's "code" of "honor," which Roth's lover bitterly contemns (358/341–42, 361/345), he betrays his youthful faith in equality and justice for which he sacrificed family and self. The mulatto's harsh censure of the old man who has forgotten about love testifies to the dimming of a once bright vision (363/346).

It is a fine irony that the "non-essential" story of Rider, a black man who is neither a McCaslin nor a possessor like them, embodies the counterforce to the dehumanizing forces of avarice and its concomitant, racial hatred. Ike's devotion to nature or Rider's to Mannie may not endure in an acquisitive world. But in Faulkner's self-inflecting tale, love emerges, through loss and failure, of highest worth.

In yet another ironic twist, the Rider story justifies some of the censure directed at old Isaac, who not only fails to mitigate injustice and exploitation but finally loses sight of "human solidarity." A tale made up of "complete antithesis," however, certifies the meaning not on one side nor the other of irreducible oppositions, but in suspended polarities. Readers who criticize the "innocent" idealist for trying "to escape" old Carothers's "doomed and fatal blood," which "seemed to destroy all it touched" (293/280), overlook the converse idea in the latter half of the sentence. Isaac knows "that even in escaping he was taking with him more of that evil and unregenerate old man who could summon, because she was his property, a human being," and get a child on her and "then dismiss her because she was of an inferior race" (294/281). Yet neither the inescapable legacy of injustice nor the prospect of failure to end it prevents his taking a moral stand.

Isaac's declaration, "I am free," which by itself appears spurious to many readers, is secured with the counterimage of bonds yoking the individual to his past: "the frail and iron thread strong as truth and impervious as evil and longer than life itself" joins "him with the lusts and passions, the hopes and dreams and griefs" of his ancestors. When Isaac reiterates, "Sam Fathers set me free" (299–300/285–86), he refers to nature's legacy, which has liberated him from an inherited rapacity antedating his grandfather and the Old People. On the other hand, Faulkner's idea of "balance" counterpoints Isaac's struggle for freedom with human covetousness from which, Isaac himself admits, "we have never been free." Snared by his wife's obsession with the farm, he concludes, *"we were all born lost"* (295/282, 314/300), and acknowledges the irrevocable hold of heritage, "impervious as evil."

Other passages explicitly contravene the self-righteousness mistakenly attributed to Isaac. With the train and lumber mill, he has helped destroy the "doomed wilderness" (321/306). Like Roth, he has killed does and shares man's "crime and guilt, and his punishment" (347/331, 349/332). Far from assuming moral superiority,

Isaac appears perplexed by his "always incomprehensible" ends (309–10/295–96): "I'm trying to explain . . . something which I have got to do which I dont quite understand myself. . . . I could say I dont know why I must do it but that I do know I have got to because I have got myself to have to live with for the rest of my life and all I want is peace to do it in" (288/275). Even this desire for "peace" has been held against him (*"Not peace but obliteration, and a little food"* is Isaac's reading of Lucas's contempt for his repudiation [109/105]). The context charts not mindless evasion, but resolve born of self-respect while acting on conscience. In "The Bear," the tattered bitch, who has "to be brave once so she could keep on calling herself a dog, and knowing beforehand what was going to happen when she done it" (199/190–91), prefigures Isaac's foolhardy attempt, "I have got to," in the face of certain defeat. "If he could have helped himself, not being the Nazarene, he would not have chosen" (310/296) his life of great privation and little gain besides his people's scorn, encoded at the start of "Was." To seekers of a redemptive strain who would proclaim him a messiah, Isaac is no savior. He has saved no son of his and, instead, has "spoiled" Roth (Roth's lover accuses him of doing so) and may have made him less human (360/343). Equally vain are his efforts to be another Sam to young hunters like Roth and Legate, who despise their mentor's views on nature and human beings.[10]

Readers who ridicule Isaac for such grandiose goals as eradicating the evils of possession and expiating the sins of the fathers miss the precise limits of his purpose: "He couldn't cure the wrong and eradicate the shame"; he "knew that he could do neither but at least he could repudiate the wrong and shame, *at least in principle, and at least the land itself in fact, for his son at least,*" and, "saving and freeing his son, lost him" (351/334–35, italics added). The reiterative "at least" signals his recognition that acting "in principle" and "in fact" effects no universal cure. Isaac's modest proposal is further undercut when his wife, bereft of the farm she covets, proscribes the marriage bed, and the son he hopes to "save and free" is never born.[11] Failure and deprivation, synopsized in the opening sentence and actualized in the rest of the novel, qualify Isaac's moral gesture with irony.

Old Uncle Ike's subsidence in "Delta Autumn" nullifies for many readers the young man's conscientious action. Faulkner's primary principle of contrariety or paradox suggests a different angle on the rise and fall trajectory of Isaac's moral history. The diminished old man typifies Faulkner's melancholy view of mutability. Lucas believes virtue wanes as ownership causes generations to decline (43–44/43–44). Boon, heroic slayer of Old Ben and Sam, degenerates to a hysterical, greedy incompetent (331/315).[12] Butch Beauchamp, who bears a "seed not only violent but dangerous and bad" (372/355), brings the dying McCaslin line to a corrupt end. Old Uncle Ike's blind spot accords with a landscape where the bad hunts for human-animal game recur, and the truths of the heart have lost currency. The gloomy scene counters unqualified optimistic readings of hope and redemption in *Go Down, Moses.*

More the apocalyptic prophet, Isaac brings no salvation to an unregenerate world, no hope for the "ruined woods" (349/332, 364/347). Still, Faulkner's equilibrated narrative poises against human failing "that thin clear quenchless lucidity which alone differed" man from bear (207/198). "Thin" but "quenchless," the drive to resist and act against iniquity reaffirms the author's faith in a "quality in man that prevails," that "will never stop trying to get rid of Snopes," the latter-day avatars of Carothers's amoral rapacity (*FU* 34). If nothing else, there are Aunt Mollie (spelled thus in "Go Down, Moses") and Miss Worsham, who keep the small flame of "human coherence and solidarity" burning and, aided by a good but deficient Gavin Stevens, help stray members of the human family *"to come home right"* (383/365). Insight and will eventually dim, but failure or folly may not extinguish the spreading *"ripples"* of that high moment of youthful aspiration for good.

The author's equivocal judgment of character balances the positive and negative aspects of Isaac's life. Instead of withdrawing, Isaac should have tried to do "something about it, . . . to change it." "I think a man ought to do more than just repudiate. He should have been more affirmative instead of shunning people" (*FU* 246, *LG* 225). But Faulkner also tempers censure with praise for Isaac's "wisdom," his capacity to recognize wrong and his efforts to do "a little better": "This story was to me a universal story of the man who, still progressing," tries to be "better than his father, hoping that his son shall be a little better than he" and "to cope" in "terms of justice and pity and compassion and strength" (*LG* 115).[13] Acting on "principle," Isaac counters those who remain insensible to misdeeds and who decline to keep inherited wrong from being passed on. "I will not profit from this which is wrong and sinful,"

Faulkner himself speaks for Isaac (*FU* 276). And again in an un-published segment of tapes at the University of Virginia: "If what I know to be evil and unjust worry me so[,] I must do something about it, . . . as failed as I am and as solitary as I am against a vast weight of public opinion" (UV T-144) "Man will always be unjust to man, yet there must always be people, men and women who are capable of the compassion toward that injustice and hatred of that injustice, and the will to risk public opprobrium, to stand up and say, This is rotten, this stinks, I won't have it" (*FU* 148). The charge to the writer applies as well to the character, for the author sees writing and resisting wrong as twin analogues of the effort to improve the human condition. Through the dichotomies of Faulk-ner's echoic narrative "emerge[s]" a measure of virtue: to try and fail is more honorable than to do nothing against evil. This creed probably underlies Faulkner's unpublished remark on the end of "The Bear": "That to me was a promise of optimism, a belief of mine that man, no matter how failed he is, is tougher than any-thing" (UV T-144).

He extols "the gallantry" of the failed effort. In tragedy, "man wishing to be braver than he is" falls short, but "the splendor, the courage of his failure" makes him a worthy "opponent" of the gods (*FU* 51). "Failure to me is the best," he concludes. "To try some-thing you can't do, because it's too much . . . , but still to try it and fail, then try it again. That to me is success" (*FN* 3–4). The flawed effort may not detract from Isaac's moral insight, which few pos-sess with more clarity and enact at greater personal cost. The mean-ing of Isaac McCaslin's life and of Bayard Sartoris's in *The Unvanquished* lies not in success or failure, but in that moment of clarity when they act on the higher impulse to do what is right. For, Faulkner contends, "out of every failure there arises always a new handfull [sic] who decline to be convinced by failure, who believe still that the human problems can be solved . . . , still irreconcilable and undismayed" (*ESPL* 166–67). A single counterforce, though deficient, keeps the Carotherses from having their way. If there were no Isaacs, "and more than" he, then the woods and human-kind too would be truly "doomed."

Against the consummation of eschatological time, Faulkner poses the free choice of human beings to damn or to redeem them-selves. An act of conscience postpones or arrests the doom prom-ised in wrongdoing and opens the future to possible melioration. In exploiting nature, humankind enacts a foreordained evil; but each individual may do so with respect and reverence or violence and rapacity, and thus be ennobled or debased. Like the biblical Isaac, who fulfills God's promise to Abraham and also contains the seeds of future nations, Isaac McCaslin, both visionary and blind, points backward and forward to fulfillment, decay, and possibility. In Faulkner's paradoxical narrative, declension contains the seed of ascension.

Conclusion

On a balmy August night in 1955 at Nagano, Japan, I walked beside William Faulkner. I was one of a group of Japanese and American professors making its way slowly along a narrow street crowded with celebrants of the summer festival, up a hill toward an ancient wooden temple and its famous cracked bell. Small booths overflowing with paper flowers, ribbons, candies, toys, and redolent incense sticks lined both sides of the street. Wind chimes tinkled over the sounds of men, women, and children, dressed in colorful summer kimonos, talking and laughing and jostling every which way. A wooden pipe stuck in his mouth, Faulkner's eyes darted in every direction, taking in every detail. I kept glancing at him, hoping he would say something, but I knew I would not hear a single word unless somehow I could get him to remove that pipe. We had forewarning of his reluctance to converse, particularly about his works, but some topics like hunting might obtain a response. I thought of "The Bear" and the boy in it, and I asked about the rite of initiation to manhood through the hunt. Sure enough, out came the pipe, though the eyes continued to rove. He was trained to hunt as a child. "That's the way it is in my country, boys grow up learning to hunt." He learned to face the challenge of the wilderness, and after a few more comments about the woods, back in went the pipe. Fearing a permanent silence, I recalled two other topics that supposedly never failed to elicit his interest, horses and his daughter. Those did open the gates somewhat. He spoke of his love for horses and indirectly of his feelings for young Jill. "I have taught her everything I know about horses. She's a pretty good horsewoman." I wondered about his calling himself a farmer. He assured me he was and talked about the land and the crops he grew, his animals, and other related matters. We soon arrived at the Zenkoji temple, and the rest of the evening we watched ancient dances and heard the old cracked bell.

William Faulkner was a representative of the Department of State at a seminar on American Literature for Japanese professors. The Japanese intelligentsia had embraced Faulkner, reading him in English and in Japanese, the latter the work of professors who vied for the prestige of translating a difficult writer in English into their difficult language. The best known among them attended the seminar. For ten days Faulkner sat at a table on an elevated platform, behind him a *tokonoma,* a delicately colored screen with an oblong silk painting hanging from the center panel, and a flower arrangement before it. The rest of us sat on the tatami floor, literally looking up at the writer who spoke for whole afternoons about his land and his people, both real and fictional; and belying the rumors, discussed at length his work and the art of writing. The sound of running water infused that serene hall, open on both sides to the rising perspectives of exquisite Japanese gardens.

Listening to the world-famous writer day after day left me certain I had met and heard a great man. The unfailing courtesy, the thoughtful response to every query, however odd, and the willingness to address any aspect of his work impressed his audience. His discourses on art were illuminating, but what struck me were his reiterations on the high purpose of art: "the strongest and most durable force man has invented" to record the fact that "he endures and hopes in spite of darkness"; and his faith in "man" who "can and does do better than he ever believed he would" (*FN* 186, 28–29; see Abbreviations for the list of Faulkner's works). Early in his career, Faulkner was the difficult writer who scoured the dregs of society. The man I heard acknowledged the human capacity for evil, but reiterated his faith in the individual responsibility to recognize wrong and, though doomed to fail, to persist against injustice. The writer he charged with the duty to promote the human struggle for good. I detected an undertone of anguish when he spoke of the problems of his "country," the South he loved and hated. He believed the future of his larger country, the United States, would be measured in its capability to acknowledge and correct its mistakes. This, I became certain, was a writer with a moral prospect. And I was curious to see if the works reflected the vision.

I discovered later that the "living voice" I heard at Nagano (*FN,* viii),[1] speaking in measured Southern accents about endurance and courage while contending with wrong, reechoes through the canon. For the writer beset with the unreliable word, Faulkner prescribed the same persistence. He discussed at length the "form," "method," "pattern," and "design" that would bring the word closer to vision. But Faulkner's commentaries on his art did not prepare me for what I would discover in the fiction, a simple enough notion about enduring misfortune and resisting evil embodied in extremely complex, self-denying form. I puzzled over the reiterative contradictions, the drive to rehearse in yet another "new way" the same tale, as though the right way were forever unattainable. After retracing the words I heard and many others through decades of study, I uncovered two clues to Faulkner's obsessive drive to try again: his distrust of language and his desire to overcome the enemy. Underlying those two motives was something close to despair at the imprecision of the art of writing. I heard him iterate his belief that "no poet, no writer, is ever satisfied with what he has done" because "it wasn't quite good enough," "it wasn't as moving as he wanted it to be, so he tries again" (*FN* 61, 53). The bleak note resounds throughout his life. Being a writer is the "worst vocation." "Demon-run," writing is "frustrating work" which is "never good enough. What the reward is for a writer, I don't know" (*LG* 220–21). The "method" seldom, if ever, matches the "dream." Perhaps, as Faulkner puts it, "the words kill it" (*ESPL* 187). The search for *the* word thus never ends.

Faulkner's recognition early in his career of the treacherous nature of his medium may have led to his break from established practice to effect a "dialogic tension" among antinomies in the language and form of fiction. Long after Nagano, I found contradiction to be Faulkner's natural mode. The words I heard in Japan counterpoise oppositions, and the "internal stratification"[2] of language, form, and substance in the fiction sustains paradox. Meaning remains suspended or deferred in the interplay of "*myriad components*" denying but also reinforcing one another. I was led to conclude that reducing a work to one polar side or the other was to break faith with the Faulkner I heard and rediscovered in his works. In division lies his wholeness.

Faulkner's bisected thought and antithetic form generate irony unlike the New Critical irony that goes beyond "mere yoking" to a "balance," that is, "a reconciliation" of mutually exclusive factors, according to Cleanth Brooks. Balance for Faulkner denotes a protracted dialectic, the interpermeation of opposites. For the New Critic, the imagination functions to "fuse the conflicting elements in a harmonious whole," to resolve "apparent discords," and thus obtain "a larger unity." The tensive "balancing of impulses" I. A. Richards would admit in poetry, Brooks turns into a "union of opposed impulses." Irony fuses the "irrelevant and discordant" and arrives at "stability."[3] Faulkner, on the other hand, thinks the imagination resists a "union" subsuming one side under the other, and instead preserves an unstable but essential engagement of discordant entities.

The New Critical doctrines on reconciliation and unity have conditioned decades of criticism, and inspired efforts to resolve inconsistencies in Faulkner or, with no little exasperation on the part of some readers, to impute incongruities to weakness of thought or artistry. Resistant to simple reduction, Faulkner's polyphonic form and design foster the dialogical play of difference, and the "layering of significance" (Roland Barthes's phrase) in fiction bypasses resolution and closure for perpetual self-qualification. If, Barthes declares, we write "ambiguously enough to suspend meaning," or proceed "as if the world signified though without saying *what,* then writing . . . gives the world an energy."[4] In Faulkner, the suspended meaning gives the *word* energy to surpass itself.

Truth for Faulkner lies in "a balance, a counterpoint" (*FN* 80) of heterogeneous components. Paradox obtains sense at neither end, but within the range of potentialities in its polar field. Barthes's formulation of a text transcending the limits of language renders precisely Faulkner's method: "In the text of pleasure, the opposing forces are no longer repressed but in a state of becoming: nothing is really antagonistic, everything is plural." The text of pleasure, Barthes adds, devalues conflict and sustains difference. "Let difference surreptitiously replace conflict." "Difference . . . is achieved over and above conflict, it is beyond and alongside conflict."

Although such a text "consists of language," it can "be outside languages" when it "destroys utterly, *to the point of contradiction,* its own discursive category," or if it attacks "the canonical structures of the language itself." "By transmutation . . . this extraordinary state, . . . outside origin and outside communication, then becomes language, and not a language." Faulkner's fiction exemplifies a form of "vocal writing" that transcends discourse. The aim of *"writing aloud,"* Barthes maintains, is "not the clarity of messages, the theatre of emotions; what it searches for . . . are the pulsional incidents, the language lined with flesh, a text where we can hear the grain of the throat," a "whole carnal stereophony . . . not that of meaning, of language," but, "in their materiality, their sensuality," the "whole presence of the human [muzzle]."[5] The "living voice" I heard at Nagano continues to live, a human presence in the "long silence of . . . notlanguage" in his work. His narrative a complex web of inexhaustible embeddings, Faulkner writes books less of statements, and more of intimations.

Notes

INTRODUCTION

1. See Abbreviations for the works of William Faulkner, cited or consulted.

2. Frank Kermode, *The Sense of an Ending* (New York: Oxford University Press, 1967/1975) 71, see also 56, 177.

3. Jean-Paul Sartre, "Time in Faulkner: *The Sound and the Fury*," in *William Faulkner: Three Decades of Criticism*, eds. Frederick J. Hoffman and Olga W. Vickery, trans. Martine Darmon (New York: Harcourt, Brace & World, 1963), 225–32.

4. "Form" refers to "all linguistic elements by which contents are expressed" (Rene Wellek and Austin Warren, *Theory of Literature*, 3rd. ed. [New York: Harvest/HBJ Books, 1977], 140), but this study distinguishes technical from structural form, the "design" or "pattern" that organizes the components of technique. Some representative studies on Faulkner's form, that is, language, technique, and structure, include: Conrad Aiken, "William Faulkner: The Novel as Form," in *William Faulkner: Three Decades of Criticism*, eds. Frederick J. Hoffman and Olga W. Vickery (New York: Harcourt, Brace & World, 1963), 135–42; and in *William Faulkner: Four Decades of Criticism* (East Lansing: Michigan State University Press, 1973); Warren Beck, "William Faulkner's Style," in *Faulkner: Essays* (Madison: University of Wisconsin Press, 1976), 34–51; J. E. Bunselmeyer, "Faulkner's Narrative Styles," *American Literature* 53, no. 3 (November 1981): 424–42; Donald M. Kartiganer, *The Fragile Thread: The Meaning of Form in Faulkner's Novels* (Amherst: University of Massachusetts Press, 1979); Arthur F. Kinney, *Faulkner's Narrative Poetics: Style as Vision* (Amherst: University of Massachusetts Press, 1978); Martin Kreiswirth, "Centers, Openings, and Endings: Some Faulknerian Constants," *American Literature* 56, no. 1 (March 1984): 38–50; Stephen M. Ross, *Fiction's Inexhaustible Voice: Speech and Writing in Faulkner* (Athens: University of Georgia Press, 1989); Hugh M. Ruppersburg, *Voice and Eye in Faulkner's Fiction* (Athens: University of Georgia Press, 1983); Walter J. Slatoff, *Quest for Failure: A Study of William Faulkner* (Ithaca: Cornell University Press, 1960).

5. The hyphen and slash (-,/) denote two kinds of sustained polarity in Faulkner's thought and art. The hyphen (except compounded words like "self-qualifying") represents a cyclic movement from one polar side to the other, as in "condensation-expansion." A slash indicates correlated terms like "time/meaning convergences" or synchronous antinomies like "synoptic/prophetic condensations."

6. Robert Scholes, "Fiction," in *Elements of Literature*, 4th ed. eds. Robert Scholes, Nancy R. Comley, Carl H. Klaus, and Michael Silverman (New York: Oxford University Press, 1991), 138.

7. Like many other writers, Michael Millgate identifies "design" in Faulkner's work with Yoknapatawpha County (*Faulkner's Place* (Athens: University of Georgia Press, 1997), 121.

8. Paul De Man, *Allegories of Reading* (New Haven: Yale University Press, 1979), 131; Jacques Derrida, *La carte postale* (Paris: Flammarion, 1980), 302, quoted in Ralph Flores, *The Rhetoric of Doubtful Authority: Deconstructive Readings of Self-Questioning Narratives, St. Augustine to Faulkner* (Ithaca: Cornell University Press, 1984), 153; Robert Penn Warren, "Introduction: Faulkner: Past and Future," in *Faulkner: A Collection of Critical Essays,* ed. Robert Penn Warren (Englewood Cliffs, N.J.: Prentice-Hall, 1966), 14.

9. Roland Barthes, *The Pleasure of the Text*, trans. Richard Miller (New York: Hill and Wang, 1975), 12.

10. Some representative studies on Faulkner's language and style include: Bunselmeyer, "Faulkner's Narrative Styles"; Flores, *The Rhetoric of Doubtful Authority*; Lothar Hönnighausen, *William Faulkner: The Art of Stylization in His Early Graphic and Literary Work* (New York: Cambridge University Press, 1987); Judith Lockyer, *Ordered by Words: Language and Narration in the Novels of William Faulkner* (Carbondale: Southern Illinois University Press, 1991); John T. Matthews, *The Play of Faulkner's Language* (Ithaca: Cornell University Press, 1982); and Patrick O'Donnell, "The Spectral Road: Metaphors of Transference in Faulkner's *As I Lay Dying*," *Papers on Language and Literature* 20, no. 1 (winter 1984): 60–79; Noel Polk, "Trying No to Say: A Primer on the Language of *The Sound and the Fury*," in *Children of the Dark House: Text and Context in Faulkner* (Jackson: University Press of Mississippi, 1996), 99–136.

Early critics like Jean-Paul Sartre, Conrad Aiken, and Robert Penn Warren began to explore Faulkner's "modernism." More recent studies based on contemporary theorists, such as Mikhail Bakhtin, Roland Barthes, Jacques Derrida, Gerard Genette, and Tzvetan Todorov, focus on Faulkner's language and the technique of loss or absence, but rarely note his structural design. Examples of these works include: Sonja Bašić, "Faulkner's Narrative Discourse: Mediation and Mimesis," in *New Directions in Faulkner Studies: Faulkner and Yoknapatawpha, 1983*, eds. Doreen Fowler and Ann J. Abadie (Jackson: University Press of Mississippi, 1984), 302–21; Bašić, "Faulkner's Narrative: Between Involvement and Distancing," in *Faulkner's Discourse: An International Symposium*, ed. Lothar H. Hönnighausen (Tubingen: Max Niemeyer Verlag, 1989), 141–48; Flores, *The Rhetoric of Doubtful Authority*; Virginia V. James Hlavsa, *Faulkner and the Thoroughly Modern Novel* (Charlottesville: University Press of Virginia, 1991); Donald M. Kartiganer, "Faulkner's Art of Repetition," in *Faulkner and the Craft of Fiction: Faulkner and Yoknapatawpha, 1987*, eds. Doreen Fowler and Ann J. Abadie (Jackson: University Press of Mississippi, 1989), 21–47; Martin Kreiswirth, "Plots and Counterplots: The Structure of *Light in August*," in *New Essays on Light in August*, ed. Michael Millgate (Cambridge: Cambridge University Press, 1987), 55–79; Richard C. Moreland, *Faulkner and Modernism: Rereading and Rewriting* (Madison: University of Wisconsin Press, 1990); Gail L. Mortimer, *Faulkner's Rhetoric of Loss: A Study in Perception and Meaning* (Austin: University of Texas Press, 1983).

11. Numerous studies explore sociology, history, philosophy, psychology, religion, and morality in Faulkner. A few representative studies include: George C. Bedell, *Kierkegaard and Faulkner: Modalities of Existence* (Baton Rouge: Louisi-

ana State University Press, 1972); Ineke Bockting, *Character and Personality in the Novels of William Faulkner: A Study in Psychostylistics* (Lanham, MD: University Press of America, 1995); Cleanth Brooks, *William Faulkner: The Yoknapatawpha Country* (New Haven: Yale University Press, 1963) and *William Faulkner: Toward Yoknapatawpha and Beyond* (New Haven: Yale University Press, 1978); Doreen Fowler, *The Return of the Repressed* (Charlottsville: University Press of Virginia, 1997); Doreen Fowler and Ann J. Abadie, eds. *Faulkner and Religion: Faulkner and Yoknapatawpha, 1989* (Jackson: University Press of Mississippi, 1991); Daniel Hoffman, *Faulkner's Country Matters: Folklore and Fable in Yoknapatawpha* (Baton Rouge: Louisiana State University Press, 1989); John T. Irwin, *Doubling & Incest/Repetition & Revenge: A Speculative Reading of Faulkner* (Baltimore: Johns Hopkins University Press, 1975); Donald M. Kartiganer and Ann J. Abadie, eds. *Faulkner and Psychology: Faulkner and Yoknapatawpha, 1991* (Jackson: University Press of Mississippi, 1994); Michael Millgate, *Faulkner's Place* (Athens: University of Georgia Press, 1997); Mortimer, *Faulkner's Rhetoric of Loss*; Max Putzel, *Genius of Place: William Faulkner's Triumphant Beginnings* (Baton Rouge: Louisiana State University Press, 1985); Kevin Railey, *History, Ideology, and the Production of William Faulkner* (Tuscaloosa: University of Alabama Press, 1999); Daniel J. Singal, *William Faulkner: The Making of a Modernist* (Chapel Hill: University of North Carolina Press, 1997); and William J. Sowder, *Existential-Phenomenological Readings on Faulkner* (Conway, AR: UCA Press, 1991).

12. In the "quest for meaning," says Tzvetan Todorov, we "search not for what the word designates, but for what it signifies" (*The Poetics of Prose*, trans. Richard Howard [Ithaca: Cornell University Press, 1977], 138).

13. The existence of theory may lead readers to assume that the writer adheres deliberately to his own prescriptions. Faulkner throws the idea in doubt when he contends in published and unpublished commentaries that "instinct" guides the writer and the story "compels its own form." Sometimes from the start it knows "exactly how it wants me to write it" (*FN* 79). The subconscious hovers over an idea until it has become "new," and the story has taken "its final shape before it ever comes into the conscious mind as an idea to write" (*FU* 238). Still, Faulkner insists, the story has to be worked through "mentally until it begins to sound right" before it is put down on paper (*FU* 55). The work takes shape in the deeper levels of mind, but some measure of what is "right," perhaps unarticulated but operative, drives the seemingly unconscious creation of story. That instinctive guide may eventually materialize in a theory. Suspended polarities in Faulkner's thought and art should dissuade us from equating theory with practice without qualification; or from dismissing inconsistencies in his thought and art as exclusive rather than mutually essential components.

The scattered sources of Faulkner's theory pose questions of accuracy and placement. The context of a pronouncement, a letter or speech, or a question and reply, and the recurrence of an idea through several decades determine its weight or place in the theoretical system outlined in chapter 1. (The author's consistently masculine terminology is observed throughout.)

14. Panthea Reid Broughton traces the beginnings of Faulkner's theory of art in his early critical readings and reviews ("An Amazing Gift: The Early Essays and Faulkner's Apprenticeship in Aesthetics and Criticism," in Fowler and Abadie, eds. *New Directions in Faulkner Studies*, 322–57).

1. THEORY OF LANGUAGE AND NARRATIVE

1. See Abbreviations for the list of Faulkner's works.
2. Faulkner in theory distinguishes voice from point of view. In fiction, voices often intermingle, while viewpoints splinter or shift. Most studies interchange the terms, narrator or voice and point of view or perspective. See for example: Norman Friedman, "Point of View in Fiction: The Development of a Critical Concept" *PMLA* 70 (1955); reprinted in *The Theory of the Novel*, ed. Philip Stevick (New York: Free Press, 1967), 108–37; and Robert Scholes and Robert Kellogg, *The Nature of Narrative* (New York: Oxford University Press, 1966/1979), 240–82. Shlomith Rimon explains Genette's distinction between point of view and voice in "A Comprehensive Theory of Narrative: Genette's Figures III and the Structuralist Studies of Fiction," *PTL: A Journal for Descriptive Poetics and Theory of Literature* 1 (1976): 33–62, see especially 50–56. Stephen M. Ross outlines a "taxonomy of voice" in Faulkner: the phenomenal voice of speech as an event or object in the fictive world, the mimetic voice of speech acts, the psychic voice of inner consciousness, and the authorial or intertextual (also labeled oratorical) voice which is "Faulknerian" (12–17, and passim). Faulkner's "written texts are fundamentally voiced" as the writer seeks "to invigorate the written with living voice" (*Fiction's Inexhaustible Voice: Speech and Writing in Faulkner* [Athens: University of Georgia Press, 1989], 236). Hugh M. Ruppersburg distinguishes point of view or perspective from narrator, and concludes that the former determines "narrative structure" (*Voice and Eye in Faulkner's Fiction* [Athens: University of Georgia Press, 1983], 14–19, 28, and passim).
3. The William Faulkner Collection at the Alderman Library, University of Virginia, includes Holograph manuscripts and Typescripts (HM,TM), as well as published and unpublished materials and tapes, marked UV with file name and number in this study. Quotations from the tapes are all unpublished. A facsimile edition of manuscripts at the Alderman, the Arents Collection, and the Albert A. and Henry W. Berg Collection at the New York Public Library has appeared under the general title, *William Faulkner Manuscripts*, a 44-volume set from Garland Publishing, New York (1986–).
4. Carvel Collins notes Faulkner's use of "regional or historical or topical" materials and mythic or psychological patterns to frame a work (29, 32–35) ("Introduction" to *Mayday* [Notre Dame, IN: University of Notre Dame Press, 1976], 3–41). Cleanth Brooks exemplifies at its best the use of background to illuminate form in *William Faulkner: The Yoknapatawpha Country* (New Haven: Yale University Press, 1963) and *William Faulkner: Toward Yoknapatawpha and Beyond* (New Haven: Yale University Press, 1978). Karl F. Zender traces "the evolution of William Faulkner's art" through "themes and motifs" on the disappearance of the traditional South and the emergence of modern America (*The Crossing of the Ways: William Faulkner, the South, and the Modern World* [New Brunswick, NJ: Rutgers University Press, 1989], ix–x). See also Michael Millgate, *Faulkner's Place* (Athens: University of Georgia Press, 1997); Max Putzel, *Genius of Place: William Faulkner's Triumphant Beginnings* (Baton Rouge: Louisiana State University Press, 1985); and Kevin Railey, *History, Ideology, and the Production of William Faulkner* (Tuscaloosa: University of Alabama Press, 1999).
5. Max Putzel, "Faulkner's Trial Preface to *Sartoris*: An Eclectic Text," *Papers of the Bibliographical Society of America* 74 (1980): 375.

6. Frank Kermode, *The Sense of an Ending* (London: Oxford University Press, 1967/1975), 45–46, 177. Jean-Paul Sartre, "Time in Faulkner: *The Sound and the Fury*," in *William Faulkner: Three Decades of Criticism*, eds. Frederick J. Hoffman and Olga W. Vickery (New York: Harcourt, Brace & World, 1963), 230; Jean Pouillon, "Time and Destiny in Faulkner," in *Faulkner: A Collection of Critical Essays*, ed. Robert Penn Warren (Englewood Cliffs, NJ: Prentice-Hall, 1966), 81–82. For a study on Faulkner's linguistic representations of synchronic time, see my "The Language of Time in Fiction: A Model in Faulkner's 'Barn Burning,' " *Journal of Narrative Technique* 24, no. 2 (spring 1994): 98–113.

7. Dorothy Commins, *What Is an Editor? Saxe Commins at Work* (Chicago: University of Chicago Press, 1978), 202. Dirk Kuyk, Jr., in *Threads Cable-Strong: William Faulkner's Go Down, Moses* (Lewisburg, PA: Bucknell University Press, 1983) distinguishes juxtaposition from condensation. Faulkner prefers the latter term, he concludes, but the two devices combined form paradox. In Faulkner's extended remarks on the subject, the two terms are interchangeable. Juxtaposition to him is a form of condensation, yoking or fusing unlike but reciprocal elements. Joseph W. Reed, Jr. (*Faulkner's Narrative* [New Haven: Yale University Press, 1973]) remarks on this ruling principle: "All of Faulkner's stated generic standards are judgments based upon condensation" (277), then illustrates it generally with elements of content rather than form or style. Francois L. Pitavy discusses the contrapuntal treatment of character and theme in the work, but he sees examples of condensation only in the "inordinate use of adjectives," in compound words, and oxymorons ("A Stylistic Approach to *Light in August* in *William Faulkner's Light in August: A Critical Casebook*, ed. Francois L. Pitavy [New York: Garland, 1982]: 177–201).

8. UV: TS of Stephen Longstreet, "William Faulkner in California," printed in *Cavalier*, 15 (April 1965), 58–61; 15 (May 1965): 50–52, 85–86; and reprinted in *Conversations with William Faulkner*, ed. M. Thomas Inge (Jackson: University Press of Mississippi, 1999): 42–57 (p. 44).

9. Ralph Flores, *The Rhetoric of Doubtful Authority: Deconstructive Readings of Self-Questioning Narratives, St. Augustine to Faulkner* (Ithaca: Cornell University Press, 1984), 153.

10. Percy A. Scholes, *The Concise Oxford Dictionary of Music*, 2d ed., ed. John Owen Ward (London: Oxford University Press, 1964), 135–36, 208–209. *The New Harvard Dictionary of Music*, ed. Don Michael Randel (Cambridge: Harvard University Press, 1986), 328. M. Carpenter Wilde, *A Loving Gentleman: The Love Story of William Faulkner and Meta Carpenter* (New York: Simon & Schuster, 1976), 65. In an unpublished segment of tapes at the University of Virginia, Faulkner states, "I heard of Bach at the moment when I needed to use counterpoint" (UV T-145).

11. Putzel, "Faulkner's Trial Preface to *Sartoris*," 378. Martin Kreiswirth, *William Faulkner: The Making of a Novelist* (Athens: University of Georgia Press, 1983). The research and editions of Carvel Collins and James B. Meriwether (see Bibliography) initiated a number of studies on the development of germs of action, character, and theme from the early to the later works. From the unfinished *Elmer* through the first three completed novels, *Soldiers' Pay, Mosquitoes*, and *Flags in the Dust*, Philip Cohen examines among several elements of narrative technique the repetition or juxtaposition of scene, character, image, and symbol, and the association of different time modes that later mark the greatest works ("Faulkner's

Early Narrative Technique and *Flags in the Dust*," *Southern Studies* 24, no. 2 (summer 1985): 202–20). Michel Gresset's psychological study of Faulkner's artistic development traces the evolution of youthful obsessions and illusions in the early poetry and fiction through the mature works written after 1935 (*Fascination: Faulkner's Fiction 1919–1936*, trans. Thomas West [Durham, NC: Duke University Press, 1989]). Other studies include: Judith Sensibar, *The Origins of Faulkner's Art* (Austin: University of Texas Press, 1984); and Judith Bryant Wittenberg, *Faulkner: The Transfiguration of Biography* (Lincoln: University of Nebraska Press, 1979).

12. *Aristotle's Theory of Poetry and Fine Art,* ed. S. H. Butcher, corrected version of the 4th ed. (1911) (New York: Macmillan, 1932), reprinted under Aristotle, *The Poetics,* in *Criticism, the Major Statements,* eds. Charles Kaplan and William Anderson, 3rd ed. (New York: St. Martin's Press, 1991), 21–53.

13. Faulkner's description of "working up to that moment, to explain why it happened or what it caused to follow," seems to trace the causal line, but the similarity is misleading. Faulkner's fractured narrative seldom proceeds in logical sequence, but rather shifts back and forth among the "pieces" of cause and effect. Surfacing intermittently through the disjunct surfaces of narrative, those segments ultimately constitute the broken but complete line of deed and retribution.

14. A discussion of the theory of language and narrative is beyond the scope of this study, but the theorists and critics cited in the notes and bibliography are among many who set the ground for this examination of Faulkner's language and form. Faulkner's reading included a broad spectrum of English, American, and European writers, from Flaubert and the French Symbolists, to Joseph Conrad, Herman Melville, James Joyce, T. S. Eliot, and Ezra Pound (Millgate, *The Achievement* 289–91. See also Joseph L. Blotner, *A Catalogue of the Library of William Faulkner.* Charlottesville: University Press of Virginia, 1964).

2. *LIGHT IN AUGUST:* BERGSON AND FAULKNER ON THE LANGUAGE OF TIME AND NARRATIVE FORM

1. See Abbreviations for the list of the works of William Faulkner and Henri Bergson. Studies on Bergson's philosophy include: H. Wildon Carr, *Henri Bergson: the Philosophy of Change* (New York: Kennikat, 1912/1970); T. E. Hulme, *Speculations: Essays on Humanism and the Philosophy of Art* (London: Routledge and Kegan Paul, 1924); William James, "The Philosophy of Bergson," in *A Pluralistic Universe* (New York: Longmans, Green, 1909); *The New Bergson,* ed. John Mullarkey (New York: Manchester University Press, 1999).

Studies on time in literature and Bergson's influence include the following: Margaret Church in *Time and Reality: Studies in Contemporary Fiction* (Chapel Hill: University of North Carolina Press, 1963) considers Faulkner's combination of transcendent and durational, or mythic and successive time "a disturbing element" (232), and concludes, his "inability to resolve this conflict lies at the basis of some of his artistic failures" (230); Melvin Friedman in *Stream of Consciousness: A Study in Literary Method* (New Haven: Yale University Press, 1955) discusses spatial and pure time, intelligence and intuition, the problem of language in artistic expression, and conjectures "a kind of poetics" may be pieced together from scattered references in Bergson's books; Shiv K. Kumar, *Bergson and the Stream of Consciousness Novel* (New York: New York University Press, 1963) provides a sketchy treatment, and the chapter on "Bergson's Theory of the Novel" touches briefly on *la duree*, rendered in the stream of consciousness novel with the "radical dislocation of normal prose syntax" (35); A. A. Mendilow in *Time and the Novel* (London: Nevill, 1952), 145–56, mentions *duree* and identifies stylistic and structural devices in fiction that evoke a sense of flow (see especially 152–55); Hans Meyerhoff in *Time in Literature* (Berkeley: University of California Press, 1955) thinks Bergson's ideas exercised "so profound an influence on literature," but limits his treatment to a few pages on duration (10, 14–18); Georges Poulet, *Studies in Human Time*, trans. Elliott Coleman (Baltimore: Johns Hopkins University Press, 1956) refers briefly to Bergson throughout the book.

2. General studies on time include: M. M. Bakhtin, "Forms of Time and Chronotope in the Novel" in *The Dialogic Imagination*, ed. Michael Holquist, trans. Caryl Emerson and Michael Holquist (Austin: University of Texas Press, 1981); Frank Kermode, *The Sense of an Ending* (London: Oxford University Press, 1967/ 1975); and Paul Ricoeur, *Time and Narrative*, 3 vols. trans. Kathleen McLaughlin and David Pellauer (Chicago: University of Chicago Press, 1984–1988).

Among the numerous studies on Faulkner's time, some representative works include : Darrel Abel, "Frozen Moment in *Light in August*" in *Twentieth-Century Interpretations of Light in August*, ed. David L. Minter (Englewood Cliffs, NJ: Prentice-Hall, 1969), 42–54; Cleanth Brooks, *William Faulkner: The Yoknapatawpha Country* (New Haven: Yale University Press, 1963); Brooks, "Faulkner on Time and History" in *William Faulkner: Toward Yoknapatawpha and Beyond* (New Haven: Yale University Press 1978), 251–82; Maurice E. Coindreau, *The Time of William Faulkner* (Columbia: University of South Carolina Press, 1971); Harold Hungerford, "Past and Present in *Light in August*," *American Literature* 55, no. 2 (May 1983): 183–98; Perrin Lowrey, "Concepts of Time in *The Sound and the Fury*," in *English Institute Essays* (New York: Columbia University Press, 1952); James H. Matlack, "The Voices of Time: Narrative Structure in *Absalom, Absalom!*" *Southern Review* 15, no. 2 (April 1979): 333–54; Douglas Messerli, "The Problem of Time in *The Sound and the Fury*: A Critical Reassessment and Reinterpretation," *Southern Literary Journal* 6, no. 2 (spring 1974): 19–41; Michael Millgate, *The Achievement of William Faulkner* (Lincoln: University of Nebraska Press, 1978); Gail Mortimer, *Faulkner's Rhetoric of Loss: A Study in Perception and Meaning* (Austin: University of Texas Press, 1983); Carolyn Porter, "The Problem of Time in *Light in August*," *Rice University Studies* 61, no. 1 (1975): 107–25; Jean Pouillon, "Time and Destiny in Faulkner," in *Faulkner: A Collection of Critical Essays*, ed. Robert Penn Warren (Englewood Cliffs, NJ: Prentice-Hall, 1966); Carl E. Rollyson, Jr. *Uses of the Past in the Novels of William Faulkner* (Ann Arbor, MI: UMI Research Press, 1984); Jean-Paul Sartre, "Time in Faulkner: *The Sound and the Fury*," in *William Faulkner: Three Decades of Criticism*, eds. Frederick J. Hoffman and Olga W. Vickery, trans. Martine Darmon (New York: Harcourt, Brace & World, 1963); Ronald Schleifer, "Faulkner's Storied Novel: *Go Down, Moses* and the Translation of Time," *Modern Fiction Studies* 28, no.1 (spring 1982): 109–27; Hyatt H. Waggoner, *William Faulkner: From Jefferson to the World* (Lexington: University of Kentucky Press, 1959); and Karl E. Zink, "Flux and the Frozen Moment: the Imagery of Stasis in Faulkner's Prose" *PMLA* 71, no. 3 (June 1956): 285–301.

3. Panthea Reid Broughton in *William Faulkner: The Abstract and the Actual* (Baton Rouge: Louisiana State University Press, 1974), typifies the usual view of Bergson's influence. The author quotes Bergson on reality as flux but takes no note of his objection to language that turns "concepts" of reality static or rigid (e.g. 54, 124, 127,157).

4. Max Putzel, "Faulkner's Trial Preface to *Sartoris:* An Eclectic Text," *Papers of the Bibliographical Society of America* 74 (1980): 375.

5. Kermode, *The Sense of an Ending*, 173. The "time of the novelist" seeks the "defeat of successiveness," says Kermode (46, 173).

6. The Holograph and Typescript manuscripts of *Light in August* are in the William Faulkner Collection at the Alderman Library, University of Virginia, under 6074 IA: 7a and 7b. See Abbreviations.

7. William Faulkner, *Light in August* (New York: Modern Library, 1968), a photographic reproduction of the first printing, 6 October 1932. All first citations are from this edition. Second page numbers are from the Corrected Text (New York: Vintage International, 1987).

8. Most studies uncover structure in patterns of action and theme, such as: Carl Benson, "Thematic Design in *Light in August*," in *William Faulkner: Four Decades of Criticism*, ed. Linda Welshimer Wagner (East Lansing: Michigan State University Press, 1973) 258–72. Phyllis Hirshleifer in "As Whirlwinds in the South: An Analysis of *Light in August*," in *William Faulkner: Four Decades of Criticism*, 244–57, declares: "The structure of the novel must surely be approached in regard to its theme and meaning" (246). The work's "contrapuntal method" by which parts "constantly combine, break apart, and then recombine in new configurations" frames a "formal structure," Martin Kreiswirth observes (59, 57). But, he concludes, the "different pieces" fail to achieve "synthesis," only an "uneasy suspension or temporary accord," and the "different narratives cannot come together but can only keep each other, as it were, in line," through a "process of mutual subversion and deconstruction" (77–78) ("Plots and Counterplots: The Structure of *Light in August*," in *New Essays on Light in August*, ed. Michael Millgate [Cambridge: Cambridge University Press, 1987]: 55–79). Faulkner believes counterpoint interlinks parts that subvert but also complete one another. Millgate singles out recurring images, analogical thematic patterns, and the character of Christmas among the work's unifying devices (*The Achievement* 136–37). Themes and characters interacting through the three segments of the book and an ending that circles back to its beginning unifies the work, Francois L. Pitavy claims (*Faulkner's Light in August*, trans. Gillian E. Cook, rev. ed. [Bloomington: Indiana University Press, 1973], 12–35). Joseph W. Reed, Jr., thinks the "strongest" of Faulkner's themes, an isolated individual against an uncaring community, structures the work (*Faulkner's Narrative* [New Haven: Yale University Press, 1973], 134–41). Hugh M. Ruppersburg considers the "external narrator" the "most pervasive structural element" (32), enhanced by multiple perspectives (42), the "interrelatedness" of events and individuals (54), and themes clustered around the individual-community conflict (*Voice and Eye in Faulkner's Fiction* [Athens: University of Georgia Press, 1983], 30–56). See also John Tucker, "William Faulkner's *Light in August*: Toward a Structuralist Reading," *Modern Language Quarterly* 43, no. 2 (June 1982): 138–55.

Michel Gresset confirms Faulkner's idea of structure when he locates the germ of the whole novel in the first chapter that initiates a "backtracking structure" of contrast, like the "numbness, stupor" of Lena (201–3) versus the violence of Joe Christmas (*Fascination: Faulkner's Fiction 1919–1936*, trans. Thomas West [Durham, NC: Duke University Press, 1989]).

9. See Regina K. Fadiman, *Faulkner's Light in August: A Description and Interpretation of the Revisions* (Charlottesville: University Press of Virginia, 1975).

10. Carole Anne Taylor in *"Light in August*: The Epistemology of Tragic Paradox," *Texas Studies in Literature and Language* 22, no. 1 (spring 1980): 48–68, reverses Faulkner's taxonomy of consciousness and assigns each mental state a specific function or quality. The child's thought or belief amounts to delusion, and the man's, a defense of an identity he does not possess. Epistemological patterns in the text show that the child "knows" without understanding (e.g., Joe "knows" about Alice and betrayal). With experience, that instinctive knowing evolves to the mature man's informed apprehension and belief. Carolyn Porter, on the other hand, observes Faulkner's hierarchy of mental states that marks in time a character's development ("The Problem of Time").

The psychological stages are distinct in Faulkner, but their functions tend to be equivocal. Belief could stem from either knowledge or delusion. Codifying the character's "evolving consciousness" under observation or knowledge, belief, and memory, as Arthur F. Kinney does, misses the ambiguity central to Faulkner's thought and art (*Faulkner's Narrative Poetics: Style as Vision* [Amherst: University of Massachussetts Press, 1978]: 33, 113). Pitavy notes the role of memory but detects no pattern of psychological development in the hierarchy of mental stages (e.g., 49–52). Reed identifies Christmas's pattern "of thinking" as a "recurrence and recapitulation" in search of cause or roots (122–32, 143). Most studies on what Reed calls the "most profound exploration of consciousness" (267) in the canon generally overlook Faulkner's translation of a psychological system into a technique of synchronic time that delineates character development and shapes narrative and theme. Stephen M. Ross says Faulkner *"goes beyond speech"* and represents consciousness in imagery, variant typography and punctuation, italics, tense forms, syntactical irregularities, and drawings or signs (*Fiction's Inexhaustible Voice: Speech and Writing in Faulkner* [Athens: University of Georgia Press, 1989], 133–47).

11. Faulkner himself considers Christmas a victim of the lack of identity: "He deliberately evicted himself from the human race because he didn't know which he was. . . . The most tragic condition a man could find himself in—not to know what he is and to know that he will never know" (*FU* 72). Carl Benson echoes Faulkner when he speaks of Christmas being "conditioned by exterior forces." Exercising "no choice," he could "never be responsible" (264–65, see note 8 above). Cleanth Brooks states on the one hand that "Joe does not know what he is" or "who he is" (*William Faulkner: The Yoknapatawpha Country*, 51, 67), but then declares Joe's persistent assertion of "his own individuality" as "heroic" ("Introduction" to *Light in August* [New York: Modern Library, 1932/1968], xx–xxi). Jean-Paul Sartre in *Being and Nothingness* (New York: Philosophical Library, 1956), calls Christmas a "victim," but finds in the dying man's eyes proof of his "absolute freedom" that nothing could take away (405–6). Versions of the victimized Christmas also appear in: Richard Chase, "Faulkner's *Light in August*," in *Twentieth-Century Interpretations of Light in August*, ed. David L. Minter (Englewood Cliffs, NJ: Prentice-Hall, 1969), 17–24; Ronald Wesley Hoag, "Ends and Loose Ends: The Triptych Conclusion of *Light in August*," *Modern Fiction Studies*

31, no. 4 (winter 1985): 675–90; Millgate, *The Achievement,* 129, 137; Pitavy, *Faulkner's Light in August*, 61, 95; James Leo Spenko, "The Death of Joe Christmas and the Power of Words," *Twentieth Century Literature* 28, no. 3 (fall 1982): 252–68; and Olga W. Vickery, *The Novels of William Faulkner: A Critical Interpretation*, rev. ed. (Baton Rouge: Louisiana State University Press, 1964), 68–69.

John L. Longley Jr. (*The Tragic Mask: A Study of Faulkner's Heroes* [Chapel Hill: University of North Carolina Press, 1963], 192–205) contends Christmas is "free to choose what he will be and his freedom is infinite" (196). "Free to the end," he chooses the "moment most filled with reconciliation" to give up his life (201).

12. Millgate, *The Achievement,* 137. Walter J. Slatoff's objection to unresolved contradictions in Faulkner reechoes through the decades (*Quest for Failure: A Study of William Faulkner* [Ithaca: Cornell University Press, 1960]), but recent criticism generally acknowledges the inherence of ambiguity and paradox in Faulkner's epistemology and form. For examples see, Ralph Flores, *The Rhetoric of Doubtful Authority: Deconstructive Readings of Self-Questioning Narratives, St. Augustine to Faulkner* (Ithaca: Cornell University Press, 1984); John T. Irwin. *Doubling & Incest/ Repetition & Revenge: A Speculative Reading of Faulkner* (Baltimore: Johns Hopkins University Press, 1975); Donald M. Kartiganer, *The Fragile Thread: The Meaning of Form in Faulkner's Novels* (Amherst: University of Massachusetts Press, 1979); Michael Millgate, *Faulkner's Place* (Athens: University of Georgia Press, 1997); Noel Polk, *Children of the Dark House*: *Text and Context in Faulkner* (Jackson: University Press of Mississippi, 1996); and Patricia Tobin, "The Time of Myth and History in *Absalom, Absalom!*" *American Literature* 45 (May 1973): 252–70.

13. Vickery, *The Novels of William Faulkner*, 72.

14. The "sense of an organic community" is a "living force" in Faulkner, maintains Brooks (*William Faulkner: The Yoknapatawpha Country*, 69, 54). Christmas, "actively repelled" by both black and white communities, becomes an outlaw (Introduction to *LIA*, xiii). Brooks, however, identifies nature with society and overlooks the bond with nature that Christmas recovers before he returns to the community to fulfill its laws. Lucas Burch-Brown, in contrast, remains an alien to both society and nature. John Tucker in "William Faulkner's *Light in August*: Toward a Structuralist Reading," *Modern Language Quarterly* 43, no. 2 (June 1982): 138–55, examines the dichotomies in form and the binary distinctions of race, gender, and class in the Jefferson community. See also Vickery, *The Novels of William Faulkner*, for social stereotypes.

A recent anthology, *Faulkner and the Natural World: Faulkner and Yoknapatawpha, 1998*, eds. Donald M. Kartiganer and Ann J. Abadie (Jackson: University Press of Mississippi, 1999), explores the subject of nature, including race and gender in Faulkner. The articles on *Light in August*, however, disregard the brief but notable passage when, after years of running, Christmas reconnects with his "native earth" where he obtains "peace" and "the true answer" he searched for all his life, and completes the recovery of his "living self" (Bergson's term) with which he faces his "death" (*LIA* 320–21/338–39). Mary Joanne Dondlinger in "Getting Around the Body: The Matter of Race and Gender in Faulkner's *Light in August*," 98–125, quotes the passage on Joe's physical shape and thought being molded by "its compulsions," but alters the contextual reference of "its," which is "his native earth," to the "regulatory law" of a racist society (109). In the passage, it is nature's "immutable laws" (of causation) that Christmas realizes he must observe to the end.

15. Writers who discuss the circle image, like Richard Chase, Francois L. Pitavy, Jean Pouillion, Olga W. Vickery, generally disregard the line counterpoised to it.

16. Spenko reflects on Faulkner's hypnotic language ("The Death of Joe Christmas and the Power of Words," 252–68). For James A. Snead (*Figures of Division: William Faulkner's Major Novels* [New York: Methuen, 1986]) the language "suggests a radical attempt to reintegrate . . . in linguistic terms, what society has sundered" (14).

3. *ABSALOM, ABSALOM!* STORY AS SELF-DECEPTION

1. The first page citation refers to William Faulkner, *Absalom, Absalom!* (New York: Random House, 1936/1964), a facsimile of the first edition, and the second page citation to the Corrected Text (New York: Vintage International, 1990). See Abbreviations for the list of Faulkner works.

Manuscripts of *Absalom, Absalom*! at the University of Virginia and University of Texas have been examined by Gerald Langford, *Faulkner's Revision of Absalom, Absalom! A Collation of the Manuscript and the Published Book* (Austin: University of Texas Press, 1971); James B. Meriwether, "Review of *Faulkner's Revision of Absalom, Absalom!* by Gerald Langford," *American Literature* 44 (January 1973): 693–95; Michael Millgate, *The Achievement of William Faulkner* (Lincoln: University of Nebraska Press, 1978); Noel E. Polk, "The Manuscript of *Absalom, Absalom!*" *Mississippi Quarterly* 25, no. 3 (summer 1972): 359–67. David Paul Ragan in his Introduction to *William Faulkner's Absalom, Absalom! A Critical Study* (Ann Arbor, MI: UMI Research Press, 1987), discusses at length the work's genetic history and the connections between *The Sound and the Fury* and *Absalom, Absalom*! and concludes that Miss Rosa's unreliable narrative "provides a metaphor for the book's structure" (29, 31, passim).

2. Studies on time and structure in *Absalom, Absalom!* include: Cleanth Brooks, "The Narrative Structure of *Absalom, Absalom!*" in *William Faulkner: Toward Yoknapatawpha and Beyond* (New Haven: Yale University Press, 1978), 301–28; Brooks, "On *Absalom, Absalom!*" *Mosaic* 7, no. 1 (fall 1973): 159–83; Patricia Drechsel Tobin, *Time and the Novel: The Genealogical Imperative* (Princeton: Princeton University Press, 1978), 107–32; Hyatt H. Waggoner, "The Historical Novel in the Southern Past: The Case of *Absalom, Absalom!*" *Southern Literary Journal* 2, no. 2 (spring 1970): 69–85. See also notes 4 and 5 below on structure in *Absalom, Absalom*!

3. Richard Forrer in "*Absalom, Absalom!*: Storytelling as a Mode of Transcendence," *Southern Literary Journal* 9, no. 1 (winter 1977): 22–46, covers in about two pages the omniscient narrator's role as evaluator of other viewpoints. John W. Hunt, *William Faulkner: Art in Theological Tension* (Syracuse: Syracuse University Press, 1965) mentions the omniscient narrator, but Lynn Gartrell Levins disregards that voice in "The Four Narrative Perspectives in *Absalom, Absalom!*" *PMLA* 85 (January 1970): 35–47. Karen McPherson thinks that speakers and listeners constantly displacing one another holds the narrative at an uncertain state of being told and being heard ("*Absalom, Absalom!*: Telling Scratches," *Modern Fic-*

tion Studies 33, no. 3 [autumn 1987]: 431–50). Olga W. Vickery, who explicates fully Rosa's voice, simply touches upon those of Mr. Compson, Quentin, and Shreve, and omits the Omniscient in *The Novels of William Faulkner: A Critical Interpretation*, rev. ed. (Baton Rouge: Louisiana State University Press, 1964). Each narrator "tells his own biography, talking about himself, in a thousand different terms, but himself," Faulkner maintains (*FU* 275); but the Omniscient, bemused by it all, subscribes to the inexplicable and, with his unadulterated voice, brings the novel to a close, though to no closure.

4. Ralph Flores thinks Quentin's mind "has been so inscribed by other tellings that it may no longer be his," and Bon, although nothing but an "enigmatic absence," plays a "key role" in all the narrators' tales (*The Rhetoric of Doubtful Authority: Deconstructive Readings of Self-Questioning Narratives, St. Augustine to Faulkner* [Ithaca: Cornell University Press, 1984] 152, 159, 162). Miss Rosa's monologues, says John A. Hodgson, are "being transmitted to us in the form of Quentin's thoughts" (" 'Logical Sequence and Continuity': Some Observations on the Typographical and Structural Consistency of *Absalom, Absalom!*" *American Literature* 43 (March 1971): 97–107. The voices of the different narrators are "filtered through the mind of a single listener," according to John T. Irwin. The "principal narrative consciousness" of Quentin "is the fixed point of view from which the reader *overhears* the various narrators" (*Doubling and Incest/Repetition and Revenge: A Speculative Reading of Faulkner* [Baltimore: Johns Hopkins University Press, 1975), 26. James H. Justus also identifies Quentin as "the central ordering narrator," and the relationship of Quentin to Shreve his audience constitutes "the frame which controls and orders each of the secondary narrations" (168–69) ("The Epic Design of *Absalom, Absalom!*," *Texas Studies in Language and Literature* 4 [summer 1962]: 157–76). James H. Matlack maintains the "whole complex of narrative materials is conveyed by Quentin's speeches alone" ("The Voices of Time: Narrative Structure in *Absalom, Absalom!*," *Southern Review* 15, no. 2 [April 1979]: 340). David Paul Ragan in William Faulkner's *Absalom, Absalom!: A Critical Study*, (92, 147, 151–52, and passim) records in detail what each narrator knows at what time, then concludes that Shreve's knowledge about people and incidents unrecorded in earlier narrations confirms the occurrence of hidden exchanges with his encyclopedic source, Quentin. Stephen M. Ross claims "an oratorical Overvoice . . . envelopes the discourse, taking up into itself all subsidiary voices." But in his role as "passive" listener, Quentin's "consciousness permeates the novel's total discourse." Even Miss Rosa's voice in Chapter 5 is "also interior to Quentin." But Ross touches only lightly on Quentin's role reversal to storyteller to Shreve, when it appears that all the other voices, including the "Overvoice" or the Omniscient converge in his voice, and finally in the storyteller Shreve as well (*Fiction's Inexhaustible Voice: Speech and Writing in Faulkner* [Athens: University of Georgia Press, 1989], 193, 220–21, 226–28.

5. Peter Brooks thinks the proairetic and hermeneutic codes in the narrative fail to "mesh," and thus obstruct the achievement of "narrative design, or plot" ("Incredulous Narration: *Absalom, Absalom!*" *Comparative Literature* 34, no. 3 (summer 1982), 248, 254). Faulkner, who insists he is not interested in "plot," relies less on a "coherent plot" and more on the interpermeation of discrete, unlike parts. Robert Dale Parker identifies in novels after *The Sound and the Fury* "two general principles of form," the "discontinuity of chaotic material" and stitching "the discontinuities back together"; but he sees the two working "separately" and against

each other rather than functioning coherently. He nonetheless concludes that the structure is framed around a "center or imaginative beginning" that "motivates everything else," as Sutpen does in *Absalom, Absalom!* (*Faulkner and the Novelistic Imagination* [Urbana: University of Illinois Press, 1985], 4, 19, 115).

6. Robert Alter, *Partial Magic: The Novel as a Self-Conscious Genre* (Berkeley: University of California Press, 1975), 129. Alter's work, read after the first draft of the chapter, corroborates a number of my observations.

Studies examining *Absalom, Absalom!* from various angles, except as a reflexive, self-denying work, include: Ralph Behrens, "Collapse of Dynasty: The Thematic Center of *Absalom, Absalom!*" *PMLA* 89, no. 3 (January 1974): 24–33; Gerhard Hoffman, "*Absalom, Absalom!*: A Postmodernist Approach," in *Faulkner's Discourse: An International Symposium*, ed. Lothar Hönnighausen (Tubingen: Max Niemeyer Verlag, 1989), 276–92; Irwin, *Doubling and Incest/Repetition and Revenge*; Dirk Kuyk, Jr., *Sutpen's Design: Interpreting Faulkner's Absalom, Absalom!* (Charlottesville: University Press of Virginia, 1990); Ilse Dusoir Lind, "The Design and Meaning of *Absalom, Absalom!*" *PMLA* 70 (December 1955): 887–912, reprinted in *William Faulkner: Three Decades of Criticism*, eds. Frederick J. Hoffman and Olga W. Vickery (New York: Harcourt, Brace & World, 1963); John T. Matthews, "The Marriage of Speaking and Hearing in *Absalom, Absalom!*" *English Literary History* 47, no. 3 (fall 1980): 575–94; Joseph W. Reed, Jr., *Faulkner's Narrative* (New Haven: Yale University Press, 1973); and Robert H. Zoellner, "Faulkner's Prose Style in *Absalom, Absalom!*" *American Literature* 30 (January 1959): 486–502. For a more extensive treatment of reflexivity in the work, see my "*Absalom, Absalom!* as a Self-Reflexive Novel," *Journal of Narrative Technique* 11, no. 2 (spring 1981): 75–90.

4. *The Sound and the Fury:* Voice and Structure

1. See Emily K. Izsak, "The Manuscript of *The Sound and the Fury*: The Revisions in the First Section," *Studies in Bibliography* 20 (1967): 189–202; James B. Meriwether, "The Textual History of The Sound and the Fury" in *Studies in The Sound and the Fury* (Columbus: Charles Merrill 1970), 1–32; and Michael Millgate, *The Achievement of William Faulkner* (Lincoln: University of Nebraska Press, 1978), 86–103.

A longer version of "An Introduction to *The Sound and the Fury*" was printed in the *Mississippi Quarterly* 26 (summer 1973): 410–15. See Abbreviations for the list of Faulkner's works.

2. Faulkner's reformulations of the germ appear in many works, including: *Faulkner in the University*, eds. Frederick L. Gwynn and Joseph L. Blotner (Charlottesville: University Press of Virginia, 1959), 1, 6, 61; *Faulkner at Nagano*, ed. Robert A Jelliffe (Tokyo: Kenkyusha Press, 1956), 102–106; "Interview with Cynthia Grenier," *Lion in the Garden*, eds. James B. Meriwether and Michael Millgate (New York: Random House, 1968), 215–27; "Interview with Jean Stein Vanden Heuvel," *Lion in the Garden*, 237–56; James B. Meriwether, "A Prefatory Note by Faulkner for the Compson Apppendix," *American Literature* 43 (May 1971): 281–84.

3. William Faulkner, *The Sound and the Fury* (New York: Modern Library, 1956). First page citations refer to this photographic reproduction of the first print-

ing (1929), and second page citations to the Corrected Text (New York: Vintage International, 1990).

4. Irena Kaluza identifies the unique syntactic pattern that embodies each primary character's mind and being. Benjy's idiocy materializes in a "primitive and monotonous" idiolect (58) composed of "the barest essentials of language" (101), which somehow turn into Benjy's poetic lexical combinations. Quentin's idiolect represents the "disintegration of the mental content" (80), or "deeper levels of uncontrolled consciousness" (100). Jason's syntax and substandard idiolect betray his "nervous restlessness" and futile efforts to be logical and rational (100). My own emphasis is on tone rather than linguistic form, but Kaluza's study of ambiguity and repetition in the work's syntactic patterns appears to corroborate my conclusions on the attributes of Faulkner's language (*The Functioning of Sentence Structure in the Stream-of-Consciousness Technique of William Faulkner's The Sound and the Fury: A Study in Linguistic Stylistics* [Folcroft, PA: Folcroft Press, 1970]).

Richard Gunter concludes Kaluza's taxonomy of ideolects exemplifies a new approach to literary study that traces the "connection between the linguistic facts of a novel" and the "response that the work induces in the reader" ("Style and Language in *The Sound and the Fury*," in *Studies in The Sound and the Fury*, ed. James B. Meriwether (Columbus, OH: Merrill, 1970, 156).

For a more recent study on stylistics, see Michael J. Toolan, *The Stylistics of Fiction: A Literary-Linguistic Approach* (New York: Routledge, 1990).

Stephen M. Ross in "The 'Loud World' of Quentin Compson," *Studies in the Novel, North Texas State* 7, no. 2 (summer 1975): 245–57, considers Quentin's speech "a linguistic equivalent of his consciousness" (251); but a more thorough treatment of the "ironies" (247) in Quentin's "myriad voices" (255) could throw more light on Faulkner's dissonant mixtures. See also *Fiction's Inexhaustible Voice: Speech and Writing in Faulkner* (Athens: University of Georgia Press, 1989), 174–76, 179–83. Other studies on language and style include: Warren Beck, *Faulkner: Essays* (Madison: University of Wisconsin Press, 1976); Noel Polk in *Children of the Dark House: Text and Context in Faulkner* (Jackson: University Press of Mississippi, 1996), 99–136, recapitulates earlier observations on language and syntax in the novel; Linda W. Wagner, "Language and Act: Caddy Compson," *Southern Literary Journal* 14, no. 2 (spring 1982): 49–61.

5. Tzvetan Todorov, *The Poetics of Prose*, trans. Richard Howard (Ithaca: Cornell University Press, 1977), 93. Todorov distinguishes voiced from unvoiced words: "Speech is constituted of words addressed to someone else, whereas thought, even verbal thought, is addressed only to oneself. The notion of speech implies the notion of others . . . ; thereby speech is profoundly linked to the other person who plays a decisive role" (94). The speechless Benjy's narrative thus transgresses all the rules observed in the other sections of the novel and in narrative generally.

Paul R. Lilly, Jr., in "Caddy and Addie: Speakers of Faulkner's Impeccable Language," *The Journal of Narrative Technique* 3 (spring 1973): 170–82, abstracts a few of Faulkner's theoretical tenets and concludes that the author regards wordless silence as the higher language. Faulkner in theory and practice values not the "wordless realm" (171), but the silence achieved beyond words, a revelation transcending language: "The thunder and the music of the prose take place in silence" (*LG* 248).

Roland Barthes maintains that when you read literature, you "consume" the "words and syntax" of "the first system" of language, but "the 'reality' of this discourse is . . . not the anecdote it transmits" but the "parasitical system" which is "principal, for it controls the final intelligibility of the whole." Literature "is a parasitical meaning which can only connote reality, not denote it" (*Critical Essays*, trans. Richard Howard [Evanston, IL: Northwestern University Press, 1972], 266–67).

6. Studies on time and other rhetorical patterns in *The Sound and the Fury* are quite extensive. A few representative works include: Beck, *Faulkner: Essays*; André Bleikasten, *The Most Splendid Failure: Faulkner's The Sound and the Fury* (Bloomington: Indiana University Press, 1976); J. E. Bunselmeyer, "Faulkner's Narrative Styles," *American Literature* 53, no. 3 (November 1981): 424–42; Albert J. Guerard, *The Triumph of the Novel* (New York: Oxford University Press, 1976); John W. Hunt, *William Faulkner: Art in Theological Tension* (Syracuse: Syracuse University Press, 1965); Perrin Lowrey, "Concepts of Time in *The Sound and the Fury, English Institute Essays* (New York: Columbia University Press, 1952): 57–82; John T. Matthews, *The Sound and the Fury: Faulkner and the Lost Cause* (Boston: Twayne, 1991); Donald Messerli, "The Problem of Time in *The Sound and the Fury: A Critical Reassessment and Reinterpretation*," *Southern Literary Journal* 6, no. 2 (spring 1974): 19–41; Millgate, *The Achievement*; Bernhard Radloff, "The Unity of Time in *The Sound and the Fury*," *The Faulkner Journal* 1, no. 2 (spring 1986): 56–68; and Olga W. Vickery, *The Novels of William Faulkner: A Critical Interpretation*, rev. ed. (Baton Rouge: Louisiana State University Press, 1964).

7. Todorov, *The Poetics of Prose*, 138.

8. See note 1 above.

9. Wagner in "Language and Act," discusses the "centrality" of Caddy to the novel (see note 4 above).

10. Fredric Jameson, *The Prison House of Language* (Princeton: Princeton University Press, 1972), 199. Todorov, *The Poetics of Prose*, 133.

11. Dilsey, Faulkner avows, "was a good human being" who held the family together not for "the hope of reward but just because it was the decent and proper thing to do" (*FU* 85). She fails, but "failure" is "the best" (*FN* 3) because it occasions endurance and a valiant spirit, a paradoxical view embodied in antithetic form and sense. Sustained polarities in Faulkner's thought and art should deter reducing his work to total pessimism or, as inaccurately, to its opposite. Millgate for one recognizes the way "uncertainty and paradox" qualify an apparent meaning or the good in Faulkner (*The Achievement*, 103).

12. The last quotation, missing in the Holograph manuscript and apparently added only to the Typescript manuscript, hypostatizes the power of silence beyond the word.

13. John W. Hunt believes Dilsey and the Easter service represent a "solid world of enduring values" with a "truly redemptive structure" (42, see note 6 above). In contrast, see John V. Hagopian, "Nihilism in Faulkner's *The Sound and the Fury*," *Modern Fiction Studies* 13, no.1 (spring 1967): 45–55. James A. Snead concludes that the first three sections chronicle "the failures of white society," while the Reverend Shegog's sermon points "a way out of language" and "racial politics"; but, since the black people have no escape from a racially divided community, the work ends in futility (*Figures of Division: William Faulkner's Major*

Novels [New York: Methuen, 1986], 37–39). Donald M. Kartiganer (*"The Sound and the Fury* and Faulkner's Quest for Form," *English Literary History* 37 [December 1970]: 613–39) thinks the novel's "irredeemably broken sequence of speakers and narrative episodes" conveys "nearly total despair" (619).

5. *As I Lay Dying:* THE VOICED AND VOICELESS/ THE SEEN AND UNSEEN

1. See Abbreviations for the list of Faulkner works.

2. William Faulkner, *As I Lay Dying* (New York: Vintage Books, 1964). This edition includes corrections based on James B. Meriwether's collation of the first edition (1930) and the original manuscript and typescript. The first page citations refer to this edition, the second page citations to the Corrected Text (New York: Vintage International, 1990).

3. Roland Barthes, *Critical Essays*, trans. Richard Howard (Evanston, IL: Northwestern University Press, 1972), 266, 270.

4. In *As I Lay Dying*, Stephen M. Ross explains, Faulkner overturns conventions of appropriate speech with "the *in*appropriate disruption of mimetic voice" through which "we discover character." The writer aims "not merely to express" consciousness, but "to constitute it out of voice" (*Fiction's Inexhaustible Voice: Speech and Writing in Faulkner* [Athens: University of Georgia Press, 1989], 112, 124).

5. Michael Millgate, *The Achievement of William Faulkner* (Lincoln: University of Nebraska Press, 1978), 107.

6. André Bleikasten, *Faulkner's As I Lay Dying*, trans. Roger Little (Bloomington: Indiana University Press, 1973), 28.

7. Tzvetan Todorov, *The Poetics of Prose*, trans. Richard Howard (Ithaca: Cornell University Press, 1977), 102. Two other "paradoxical affirmations" abstract the contrary functions of language: "Words do not signify the presence of things but their absence"; and "Words do not designate things but the contrary of things." Todorov thus concludes, in the "quest for meaning" one looks "not for what the word designates, but for what it signifies" (101–2, 138).

8. Bleikasten, *Faulkner's As I Lay Dying*, 135. Bleikasten, like many critics, reduces Addie's objections to the separation of word from deed. Addie's views, in fact, echo her author's concerns over the power of the word to falsify or obstruct human relating and communication. Joseph R. Urgo (*Faulkner's Apocrypha: A Fable, Snopes, and the Spirit of Human Rebellion* [Jackson: University Press of Mississippi, 1989], 62) considers Addie's "attack on words" as "essentially specious," for she assumes "a fixed dichotomy between empty word and significant act," a view Olga W. Vickery holds as well (*The Novels of William Faulkner: A Critical Interpretation*, rev. ed. [Baton Rouge: Louisiana University Press, 1964], 53–54). Patrick O'Donnell notes the self-denying yet sustained "contraries" in the tropes and language of the novel but, like most readers, misses Addie's (and Faulkner's) faith in the power of word to speak past itself in silence, which Darl and Dewey Dell and Cash experience ("The Spectral Road: Metaphors of Transference in Faulkner's *As I Lay Dying*," *Papers on Language and Literature* 20, no. 1 [winter 1984]: 61, 65, 76–77).

Richard Godden in "William Faulkner, Addie Bundren, and Language" (*Studies in English* 15 [1978]: 101–23), reduces Addie's views to polar formulas: "Eden = virginity = silence" versus "The Fall = fertility = language" (109), and concludes that Addie, who prefers virginity to fertility, reduces silence to "a negative value" (104), and, erroneously believing in the origin of words, wants "to cure rather than mistrust" words (112). Addie's paradoxes in fact strain such reductive categories. To accuse Addie of believing in the origin of words or of trying to "cure" words disregards her cynicism over word-deceived deceivers, and her rejection of the duplicitous "   " = Anse = word = "significant shape profoundly without life" for the silence of God's "dark voicelessness" where the Word is true. Addie emblematizes the nostalgia lurking behind modern theories of language. (The idea of "nostalgia" in contemporary theory comes from Goeffrey Hartman, during an informal discussion at Yale University in the summer, 1977).

9. Cleanth Brooks in *William Faulkner: The Yoknapatawpha Country* (New Haven: Yale University Press, 1963), 152, 155. Vickery in *The Novels of William Faulkner,* on the other hand, considers the journey from beginning to end "a travesty of the ritual" (52). Faulkner's antithetic form sets the matter within suspended polarities.

10. Bleikasten, *Faulkner's As I Lay Dying,* 54. But see pages 47–48 where Bleikasten traces a circular pattern brought about by the "reciprocal illumination" between Addie's monologue and those of the other characters.

11. Donald M. Kartiganer assumes the opposite view of form in *As I Lay Dying:* "The meaning of its form, of its internal relations, suggests . . . the failure of coherence . . . ; some failure of the imagination to reconcile form and vision, to create a shape that is not a stasis, a change that is not chaos" (*The Fragile Thread: The Meaning of Form in Faulkner's Novels* [Amherst: University of Massachusetts Press, 1979], 32–33). Vickery, (*The Novels of William Faulkner*), echoes Faulkner's antithetic mode when she characterizes structure as both "centrifugal" (each section relates to the Addie section) and "linear" (each section contributes to sequence that constitutes plot) (55).

12. See for example, Bleikasten, *Faulkner's As I Lay Dying,* 22. Pauline E. Degenfelder concludes the high style defies verisimilitude but functions to communicate complex insights into reality that characters are incapable of articulating ("Yoknapatawphan Baroque: A Stylistic Analysis of *As I Lay Dying,*" in *William Faulkner's As I Lay Dying: A Critical Casebook,* ed. Dianne L. Cox [New York: Garland, 1985], 71, 81–82). Mary Jane Hurst shows a direct correlation between each character's "distinct language patterns" and his/her personality and behavior ("Characterization and Language: A Case-Grammar Study of *As I Lay Dying,*" *Language and Style: An International Journal* 20, no. 1 [winter 1987]: 71–87).

13. Some of Darl's brief telepathic narrations occur in pages 11–13/11–13, 129/ 136, 174/182–83.

14. Brooks, *William Faulkner,* 146. See Watson G. Branch, "Darl Bundren's 'Cubistic' Vision," *Texas Studies in Literature and Language* 19 (spring 1977), 42–59, for a list of critical studies on Darl's relationship to Addie.

15. Robert Hemenway in "Enigmas of Being in *As I Lay Dying,*" *Modern Fiction Studies* 16 (summer 1970): 133–46, finds the key to this passage in "Darl's attempt to determine Addie's tense—the location of her humanity in relation to time" (141).

16. See Dorritt Cohn, *Transparent Minds: Narrative Modes for Presenting Consciousness in Fiction* (Princeton: Princeton University Press, 1978), 12–15, 72, 171–78.

17. This example of irregular syntax is missing from the Holograph manuscript (at UV), and was apparently added during a later revision. Katë Hamburger, who considers the preterite the norm of fiction (*The Logic of Literature* [Bloomington: Indiana University Press, 1973], 64–134, see especially 89–93]), thinks the aberrant present tense has a "disquieting effect" for it "draws attention to the fact that only in a novel, and nowhere else, can we experience what a person is thinking right now, and thereby it destroys in the same measure the illusion of fictive life which the novel produces" (108). Her objection reenforces my argument that, in transgressing the canons of form and verisimilitude, Faulkner deliberately undoes the "illusion of fictive life" so as to empower the word beyond its discursive sense.

18. The shifts to past tense in Darl's monologues "suggest a detachment from whatever he describes," Stephen M. Ross claims, and signal the "psychological disengagement" of Vardaman from events (122–23). Dorritt Cohn notes an "impassiveness," a "removal of affect" in Darl's narration of the river crossing, but overlooks the shift to the subjective/affective in the italicized past tense paragraph (205–6). Joseph M. Garrison, Jr., thinks Darl's precise, "mathematical" style (in contrast to his "synesthetic" impressionistic style) indicates the brothers do not see the flood as "terribly threatening" ("Perception, Language, and Reality in *As I Lay Dying*," in Cox, ed. *William Faulkner's As I Lay Dying*, 50–51).

6. *The Unvanquished:* The Doubling Voice

1. Franz K. Stanzel in *Narrative Situations in the Novel*, trans. James P. Pusack (Bloomington: Indiana University Press, 1971), 46, believes a temporally distant viewpoint compresses narrative matter and also interprets the fictive world. Floyd C. Watkins in *The Flesh and the Word: Eliot, Hemingway, Faulkner* (Nashville: Vanderbilt University Press, 1971) finds the layered voices and viewpoints problematic. What could not be attributed to the boy he dismisses as the author intruding "to express his own opinions" and to "moralize" about events (236–37). On the other hand, Watkins also notes that Bayard's "integrity, honor and courage" are not articulated, but rather evoked through "remarkably concrete imagery which in some inexplicable way reveals his strength and agitation by seeming irrelevance" (235). That seemingly irrelevant (unconventional, that is) imagery and style advance Faulkner's end, to disclose the child's maturing self.

Other readers object to the ambiguity generated by the mixed styles. Alfred Kazin censures the "polar extremes" in Faulkner's "polyphonic rhetoric" that records "the outrageous confusions of the ineffable" (*On Native Grounds* [New York: Doubleday Anchor Books, 1956], 350–61, in particular, 355–58). Walter J. Slatoff decries the disorder and inconclusiveness the author welcomes "too easily," and the oxymoron and paradox and the "unresolved suspensions" permeating the fiction (*Quest for Failure: A Study of William Faulkner* [Ithaca: Cornell University Press, 1960], 83, 86, 248, 263–65, and passim). James Guetti, in *The Limits of Metaphor* (Ithaca: Cornell University Press, 1967), thinks the "permanent unresolution" and "verbal suspensions . . . that never come to issue" indicates, as in *Absalom, Absalom!*, an "incapacity to compose language itself" (163, 3). John T.

Irwin, on the other hand, welcomes the "irreducibly ambiguous" events that add complexity and depth to works like *Absalom, Absalom!* and *The Sound and the Fury* (*Doubling and Incest/Repetition and Revenge: A Speculative Reading of William Faulkner* [Baltimore: Johns Hopkins University Press, 1975], 124 and passim).

2. Most readings concentrate on the substance or theme and miss the equipoise and self-corrrective irony in the language, technique, and structure of the work. Irving Howe contends the "slick and jolly" treatment of weighty events makes *The Unvanquished* "too feeble" to be taken seriously (*William Faulkner: A Critical Study*, 3d ed. [Chicago: University of Chicago Press, 1975], 44–45). Forrest L. Ingram thinks the work is not a novel since each story is "self-contained, complete, and for the most part simple," and therefore not "an integral part of some larger action," like the chapters of a traditional novel (*Representative Short Story Cycles of the Twentieth Century* [The Hague: Mouton, 1971], 138). Michael Millgate thinks the last story, "An Odor of Verbena," sounds a jarring note with its unprepared reversal of values, the Sartoris code revaluated, and Colonel John Sartoris's "heroic stature" reduced. The disjointed work, lacking "serious moral complication," appears "as romanticized 'tall tales' of heroic Southern resistance to the North" (*The Achievement of William Faulkner* [Lincoln: University of Nebraska Press, 1978], 167, 170). Daniel J. Singal labels the work a "Civil War potboiler" in which Faulkner regresses to Victorian values celebrating "the innate moral superiority of the old planter class" (*William Faulkner: The Making of a Modernist* [Chapel Hill: University of North Carolina Press, 1997], 221.

Cleanth Brooks, in contrast, argues that Faulkner assays his characters' motives and moral values and, in the process, deromanticizes them (*William Faulkner: The Yoknapatawpha Country* [New Haven: Yale University Press, 1963], 79. See also 84, 88). Andrew Lytle ranks *The Unvanquished* as the "most successful and the least understood" (130) of Faulkner's books ("The Son of Man: He will Prevail," *Sewanee Review* 63 [1955]: 114–37). James B. Meriwether, in an unpublished dissertation ("The Place of *The Unvanquished* in William Faulkner's Yoknapatawpha Series" [Princeton University, May 1958]), declares it "technically, stylistically and structurally a single book" (132). Hyatt H. Waggoner makes a strong case for *The Unvanquished* as a novel in *William Faulkner: From Jefferson to the World* (Lexington: University of Kentucky Press, 1959), 170–83.

3. Joanne V. Creighton, in *William Faulkner's Craft of Revision: The Snopes Trilogy, The Unvanquished, and Go Down, Moses* (Detroit, MI: Wayne State University Press, 1977), 73–84, concludes the changes create a "double perspective" when the man's "qualification and critical evaluation" and the boy's "sentimental distortion" are combined (75–76, 78). But beyond noting the altered tone and improved characterization and style, Creighton generally overlooks the transformation of the juvenile adventures into polytonal form that simultaneously undermines what it affirms. James B. Meriwether thinks the additions to "Ambuscade" set down the "unifying" themes of black-white relationship and man's relation to the land (61).

4. William Faulkner, *The Unvanquished* (New York: Vintage Books, 1938). The first page citations are from this edition, a collation of the first edition and the original manuscript and typescript. The second page citations are from the Corrected Text (New York: Vintage International, 1991). The first five stories originally appeared in *Saturday Evening Post*: "Ambuscade" (29 September 1934); "Retreat"

(13 October 1934); "Raid" (3 November 1934); "The Unvanquished" (14 November 1936, retitled "Riposte in Tertio"; "Vendée" (5 December 1936). The sixth story, "Skirmish at Sartoris" (originally titled "Drusilla"), appeared in *Scribner's Magazine* (April 1935).

5. Bayard's attitude and language, nonetheless, betray unconscious enculturation when he asserts authority over Ringo, forcing him to play the Yankee general twice to his once, and ironically putting himself in the role of the defeated, while Ringo plays victor twice. (In Faulkner's antonymous universe, it is the defeated who gains the greater glory.) The grown Bayard falls back on the stereotypic term, "boy," for his friend. The children's "brotherhood," however, inculcates a sense of human kinship that guides Bayard's future action.

6. Jean Pouillon, "Time and Destiny in Faulkner," in *Faulkner, A Collection of Critical Essays*, ed. Robert Penn Warren (Englewood Cliffs, NJ: Prentice-Hall, 1966), 81.

7. Mircea Eliade, *Rites and Symbols of Initiation: The Mysteries of Birth and Rebirth*, trans. Willard R. Trask (New York: Harper Torchbooks, 1958), xiii.

7. STRUCTURE AND MEANING IN *GO DOWN, MOSES*

1. William Faulkner, *Go Down, Moses* (New York: Modern Library, 1942). All citations refer to this edition (First Printing); second page citations refer to the Corrected Text (New York: Vintage International, 1990). The quotations observe Faulkner's inconsistent typography, including omitted capitals and punctuations. The separate stories are abbreviated as follows: "Was" ("W"), "The Fire and the Hearth" ("FH"), "Pantaloon in Black" ("PB"), "The Old People" ("TOP"), "The Bear" ("TB"), "Delta Autumn" ("DA"), "Go Down, Moses" ("GDM"). Other Faulkner works cited are listed in Abbreviations.

For the genetic history of *Go Down, Moses* see Joanne V. Creighton, *William Faulkner's Craft of Revision: The Snopes Trilogy, The Unvanquished, and Go Down, Moses* (Detroit, MI: Wayne State University Press, 1977); James Early, *The Making of Go Down, Moses* (Dallas, TX: Southern Methodist University Press, 1972); Carol Clancey Harter, "The Winter of Isaac McCaslin: Revisions and Irony in Faulkner's 'Delta Autumn,' " *Journal of Modern Literature* 1 (winter 1970): 209–25; James B. Meriwether, *The Literary Career of William Faulkner* (Princeton: Princeton University Library, 1961); Russell Roth, "The Brennan Papers: Faulkner in Manuscript," *Perspective* 2 (summer 1949): 219–24.

2. A student's handwritten notes of an interview with Faulkner, with "possible . . . errors" in it, quotes him as saying about *Go Down, Moses*, "I started this out as a collection of short stories. After reworking it became seven different facets of one field. It is simply a collection of short stories" (*LG* 52–54). The first two sentences specify the change the writer made from a "collection" to a unified work. The final sentence may therefore be considered one of possible "errors" in the notes, a conclusion verified by Faulkner's insistence throughout his life that *Go Down, Moses*, rather than "a collection of short stories," is "indeed a novel." Another version of the interview repeats the quotation above (Lavon Rascoe, "An Interview with William Faulkner," in *Conversations with William Faulkner*, ed. M. Thomas Inge [Jackson: University Press of Mississippi, 1999)], 66–72. But A. Wigfall Green's transcription of the student's notes deletes the third sentence, un-

derscoring Faulkner's pleasure in transforming what "started as a collection of short stories" into "seven different facets of one idea" (in *William Faulkner of Oxford*, eds. James W. Webb and A. Wigfall Green [Baton Rouge: Louisiana State University Press, 1965], 127–39). Reprinted in Inge, ed., *Conversations with William Faulkner*, 73–82.

3. Creighton thinks the story is "filtered through the perspective of the boy" Cass, but the boy Ike's "hearing" and "listening," specified at the start, superimposes over it another filter. She considers the "capsule characterization of Isaac McCaslin" in part 1 of "Was," and part 4 of "The Bear" the "key unifying devices" (*William Faulkner's Craft of Revision*, 87–88), but offers limited proof on the way the germinal addition and its modulations, and the countermotions to and from part 4 of "The Bear" frame the work's total design. Warren Beck considers "the major events coded within the book's cryptic opening" to be a "prophecy or even annunciation" of Isaac's presence, which will "dominate" the work, although he hardly features Isaac's "preeminence" over the first story and the succeeding ones (*Faulkner: Essays* [Madison: University of Wisconsin University Press, 1976], 349–50). John Limon ("The Integration of Faulkner's *Go Down, Moses*" *Critical Inquiry* [winter 1986], 422–38) argues that Rider cannot be understood, and the work "cannot be made to cohere" and is therefore "a collection of stories and not a novel" (422–23). Joseph W. Reed, Jr., thinks "every cause" and "every pattern" developed through the other stories "can be found there" in the first story, except for the introduction to "Was" and part 4 of "The Bear," which are "misfits" in a novel otherwise "coherent in its parts" (*Faulkner's Narrative* [New Haven: Yale University Press, 1973], 186–87, 195–96). "Everything else grows out" of "Was," James A. Snead avers, although he fails to note how Isaac's creed at the head of the story qualifies "Cass's whitewashed storytelling" (*Figures of Division: William Faulkner's Major Novels* [New York: Methuen, 1986*]*, 202–4). The whole novel, Stephen M. Ross declares, constitutes the "total discourse" of one character, Isaac McCaslin. His "psyche" is "the fixed ground from which the reader's experience derives" (*Fiction's Inexhaustible Voice: Speech and Writing in Faulkner* [Athens: University of Georgia Press, 1989], 154–55). Isaac's dual creed, this study shows, sets the catalyst for succeeding action through the work.

Other studies on time and structure in *Go Down, Moses* include: Thomas C. Foster, "History, Private Consciousness, and Narrative Form in *Go Down, Moses*," *Centennial Review* 24, no.1 (winter 1984): 61–76; Ronald Schleifer, "Faulkner's Storied Novel: *Go Down, Moses* and the Translation of Time," *Modern Fiction Studies* 28, no. 1 (spring 1982):109–27; A. Bruce Southard, "Syntax and Time in Faulkner's *Go Down Moses*," *Language and Style* 14, no.2 (spring 1981), 107–15; and Weldon Thornton, "Structure and Theme in Faulkner's *Go Down, Moses*," in *William Faulkner: A Critical Collection*, ed. Leland H. Cox (Detroit, MI: Gale Research, 1982).

4. In the spring, 1940, Faulkner put together six published stories about black people and their relationship with white people. In the fall, he changed the original protagonist to Isaac McCaslin, added an extensively revised story that became "Delta Autumn," and composed part 1 of "Was" and part 4 of "The Bear," shifting the focus to the hunt and man's relationship with nature. Daniel J. Singal represents readers who think "the two halves of this novel" fail to cohere (*The Making of a Modernist* [Chapel Hill: University of North Carolina Press, 1997], 283). He praises the "Modernist" theme of racial relations in the early version of the novel,

but the addition of the wilderness-hunting theme in the later version throws "the design of the novel well out of kilter" (279–80).

5. Isaac's repudiation of patrimony marks the "central moral issue" that unites the separate stories, Creighton concludes (*William Faulkner's Craft of Revision* 127). That moral action, however, appears to be only one of several comprehensive issues around the joint legacies from nature and society. Faulkner himself links human exploitation with the destruction of nature. He wants to evoke in "The Bear" "compassion" for the wilderness so "ruthlessly destroyed . . . by men who simply wanted to make that earth grow something they could sell for a profit, which brought into it a condition based on an evil like human bondage" (*FU* 277).

6. Stanley Tick ("The Unity of *Go Down, Moses*," in *William Faulkner: Four Decades of Criticism* [East Lansing: Michigan State University Press, 1973], 327–34) regards the story of Rider not only "non-essential" to the structure, but "irrelevant" to the McCaslin saga (329–30).

Among the many substantial studies on patterns of plot and theme in *Go Down, Moses* are: Beck, *Faulkner: Essays*; Cleanth Brooks, *William Faulkner: The Yoknapatawpha Country* (New Haven: Yale University Press, 1963); Dirk Kuyk, Jr., *Threads Cable-Strong: William Faulkner's Go Down, Moses* (Lewisburg, PA: Bucknell University Press, 1983); Michael Millgate, *The Achievement of William Faulkner* (Lincoln: University of Nebraska Press, 1978); Olga W. Vickery, *The Novels of William Faulkner: A Critical Interpretation* (Baton Rouge: Louisiana State University Press, 1964). Beck thinks the "general theme" of racial relations creates a "tonal-thematic unity" (343–44). "The varying fortunes" of the McCaslin family (excepting Rider in "PB" who is not a McCaslin) provide the novel's "over-all unity," Brooks contends (244). Paradoxical juxtaposition and condensation, the equivalent of linear and cyclic motions, frame a pattern of structural form, Kuyk observes, but his discussion focuses on ritual, plot, fabula, history, myth, and motivic patterns that unify the substance of story (22–31, 76–78, and passim). Millgate identifies white-black relations and the destruction of the wilderness among the themes tying the stories together (204, 212), but ultimately all the motifs converge around moral responsibility for action (287). He detects a "centripetal . . . structural tendency" in Faulkner's works brought about by condensation, suspension, and fragmentation (286–87). Vickery identifies a single structural framework in each story, the "ritual hunt" (124). See also Singal, *The Making of a Modernist*, and Thornton, "Structure and Theme in Faulkner's *Go Down, Moses*."

7. Beck devotes over fifty pages of his book to part 4 of "The Bear" (*Faulkner: Essays*, 395–449); Creighton (*William Faulkner's Craft of Revision*), and Millgate (*The Achievement*), among many others, also locate the novel's center in that section. Ross argues that part 4, a "textual" representation of Isaac's consciousness" and of the "moral knowledge" he has gained, coalesces "the entire novel into a coherent whole" (*Fiction's Inexhaustible Voice*, 158–59). See also notes 3 and 4 above.

8. "These twin brothers," says Faulkner of Uncles Buck and Buddy, "had believed that there was something outrageous and wrong in slavery and they had done what they could," but "in daily life, they would use the terms in which the Negro was on a level with the dog or the animal they ran" (*FU* 39–40).

9. The deputy who is "trying to make sense of his actual experience of Rider," is not "devastatingly different from the redneck we have all presumed to know," Noel Polk argues, but the man's dehumanizing attitude impugns that whole class (*Children of the Dark House: Text and Context in Faulkner* [Jackson: University Press of Mississippi, 1996]), 240).

10. Panthea Reid Broughton decries Isaac's belief that "he may escape" his past (*William Faulkner: The Abstract and the Actual* [Baton Rouge: Louisiana State University Press, 1974], 111); and Leonard Gilley, his blindness to nature's violence and his own destructiveness ("The Wilderness Theme in Faulkner's 'The Bear,' " *Midwest Quarterly* 6 (July 1965): 379–85). Millgate (*The Achievement*) objects to his "idealism" and "withdrawal and escape" from difficult realities (208–10). Singal accuses Isaac of regressing to the "mindless chauvinism" of his ancestors (*The Making of a Modernist*, 282), while Vickery reprehends Isaac's "withdrawal" from humanity, and his evasion of "guilt" and "responsibilities" (*The Novels of William Faulkner*, 133). In contrast, R. W. B. Lewis would make Isaac a saint or redemptive savior in "The Hero in the New World: William Faulkner's 'The Bear,' " in *Bear, Man, and God: Seven Approaches to William Faulkner's "The Bear,"* 2d. ed. eds. Francis Lee Utley, Lynn Z. Bloom, and Arthur F. Kinney (New York: Random House, 1964, 188–201).

11. In "Lion," a prototpe of "The Bear," Isaac has a grandson (*Uncollected Stories of William Faulkner*, ed. Joseph Blotner [New York: Vintage Books, 1981], 184–200). When Faulkner turns him childless in the novel, he nullifies one of Isaac's principal reasons for repudiating property and further weights the cost Isaac pays for moral action.

12. Boon's behavior at the conclusion of "The Bear" has been attributed to injured pride and greed, frustration, madness, or corruption by technology. Bisected like other prominent characters, Boon has a converse, strangely protective side. He sits two nights under a sapling to protect a bear cub terrified by the new train. He cares lovingly for Lion after Sam has made him approachable. He enacts a killing ritual worthy of venerable Old Ben. Afterward, he ignores his own wounds to get help for Lion. He gives Sam the death he wants, then with Ike, protects the body in its frame. In an unpublished segment of tapes at the University of Virginia, Faulkner remarks on Boon's "godlike attribute . . . , his strength and his capacity to be brave, to save, to protect the weak and the small," even "just a dog" (UV T-144). Yoking these two sides of Boon casts a different hue on the final scene.

13. Faulkner's inconsistent comments (like those of his readers) attest to the bifurcated nature and deeds of his protagonist. Isaac, he says, decides not to "participate" in something "rotten" that he "can't do anything about," but in the novel, he acts on inherited "wrong and shame" at great personal cost and thus belies his creator's words. Faulkner, on the other hand, recognizes that, acting on principle, Isaac gains not "success," but "something a lot more important," "serenity" and "wisdom" (*FU* 246, 54). His character appears to fulfill the writer's purpose: to encourage people to adhere to "honor, truth, pity, consideration," and "endure well grief and misfortune and injustice . . . not for reward but for virtue's own sake" so they could live with themselves (*SL* 142).

CONCLUSION

1. Robert A. Jelliffe, Fulbright Professor to Japan and director of the Seminar on American Literature at Nagano, compiled, edited, and wrote an introduction for Faulkner's talks and speeches in *Faulkner at Nagano* (Tokyo: Kenkyusha, 1956). See Abbreviations for the list of Faulkner's works.

2. M. M. Bakhtin, *The Dialogic Imagination*, ed. Michael Holquist, trans. Caryl

Emerson and Michael Holquist (Austin: University of Texas Press, 1981), 314, 263.

3. Cleanth Brooks, *Modern Poetry and the Tradition* (New York: Oxford University Press, 1965), 37, 40, 41–42; and "Irony as a Principle of Structure" in *Literary Opinion in America*, ed. Morton Dauwen Zabel, vol. 2, 3d. ed. (New York: Harper Torchbooks, 1962), 736, 732–33; I. A. Richards, quoted by Brooks in *Modern Poetry*, 48.

4. Roland Barthes, *The Pleasure of the Text*, trans. Richard Miller (New York: Hill and Wang, 1975), 12; and *Critical Essays*, trans. Richard Howard (Evanston, IL: Northwestern University Press, 1972), 267.

5. Barthes, *The Pleasure of the Text*, 15, 30–31, 66–67.

Bibliography

A selected list of works cited or consulted.

MANUSCRIPTS BY WILLIAM FAULKNER

William Faulkner Collection at the Alderman Library, University of Virginia, under file name or number in text.
William Faulkner Manuscripts. 44 vols. New York: Garland, 1986–.

NOVELS BY WILLIAM FAULKNER

Absalom, Absalom! New York: Random House, 1936/1964; The Corrected Text. New York: Vintage International, 1990.

As I Lay Dying. New York: Vintage Books, 1930/1964; The Corrected Text. New York: Vintage International, 1990.

A Fable. New York: Vintage Books, 1950/1978.

Flags in the Dust. Edited by Douglas Day. New York: Vintage Books, 1974.

Go Down, Moses. New York: Modern Library, 1942; The Corrected Text. New York: Vintage International, 1990.

The Hamlet. New York: Vintage Books, 1940/1958; The Corrected Text. New York: Vintage International, 1991.

Intruder in the Dust. New York: Modern Library, 1948; The Corrected Text. New York: Vintage International, 1991.

Light in August. New York: Modern Library, 1932/1968; The Corrected Text. New York: Vintage International, 1987.

The Mansion. New York: Vintage Books, 1955/1965.

Mayday. Notre Dame, IN: University of Notre Dame Press, 1976.

Mosquitoes. New York: Boni and Liveright, 1927.

Pylon. New York: Smith and Haas, 1935.

The Reivers. New York: Random House, 1962/1992.

Requiem for a Nun. New York: Vintage Books, 1951/1975.

Sartoris. New York: Random House, 1929/1956.

Soldier's Pay. New York: Boni and Liveright, 1927.

The Sound and the Fury. New York: Modern Library, 1929/1956; The Corrected Text. New York: Vintage International, 1990.

The Town. New York: Vintage Books, 1957/1961.

The Unvanquished. New York: Vintage Books, 1938/1965; The Corrected Text. New York: Vintage International, 1991.

The Wild Palms. New York: Vintage Books, 1939/1964.

SHORT STORIES AND NONFICTION MATERIALS BY WILLIAM FAULKNER, INCLUDING INTERVIEWS, LECTURES, LETTERS, SKETCHES, AND REVIEWS

Collected Stories of William Faulkner. New York:Vintage Books, 1977.

Conversations with William Faulkner. Edited by M. Thomas Inge. Jackson: University Press of Mississippi, 1999.

William Faulkner: Early Prose and Poetry. Edited by Carvel Collins. Boston: Little, Brown, 1962.

Essays, Speeches, and Public Letters. Edited by James B. Meriwether. New York: Random House, 1965.

Faulkner-Cowley File: Letters and Memories, 1944–1962. Edited by Malcolm Cowley. New York: Viking, 1966.

A Faulkner Miscellany. Edited by James B. Meriwether. Jackson: University Press of Mississippi, 1974.

Faulkner at Nagano. Edited by Robert A. Jelliffe. Tokyo: Kenkyusha, 1956.

Faulkner in the University. Edited by Frederick L. Gwynn and Joseph L. Blotner. Charlottesville: University of Virginia Press, 1959.

Faulkner at West Point. Edited by Joseph L. Fant III and Robert Ashley. New York: Random House, 1964.

"An Introduction to *The Sound and the Fury*." *Mississippi Quarterly* 26 (summer 1973): 410–15.

Lion in the Garden: Interviews with William Faulkner, 1926–1962. Edited by James B. Meriwether and Michael Millgate. New York: Random House, 1968.

New Orleans Sketches. Edited by Carvel Collins. New York: Random House, 1968.

Selected Letters of William Faulkner. Edited by Joseph L. Blotner. New York: Random House, 1977.

Thinking of Home; William Faulkner's Letters to His Mother and Father, 1918–1925. Edited by James G. Watson. New York: Norton, 1992.

Uncollected Stories of William Faulkner. Edited by Joseph L. Blotner. New York: Vintage Books, 1981.

William Faulkner: Letters and Fictions. James G. Watson. Austin: University of Texas Press, 1987.

William Faulkner of Oxford. Edited by James W. Webb and A. Wigfall Green. Baton Rouge: Louisiana State University Press, 1965.

THEORY, CRITICISM, AND BIOGRAPHY

Abel, Darrel. "Frozen Moment in *Light in August*." In *Twentieth-Century Interpretations of Light in August*. Edited by David L. Minter. Englewood Cliffs, NJ: Prentice-Hall, 1969.

Aiken, Conrad. "William Faulkner: The Novel as Form." *The Atlantic Monthly* 164 (November 1939), 650–54. Reprinted in *William Faulkner: Three Decades of Criticism*. Edited by Frederick J. Hoffman and Olga W. Vickery. New York: Harcourt, Brace & World, 1960/1963; and in *William Faulkner: Four Decades of Criticism*. East Lansing: Michigan State University Press, 1973.

Alter, Robert. *Partial Magic: The Novel as a Self-Conscious Genre*. Berkeley: University of California Press, 1975.

Aristotle. *Aristotle's Theory of Poetry and Fine Art*. Edited by S. H. Butcher. Corrected version of the 4th ed. (1911). New York: Macmillan, 1932. Reprinted, Aristotle, *The Poetics*, in *Criticism, the Major Statements*. Edited by Charles Kaplan and William Anderson, 3rd ed. New York: St. Martin's Press, 1991.

Bachelard, Gaston. *The Poetics of Space*. Trans. Maria Jolas. New York: Orion, 1964.

Bakhtin, M. M. *The Dialogic Imagination*. Edited by Michael Holquist. Trans. Caryl Emerson and Michael Holquist. Austin: University of Texas Press, 1981.

Barthes, Roland. *Critical Essays*. Trans. Richard Howard. Evanston, IL: Northwestern University Press, 1972.

———. *The Pleasure of the Text*. Trans. Richard Miller. New York: Hill and Wang, 1975.

Bašić, Sonja. "Faulkner's Narrative Discourse: Mediation and Mimesis." In *New Directions in Faulkner Studies: Faulkner and Yoknapatawpha, 1983*. Edited by Doreen Fowler and Ann J. Abadie. Jackson: University Press of Mississippi, 1984.

———. "Faulkner's Narrative: Between Involvement and Distancing." In *Faulkner's Discourse: An International Symposium*. Edited by Lothar H. Hönnighausen. Tubingen: Max Niemeyer Verlag, 1989.

Beck, Warren. *Faulkner: Essays*. Madison: University of Wisconsin Press, 1976).

Bedell, George C. *Kierkegaard and Faulkner: Modalities of Existence*. Baton Rouge: Louisiana State University Press, 1972.

Behrens, Ralph. "Collapse of Dynasty: The Thematic Center of *Absalom, Absalom!*" *PMLA* 89, no. 3 (January 1974): 24–33.

Benson, Carl. "Thematic Design in *Light in August*." Reprinted in *William Faulkner: Four Decades of Criticism*. Edited by Linda Welshimer Wagner. East Lansing: Michigan State University Press, 1973.

Bergson, Henri. *Creative Evolution*. Trans. Arthur Mitchell. New York: Holt, 1907/1911.

———. *An Introduction to Metaphysics: The Creative Mind*. Trans. Mabelle L. Andison. Totowa, NJ: Littlefield, 1903–1923/1965.

———. *The Introduction to a New Philosophy*. Trans. Sidney Littman. Boston: Luce, 1903/1912.

———. *Laughter*. Trans. Cloudesley Brereton and Fred Rothwell. New York: Macmillan, 1911/1928.

———. *Matter and Memory*. Trans. Nancy Margaret Paul and W. Scott Palmer. London: G. Allen and Unwin, 1896/1911.

———. *Time and Free Will*. Trans. F. S. Pogson. New York: Harper, 1889/1960.

———. *The Two Sources of Morality and Religion*. Trans. R. Ashley Audra and Cloudesley Brereton. New York: Doubleday, 1932/1935.

Bleikasten, André. *Faulkner's As I Lay Dying*. Trans. Roger Little. Bloomington: Indiana University Press, 1973.

———. *The Ink of Melancholy*. Bloomington: Indiana University Press, 1990.

———. *The Most Splendid Failure: Faulkner's The Sound and the Fury*. Bloomington: Indiana University Press, 1976.

Bloom, Harold, ed. *Faulkner's Light in August: Modern Critical Interpretations*. New York: Chelsea House, 1988.

Blotner, Joseph L. *Faulkner: A Biography*. 2 vols. New York: Random House, 1974.

———. *Faulkner: A Biography*. 1 vol. rev. New York: Random House, 1984.

———. *A Catalogue of the Library of William Faulkner*. Charlottesville: University Press of Virginia, 1964.

———, ed. *Uncollected Stories of William Faulkner*. New York: Vintage Books, 1981.

Bockting, Ineke. *Character and Personality in the Novels of William Faulkner: A Study in Psychostylistics*. Lanham, MD: University Press of America, 1995.

Branch, Watson G. "Darl Bundren's 'Cubistic' Vision." *Texas Studies in Literature and Language* 19 (spring 1977): 42–59.

Brooks, Cleanth. "On *Absalom, Absalom!*" *Mosaic* 7, no. 1 (fall 1973): 159–83.

———. "Introduction" to *Light in August*. New York: Modern Library, 1932/1968.

———. "Irony as a Principle of Structure." In *Literary Opinion in America*, vol. 2, 3d. ed. Edited by Morton Dauwen Zabel. New York: Harper Torchbooks, 1962.

———. *Modern Poetry and the Tradition*. New York: Oxford University Press, 1965.

———. *William Faulkner: The Yoknapatawpha Country*. New Haven: Yale University Press, 1963.

———. *William Faulkner: Toward Yoknapatawpha and Beyond*. New Haven: Yale University Press, 1978.

Brooks, Peter. "Incredulous Narration: *Absalom, Absalom!*" *Comparative Literature* 34, no. 3 (summer 1982): 247–68.

Broughton, Panthea Reid. "An Amazing Gift: The Early Essays and Faulkner's Apprenticeship in Aesthetics and Criticism." In *New Directions in Faulkner Studies: Faulkner and Yoknapatawpha, 1983*. Edited by Doreen Fowler and Ann J. Abadie. Jackson: University Press of Mississippi, 1984.

———. *William Faulkner: The Abstract and the Actual*. Baton Rouge: Louisiana State University Press, 1974.

Bunselmeyer, J. E. "Faulkner's Narrative Styles." *American Literature* 53, no. 3 (November 1981): 424–42.

Carr, H. Wildon. *Henri Bergson: The Philosophy of Change*. New York: Kennikat Press, 1970. Reprint of 1912 ed.

Chase, Richard. "Faulkner's *Light in August*." In *Twentieth-Century Interpreta-*

tions of Light in August. Edited by David L. Minter. Englewood Cliffs: Prentice-Hall, 1969.

Church, Margaret. *Time and Reality: Studies in Contemporary Fiction*. Chapel Hill: University of North Carolina Press, 1963.

Cohen, Philip. "Faulkner's Early Narrative Technique and *Flags in the Dust*" *Southern Studies* 24, no. 2 (summer 1985): 202–20.

Cohn, Dorritt. *Transparent Minds: Narrative Modes for Presenting Consciousness in Fiction*. Princeton: Princeton University Press, 1978.

Coindreau, Maurice E. *The Time of William Faulkner*. Columbia: University of South Carolina Press, 1971.

Collins, Carvel. "Introduction," *Mayday*. Notre Dame, IN: University of Notre Dame Press, 1976.

Commins, Dorothy. *What Is an Editor? Saxe Commins at Work*. Chicago: University of Chicago Press, 1978.

Creighton, Joanne V. *William Faulkner's Craft of Revision: The Snopes Trilogy, The Unvanquished, and Go Down, Moses*. Detroit: Wayne State University Press, 1977.

Degenfelder, Pauline E. "Yoknapatawphan Baroque: A Stylistic Analysis of *As I Lay Dying*." In *William Faulkner's As I Lay Dying: A Critical Casebook*. Edited by Dianne L. Cox. New York: Garland, 1985.

De Man, Paul. *Allegories of Reading*. New Haven: Yale University Press, 1979.

Derrida, Jacques. *Of Grammatology*. Trans. Gayatri Chakravorty Spivak. Baltimore: Johns Hopkins University Press, 1976.

———. La carte postal. Paris: Flammarion, 1980. See also: *The Post Card: From Socrates to Freud*. Trans. Alan Bass. Chicago: University of Chicago Press, 1987.

———. *Writing and Difference*. Trans. Alan Bass. Chicago: University of Chicago Press, 1978.

———. "Structure, Sign, and Play in the Discourse of the Human Sciences." In *The Structuralist Controversy*. Edited by Richard Macksey and Eugenio Donato. Baltimore: Johns Hopkins University Press, 1972.

De Saussure, Ferdinand. *Course in General Linguistics*. trans. Wade Baskin. New York: Philosophical Library, 1956.

Dondlinger, Mary Joanne. "Getting Around the Body: The Matter of Race and Gender in Faulkner's *Light in August*." In *Faulkner and the Natural World: Faulkner and Yoknapatawpha, 1998*. Edited by Donald M. Kartiganer and Ann J. Abadie. Jackson: University Press of Mississippi, 1999.

Early, James. *The Making of Go Down, Moses*. Dallas: Southern Methodist University Press, 1972.

Edel, Leon. *The Psychological Novel*. Philadephia: Lippincott, 1955.

Eliade, Mircea. *Rites and Symbols of Initiation: The Mysteries of Birth and Rebirth*. Trans. Willard R. Trask. New York: Harper Torchbooks, 1958.

Fadiman, Regina K. *Faulkner's Light in August: A Description and Interpretation of the Revisions*. Charlottesville: University Press of Virginia, 1975.

Faulkner, John. *My Brother Bill*. New York: Trident, 1963.

Flores, Ralph. *The Rhetoric of Doubtful Authority: Deconstructive Readings of Self-Questioning Narratives, St. Augustine to Faulkner.* Ithaca: Cornell University Press, 1984.

Forrer, Richard. "*Absalom, Absalom!*: Storytelling as a Mode of Transcendence." *Southern Literary Journal* 9 (winter 1977): 22–46.

Foster, Thomas C. "History, Private Consciousness, and Narrative Form in *Go Down, Moses.*" *Centennial Review* 28, no. 1 (winter 1984): 61–76.

Fowler, Doreen. *The Return of the Repressed.* Charlottesville: University Press of Virginia, 1997.

Fowler, Doreen, and Ann J. Abadie, eds. *A Cosmos of My Own: Faulkner and Yoknapatawpha, 1980.* Jackson: University Press of Mississippi, 1981.

———. *Faulkner and the Craft of Fiction: Faulkner and Yoknapatawpha, 1987.* Jackson: University Press of Mississippi, 1989.

———. *Faulkner and Religion: Faulkner and Yoknapatawpha, 1989.* Jackson: University Press of Mississippi, 1991.

———. *New Directions in Faulkner Studies: Faulkner and Yoknapatawpha, 1983.* Jackson: University Press of Mississippi, 1984.

Friedman, Melvin. *Stream of Consciousness: A Study in Literary Method.* New Haven: Yale University Press, 1955.

Friedman, Norman. "Point of View in Fiction: The Development of a Critical Concept." *PMLA* 70 (1955). Reprinted in *The Theory of the Novel.* Edited by Philip Stevick. New York: Free Press, 1967.

Garrison, Joseph M., Jr. "Perception, Language, and Reality in *As I Lay Dying.*" In *William Faulkner's As I Lay Dying: A Critical Casebook.* Edited by Dianne L. Cox. New York: Garland, 1985.

Genette, Gerard. *Narrative Discourse: An Essay in Method.* Trans. Jane E. Lewin. Ithaca: Cornell University Press, 1980.

Gilley, Leonard. "The Wilderness Theme in Faulkner's 'The Bear.' " *Midwest Quarterly* 6 (July 1965): 379–85.

Godden, Richard. "William Faulkner, Addie Bundren, and Language." *Studies in English* 15 (1978): 101–23.

Gresset, Michel. *Fascination: Faulkner's Fiction 1919–1936.* Trans. Thomas West. Durham, NC: Duke University Press, 1989.

Guerard, Albert J. *The Triumph of the Novel.* New York: Oxford University Press, 1976.

Guetti, James. *The Limits of Metaphor.* Ithaca: Cornell University Press, 1967.

Gunter, Richard. "Style and Language in *The Sound and the Fury.*" In *Studies in The Sound and the Fury.* Edited by James B. Meriwether. Columbus, OH: Merrill, 1970.

Gwin, Minrose C. *The Feminine and Faulkner: Reading (Beyond) Sexual Difference.* Knoxville: University of Tennessee Press, 1990.

Gwynn, Frederick L. and Joseph L. Blotner, eds. *Faulkner in the University.* Charlottesville: University Press of Virginia , 1959.

Hagopian, John V. "Nihilism in Faulkner's *The Sound and the Fury.*" *Modern Fiction Studies* 13, no. 1 (spring 1967): 45–55.

Hamburger, Katë. *The Logic of Literature*. Bloomington: Indiana University Press, 1973.

Harrington, Evans, and Ann J. Abadie, eds. *Faulkner and the Short Story: Faulkner and Yoknapatawpha, 1990*. Jackson: University Press of Mississippi, 1992.

Harter, Carol Clancey. "The Winter of Isaac McCaslin: Revisions and Irony in Faulkner's 'Delta Autumn.' " *Journal of Modern Literature* 1 (winter 1970): 209–25.

Hedeen, Paul M. "A Symbolic Center in a Conceptual Country: A Gassian Rubric for *The Sound and the Fury*." *Modern Fiction Studies* 31, no. 4 (winter 1985): 623–43.

Heidegger, Martin. *Being and Time*. London: Harper, 1962.

Hemenway, Robert. "Enigmas of Being in *As I Lay Dying*." *Modern Fiction Studies* 16 (summer 1970): 133–46.

Hirshleifer, Phyllis. "As Whirlwinds in the South: An Analysis of *Light in August*." In *William Faulkner: Four Decades of Criticism*. Edited by Linda Welshimer Wagner. East Lansing: Michigan State University Press, 1973.

Hlavsa, Virginia V. James. *Faulkner and the Thoroughly Modern Novel*. Charlottesville: University Press of Virginia, 1991.

Hoag, Ronald Wesley. "Ends and Loose Ends: The Triptych Conclusion of *Light in August*." *Modern Fiction Studies* 31, no. 4 (winter 1985): 675–90.

Hodgson, John A. " 'Logical Sequence and Continuity': Some Observations on the Typographical and Structural Consistency of *Absalom, Absalom!*" *American Literature* 43 (March 1971): 97–107.

Hoffman, Daniel. *Faulkner's Country Matters: Folklore and Fable in Yoknapatawpha*. Baton Rouge: Louisiana State University Press, 1989.

Hoffman, Frederick J. *The Art of Southern Fiction: A Study of Some Modern Novelists*. Carbondale: Southern Illinois University Press, 1967.

Hoffman, Frederick J., and Olga W. Vickery, eds. *William Faulkner: Two Decades of Criticism*. East Lansing: Michigan State College Press, 1951.

———. *William Faulkner: Three Decades of Criticism*. New York: Harcourt, Brace & World, 1963.

Hoffman, Gerhard. "*Absalom, Absalom!: A Postmodernist Approach*." In *Faulkner's Discourse: An International Symposium*. Edited by Lothar Hönnighausen. Tubingen: Max Niemeyer Verlag, 1989.

Hönnighausen, Lothar. *Faulkner: Masks and Metaphors*. Jackson: University Press of Mississippi, 1997.

———. *William Faulkner: The Art of Stylization in His Early Graphic and Literary Work*. New York: Cambridge University Press, 1987.

———, ed. *Faulkner's Discourse: An International Symposium*. Tubingen: Max Niemeyer Verlag, 1989.

Howe, Irving. *William Faulkner: A Critical Study*. 3rd ed. Chicago: University of Chicago Press, 1975.

Hulme, T. E. *Speculations: Essays on Humanism and the Philosophy of Art*. London: Routledge and Kegan Paul, 1924.

Humphrey, Robert. *Stream of Consciousness in the Modern Novel*. Berkeley: University of California Press, 1954.

Hungerford, Harold. "Past and Present in *Light in August*." *American Literature* 55, no. 2 (May 1983): 183–98.

Hunt, John W. *William Faulkner: Art in Theological Tension*. Syracuse, NY: Syracuse University Press, 1965.

Hurst, Mary Jane. "Characterization and Language: A Case-Grammar Study of *As I Lay Dying*." *Language and Style: An International Journal* 20, no. 1 (winter 1987): 71–87.

Hutcheon, Linda. *A Poetics of Postmodernism: History, Theory, Fiction*. New York: Routledge, 1988.

Ingarden, Roman. *The Literary Work of Art*. Trans. George C. Grabowicz. Evanston, IL: Northwestern University Press, 1973.

Inge, M. Thomas, ed. *Conversations with William Faulkner*. Jackson: University Press of Mississippi, 1999.

Ingram, Forrest L. *Representative Short Story Cycles of the Twentieth Century*. The Hague: Mouton, 1971.

Irwin, John T. *Doubling & Incest/Repetition & Revenge: A Speculative Reading of Faulkner*. Baltimore: Johns Hopkins University Press, 1975.

Iser, Wolfgang. *The Implied Reader*. Baltimore: Johns Hopkins University Press, 1974.

Izsak, Emily K. "The Manuscript of *The Sound and the Fury*: The Revisions in the First Section." *Studies in Bibliography* 20 (1967): 189–202.

Jacobson, Roman, and Morris Hallen. *Fundamentals of Language*. The Hague: Mouton, 1971.

James, Henry. *The Art of the Novel: Critical Prefaces*. New York: Charles Scribner's Sons, 1934.

James, William. "The Philosophy of Bergson." In *A Pluralistic Universe*. New York: Longmans, Green, 1909.

Jameson, Fredric. *The Prison House of Language: A Critical Account of Structuralism and Russian Formalism*. Princeton: Princeton University Press, 1972.

Jelliffe, Robert A., ed. *Faulkner at Nagano*. Tokyo: Kenkyusha, 1956.

Justus, James H. "The Epic Design of *Absalom, Absalom!*" *Texas Studies in Language and Literature* 4 (summer 1962): 157–76.

Kahler, Erich. *The Inward Turn of Narrative*. Trans. Richard and Clara Winston. Princeton: Princeton University Press, 1973.

Kaluza, Irena. *The Functioning of Sentence Structure in the Stream-of-Consciousness Technique of William Faulkner's The Sound and the Fury: A Study in Linguistic Stylistics*. Folcroft, PA: Folcroft Press, 1970.

Kartiganer, Donald M. "Faulkner's Art of Repetition." In *Faulkner and the Craft of Fiction: Faulkner and Yoknapatawpha, 1987*. Edited by Doreen Fowler and Ann J. Abadie. Jackson: University Press of Mississippi, 1989.

———. *The Fragile Thread: The Meaning of Form in Faulkner's Novels*. Amherst: University of Massachusetts Press, 1979.

———. "*The Sound and the Fury* and Faulkner's Quest for Form." *English Literary History* 37 (December 1970): 613–39.

Kartiganer, Donald M., and Ann J. Abadie, eds. *Faulkner in Cultural Context:*

Faulkner and Yoknapatawpha, 1995. Jackson: University Press of Mississippi, 1997.

————. *Faulkner and the Natural World: Faulkner and Yoknapatawpha, 1998*. Jackson: University Press of Mississippi, 1999.

————. *Faulkner and Psychology: Faulkner and Yoknapatawpha, 1991*. Jackson: University Press of Mississippi, 1994.

Kawin, Bruce F. *Telling It Again and Again*. Ithaca: Cornell University Press, 1972.

Kazin, Alfred. *On Native Grounds*. New York: Doubleday Anchor Books, 1956.

Kermode, Frank. *The Sense of an Ending*. New York: Oxford University Press, 1967/1975.

Kerr, Elizabeth M. *Yoknapatawpha: Faulkner's "Little Postage Stamp of Native Soil."* rev. ed. New York: Fordham University Press, 1976.

Kierkegaard, Soren. *Repetition*. Princeton: Princeton University Press, 1946.

Kinney, Arthur F. *Faulkner's Narrative Poetics: Style as Vision*. Amherst: University of Massachusetts Press, 1978.

Kreiswirth, Martin. "Centers, Openings, and Endings: Some Faulknerian Constants." *American Literature* 56, no. 1 (March 1984): 38–50.

————. "Plots and Counterplots: The Structure of *Light in August*." In *New Essays on Light in August*. Edited by Michael Millgate. Cambridge: Cambridge University Press, 1987.

————. *William Faulkner: The Making of a Novelist*. Athens: University of Georgia Press, 1983.

Kumar, Shiv K. *Bergson and the Stream of Consciousness Novel*. New York: New York University Press, 1963.

Kuyk, Dirk, Jr. *Sutpen's Design: Interpreting Faulkner's Absalom, Absalom!* Charlottesville: University Press of Virginia, 1990.

————. *Threads Cable-Strong: William Faulkner's Go Down, Moses*. Lewisburg, PA: Bucknell University Press, 1983.

Langford, Gerald. *Faulkner's Revision of Absalom, Absalom! A Collation of the Manuscript and the Published Book*. Austin: University of Texas Press, 1971.

Larsen, Eric. "The Barrier of Language: the Irony of Language in Faulkner." *Modern Fiction Studies* 13 (spring 1967): 19–31.

Levins, Lynn Gartrell. "The Four Narrative Perspectives in *Absalom, Absalom!*" *PMLA* 85 (January 1970): 35–47.

————. *Faulkner's Heroic Design: The Yoknapatawpha Novels*. Athens: University of Georgia Press, 1976.

Lewis, R. W. B. "The Hero in the New World: William Faulkner's 'The Bear.' " In *Bear, Man, and God: Seven Approaches to William Faulkner's "The Bear."* 2d. ed. Edited by Francis Lee Utley, Lynn Z. Bloom, and Arthur F. Kinney. New York: Random House, 1964.

Lilly, Paul R., Jr. "Caddy and Addie: Speakers of Faulkner's Impeccable Language." *The Journal of Narrative Technique* 3 (spring 1973): 170–82.

Limon, John. "The Integration of Faulkner's *Go Down, Moses*." *Critical Inquiry* (winter 1986): 422–38.

Lind, Ilse Dusoir. "The Design and Meaning of *Absalom, Absalom!*" *PMLA* 70

(December 1955): 887–912. Reprinted in *William Faulkner: Three Decades of Criticism*. Edited by Frederick J. Hoffman and Olga W. Vickery. New York: Harcourt, Brace & World, 1963.

Lockyer, Judith. *Ordered By Words: Language and Narration in the Novels of William Faulkner*. Carbondale: Southern Illinois University Press, 1991.

Lodge, David. *The Modes of Modern Writing: Metaphor, Metonymy and the Typology of Modern Literature*. Ithaca: Cornell University Press, 1977.

Longley, John L., Jr. *The Tragic Mask: A Study of Faulkner's Heroes*. Chapel Hill: University of North Carolina Press, 1963.

Longstreet, Stephen. "William Faulkner in California." Typescript in the William Faulkner Collection, Alderman Library, University of Virginia (1936). Printed in *Cavalier* 15 (April 1965): 58–61; 15 (May 1965): 50–52, 85–86; and reprinted in *Conversations with William Faulkner*. Edited by M. Thomas Inge. Jackson: University Press of Mississippi, 1999.

Lowrey, Perrin. "Concepts of Time in *The Sound and the Fury*." In *English Institute Essays*. New York: Columbia University Press, 1952.

Lytle, Andrew. "The Son of Man: He will Prevail." *Sewanee Review* 63 (1955): 114–37.

Matlack, James H. "The Voices of Time: Narrative Structure in *Absalom, Absalom!*" *Southern Review* 15, no. 2 (April 1979): 333–54.

Matthews, John T. "The Marriage of Speaking and Hearing in *Absalom, Absalom!*" *English Literary History* 47, no. 3 (fall 1980): 575–94.

———. *The Play of Faulkner's Language*. Ithaca: Cornell University Press, 1982.

———. *The Sound and the Fury: Faulkner and the Lost Cause*. Boston: Twayne, 1991.

McPherson, Karen. "*Absalom, Absalom!*: Telling Scratches." *Modern Fiction Studies* 33, no. 3 (autumn 1987): 431–50.

Mendilow. A. A. *Time and the Novel*. London: Nevill, 1952.

Meriwether, James B. *The Literary Career of William Faulkner*. Princeton: Princeton University Library, 1961.

———. "The Place of *The Unvanquished* in William Faulkner's Yoknapatawpha Series." Ph.D. diss., Princeton University, 1958.

———. "A Prefatory Note by Faulkner for the Compson Appendix." *American Literature* 42 (May 1971): 281–84.

———. Review of *Faulkner's Revision of Absalom, Absalom! A Collation of the Manuscript and the Published Book*, by Gerald Langford. *American Literature* 44 (January 1973): 693–95.

———. "The Textual History of *The Sound and the Fury*." In *Studies on The Sound and the Fury*. Columbus, OH: Charles Merrill, 1970.

Merleau-Ponty, Maurice. *Phenomenology of Perception*. Trans. Colin Smith. New York: Humanities Press, 1962.

Messerli, Douglas. "The Problem of Time in *The Sound and the Fury*: A Critical Reassessment and Reinterpretation." *Southern Literary Journal* 6, no. 2 (April 1974): 19–41.

Meyerhoff, Hans. *Time in Literature*. Berkeley: University of California Press, 1955.

Miller, J. Hillis. *Fiction and Repetition: Seven English Novels*. Cambridge: Harvard University Press, 1982.

———. "The Two Relativisms: Point of View and Indeterminacy in the Novel *Absalom, Absalom!*" In *Relativism in the Arts*. Edited by Betty Joan Craige. Athens: University of Georgia Press, 1983.

Millgate, Michael. *The Achievement of William Faulkner*. Lincoln: University of Nebraska Press, 1978.

———. *Faulkner's Place*. Athens: University of Georgia Press, 1997.

———, ed. *New Essays on Light in August*. Cambridge: Cambridge University Press, 1987.

Minter, David L. *William Faulkner: His Life and Work*. Baltimore: Johns Hopkins University Press, 1980.

———, ed. *Twentieth-Century Interpretations of Light in August*. Englewood Cliffs, NJ: Prentice-Hall, 1969.

Moreland, Richard C. *Faulkner and Modernism: Rereading and Rewriting*. Madison: University of Wisconsin Press, 1990.

Mortimer, Gail L. *Faulkner's Rhetoric of Loss: A Study in Perception and Meaning*. Austin: University of Texas Press, 1983.

Mullarkey, John, ed. *The New Bergson*. New York: Manchester University Press, 1999.

O'Donnell, Patrick. "The Spectral Road: Metaphors of Transference in Faulkner's *As I Lay Dying*." *Papers on Language and Literature* 20, no. 1 (winter 1984): 60–79.

Parker, Robert Dale. *Faulkner and the Novelistic Imagination*. Urbana: University of Illinois Press, 1985.

Patrides, C. A. *Aspects of Time*. Toronto: University of Toronto Press, 1976.

Pilkington, John. *The Heart of Yoknapatawpha*. Jackson: University Press of Mississippi, 1981.

Pitavy, Francois L. *Faulkner's Light in August*. Trans. Gillian E. Cook, rev. ed. Bloomington: Indiana University Press, 1973.

———. "A Stylistic Approach to *Light in August*." In *William Faulkner's Light in August: A Critical Casebook*. Edited by Francois L. Pitavy. New York: Garland, 1982.

Poirier, Richard. *A World Elsewhere: The Place of Style in American Literature*. New York: Oxford University Press, 1966.

Polk, Noel. *Children of the Dark House: Text and Context in Faulkner*. Jackson: University Press of Mississippi, 1996.

———. "The Manuscripts of *Absalom, Absalom!*" *Mississippi Quarterly* 25, no. 3 (summer 1972): 359–67.

Porter, Carolyn. "The Problem of Time in *Light in August*." *Rice University Studies* 61, no. 1 (1975): 107–25.

Pouillon, Jean. "Time and Destiny in Faulkner." In *Faulkner: A Collection of Critical Essays*. Edited by Robert Penn Warren. Englewood Cliffs, NJ: Prentice-Hall, 1966.

Poulet, Georges. *Studies in Human Time*. Trans. Elliott Coleman. Baltimore: Johns Hopkins University Press, 1956.

———. *The Metamorphoses of the Circle*. Baltimore: Johns Hopkins University Press, 1966.

Putzel, Max. "Faulkner's Trial Preface to *Sartoris*: An Eclectic Text." *Papers of the Bibliographical Society of America* 74 (1980): 361–78.

———. *Genius of Place: William Faulkner's Triumphant Beginnings*. Baton Rouge: Louisiana State University Press, 1985.

Radloff, Bernhard. "The Unity of Time in *The Sound and the Fury*." *The Faulkner Journal* 1, no. 2 (spring 1986): 56–68.

Ragan, David Paul. *William Faulkner's Absalom, Absalom! A Critical Study*. Ann Arbor: UMI Research Press, 1987.

Railey, Kevin. *History, Ideology, and the Production of William Faulkner*. Tuscaloosa: University of Alabama Press, 1999.

Randel, Don Michael, ed. *The New Harvard Dictionary of Music*. Cambridge: Harvard University Press, 1986.

Reed, Joseph W., Jr. *Faulkner's Narrative* New Haven: Yale University Press, 1973.

Ricoeur, Paul. *Time and Narrative*, 3 vols. Trans. Kathleen McLaughlin and David Pellauer. Chicago: University of Chicago Press, 1984–1988.

Rimon, Shlomith. "A Comprehensive Theory of Narrative: Genette's *Figure III* and the Structuralist Studies of Fiction." *PTL: A Journal for Descriptive Poetics and Theory of Literature* 1 (1976): 33–62.

Rio-Jelliffe, R. "*Absalom, Absalom! as a Self-Reflexive Novel*." *Journal of Narrative Technique* 11, no. 2 (spring 1981): 75–90.

———. "The Language of Time in Fiction: A Model in Faulkner's 'Barn Burning.' " *Journal of Narrative Technique* 24, no. 2 (spring 1994): 98–113.

Rollyson, Carl E., Jr. *Uses of the Past in the Novels of William Faulkner*. Ann Arbor: UMI Research Press, 1984.

Ross, Stephen M. *Fiction's Inexhaustible Voice: Speech and Writing in Faulkner*. Athens: University of Georgia Press, 1989.

———. "The 'Loud World' of Quentin Compson." *Studies in the Novel, North Texas State* 7, no. 2 (summer 1975): 245–57.

Roth, Russell. "The Brennan Papers: Faulkner in Manuscript." *Perspective* 2 (summer 1949): 219–24.

Rubin, Louis D., Jr. *The Writer in the South: Studies in a Literary Community*. Athens: University of Georgia Press, 1972.

Ruppersburg, Hugh M. *Voice and Eye in Faulkner's Fiction*. Athens: University of Georgia Press, 1983.

Sartre, Jean-Paul. *Being and Nothingness*. New York: Philosophical Library, 1956.

———. "Time in Faulkner: *The Sound and the Fury*." Originally published in *La Nouvelle Revue Francaise*, 1939. Reprinted in *William Faulkner: Three Decades of Criticism*. Edited by Frederick J. Hoffman and Olga W. Vickery. Trans. Martine Darmon. New York: Harcourt, Brace & World, 1963.

Schleifer, Ronald. "Faulkner's Storied Novel: *Go Down, Moses* and the Translation of Time." *Modern Fiction Studies* 28, no. 1 (spring 1982): 109–27.

Scholes, Percy A. *The Concise Oxford Dictionary of Music*, 2nd ed. Edited by John Owen Ward. London: Oxford University Press, 1964.

Scholes, Robert, and Robert Kellogg. *The Nature of Narrative*. New York: Oxford University Press, 1966/1979.

Scholes, Robert, Nancy R. Comley, Carl H. Klaus, Michael Silverman, eds. *Elements of Literature*, 4th ed. New York: Oxford University Press, 1991.

Sensibar, Judith. *The Origins of Faulkner's Art*. Austin: University of Texas Press, 1984.

Singal, Daniel J. *William Faulkner: The Making of a Modernist*. Chapel Hill: University of North Carolina Press, 1997.

Skei, Hans H. *William Faulkner: The Novelist as Short Story Writer*. Oslo: Universtetforlaget, 1985.

———. *Reading Faulkner's Best Short Stories*. Columbia: University of South Carolina Press, 1999.

Slatoff, Walter J. *Quest for Failure: A Study of William Faulkner*. Ithaca: Cornell University Press, 1960.

Smith, Barbara Herrnstein. *On the Margins of Discourse: the Relation of Literature to Discourse*. Chicago: University of Chicago Press, 1978.

Snead, James A. *Figures of Division: William Faulkner's Major Novels*. New York: Methuen, 1986.

Southard, A. Bruce. "Syntax and Time in Faulkner's *Go Down, Moses*." *Language and Style* 14, no. 2 (spring 1981): 107–15.

Sowder, William J. *Existential-Phenomenological Readings on Faulkner*. Conway, AR: UCA Press, 1991.

Spencer, Sharon. *Space, Time, and Structure in the Modern Novel*. New York: New York University Press, 1971.

Spenko, James Leo. "The Death of Joe Christmas and the Power of Words." *Twentieth-Century Literature* 28, no. 3 (fall 1982): 252–68.

Stanzel, Franz K. *Narrative Situations in the Novel*. Trans. James P. Pusack. Bloomington: Indiana University Press, 1971.

Stevick, Philip, ed. *The Theory of the Novel*. New York: Free Press, 1967.

Taylor, Carole Anne. "*Light in August*: The Epistemology of Tragic Paradox." *Texas Studies in Literature and Language* 22, no. 1 (spring 1980): 48–68.

Thornton, Weldon. "Structure and Theme in Faulkner's *Go Down, Moses*." In *William Faulkner: A Critical Collection*. Edited by Leland H. Cox. Detroit: Gale Research, 1962.

Tick, Stanley. "The Unity of *Go Down, Moses*." *Twentieth-Century Literature* 8 (July 1962): 62–76. Reprinted in *William Faulkner: Four Decades of Criticism*. Edited by Linda Welshimer Wagner. East Lansing: Michigan State University Press, 1973.

Tobin, Patricia Drechsel. *Time and the Novel: The Genealogical Imperative*. Princeton: Princeton University Press, 1978.

Todorov, Tzvetan. *The Poetics of Prose*. Trans. Richard Howard. Ithaca: Cornell University Press, 1977.

Toliver, Harold. *Animate Illusions: Explorations of Narrative Structure*. Lincoln: University of Nebraska Press, 1974.

Toolan, Michael J. *The Stylistics of Fiction: A Literary-Linguistic Approach*. New York: Routledge, 1990.

Tucker, John. "William Faulkner's *Light in August*: Toward a Structuralist Reading." *Modern Language Quarterly* 43, no. 2 (June 1982): 138–55.

Urgo, Joseph R. *Faulkner's Apocrypha: A Fable, Snopes, and the Spirit of Human Rebellion*. Jackson: University Press of Mississippi, 1989.

Uspensky, Boris. *A Poetics of Composition*. Trans. Valentina Zavarin and Susan Wittig. Berkeley: University of California Press, 1974.

Utley, Francis Lee, Lynn Z. Bloom, and Arthur F. Kinney, eds. *Bear, Man, and God: Eight Approaches to William Faulkner's "The Bear,"* 2d. ed. New York: Random House, 1971.

Vickery, Olga W. *The Novels of William Faulkner: A Critical Interpretation*, rev. ed. Baton Rouge: Louisiana State University Press, 1964.

Waggoner, Hyatt H. "The Historical Novel in the Southern Past: The Case of *Absalom, Absalom!*" *Southern Literary Journal* 2 (spring 1979): 69–85.

———. *William Faulkner: From Jefferson to the World*. Lexington: University of Kentucky Press, 1959.

Wagner, Linda W. "Language and Act: Caddy Compson," *Southern Literary Journal* 14, no. 2 (spring 1982): 49–61.

Wagner, Linda Welshimer, ed. *William Faulkner: Four Decades of Criticism*. East Lansing: Michigan State University Press, 1973.

Warren, Robert Penn. "Introduction: Faulkner: Past and Future." In *Faulkner: A Collection of Critical Essays*. Edited by Robert Penn Warren. Englewood Cliffs, NJ: Prentice-Hall, 1966.

Wasson, Ben. *Count No 'Count: Flashbacks to Faulkner*. Jackson: University Press of Mississippi, 1983.

Watkins, Floyd C. *The Flesh and the Word: Eliot, Hemingway, Faulkner*. Nashville: Vanderbilt University Press, 1971.

Watson, James G. *William Faulkner: Letters and Fictions*. Austin: University of Texas Press, 1987.

———, ed. *Thinking of Home: William Faulkner's Letters to His Mother and Father, 1918–1925*. New York: Norton, 1992.

Wellek, Rene, and Austin Warren. *Theory of Literature*, 3d. ed. New York: Harvest/HBJ Books, 1977.

Wilde, M. Carpenter. *A Loving Gentleman: The Love Story of William Faulkner and Meta Carpenter*. New York: Simon & Schuster, 1976.

Wittenberg, Judith Bryant. *Faulkner: The Transfiguration of Biography*. Lincoln: University of Nebraska Press, 1979.

Wolff, Sally, and Floyd C. Watkins, eds. *Talking About William Faulkner: Interviews with Jimmy Faulkner and Others*. Baton Rouge: Louisiana State University Press, 1996.

Zabel, Morton Dauwen, ed. *Literary Opinion in America*, vol. 2, 3d. ed. New York: Harper Torchbooks, 1962.

Zender, Karl F. *The Crossing of the Ways: William Faulkner, The South, and the Modern World*. New Brunswick, NJ: Rutgers University Press, 1989.

———. "Faulkner and the Power of Sound." *PMLA* 99, no.1 (January 1984): 89–108.

Zink, Karl E. "Flux and the Frozen Moment: The Imagery of Stasis in Faulkner's Prose." *PMLA* 71, no. 3 (June 1956): 285–301.

Zoellner, Robert H. "Faulkner's Prose Style in *Absalom, Absalom!*" *American Literature* 30 (January 1959): 486–502.

Index

Abraham, 148

Absalom, Absalom! 20, 24, 27, 28, 38, 39, 48, 50, 57, 74–85, 87, 93, 94, 102, 106, 115, 127;

causality in a fractured tale, 74–76, 79–80; "elapsed and yet-elapsing" time in, 75–85; germs and contrapuntal structure in, 74, 75–85; implausible form tells a credible "implied story," 74–76, 78–85; layered voices tell a truth/lie, 74, 77–79, 81–85; "notlanguage" tells in silence, 78, 79; the Omniscient (narrator), 77–78, 164–65 n. 3; paradox in the reflexive novel, 74, 80, 83–84; Quentin and Shreve as incredible co-tellers, 80–83; Quentin as listener and teller, 77–79, 165 n. 4; Quentin's strategies against the unreliable word, 74–78, 79–80; Sutpen trusts words, 75; theme of, 80, 84–85; uniform style in, 83; words and deeds ripple on, 75–76, 82, 84–85

Alice, 62–63

Ames, Dalton, 96, 102

Aristotle, 47–49

As I Lay Dying: 20, 24, 27, 30, 32, 38, 39, 40, 44, 50, 57, 83, 103–17; Addie Bundren on the treacherous word, 103–4, 106–9; the Addie or Darl "moment" and structure in, 50, 105–17; Bergson on "external" language, 104; on deeper mind, 110; the Bundren journey as subverted quest myth, 108; the disjunct plot and modulant structure in, 105–16; duration in Darl's mixed styles, voices, and viewpoints, 104–5, 109–13, 114–16; Faulkner contends Darl "wasn't mad," 116; on *AILD,* 44; an implausible form speaks a "dark voicelessness," 103–7, 109–17; tense shifts and perspective in, 115–16; Vardaman's mixed styles, 113–14; the voiced word and "voiceless speech," 104, 107, 109–10, 112, 114–15, 116–17; "writing" both potent and treacherous, 116–17

Balzac, Honoré de, 45, 52

"Barn Burning," 37–38, 39

Barthes, Roland, 22, 104, 152–53, 167–168 n. 5

Bascomb, Maury (Uncle Maury), 92, 102

Beauchamp, Hubert (Uncle Hubert), 138

Beauchamp, Lucas, 133, 142–43, 146

Beauchamp, Molly (Aunt Mollie), 142, 146

Beauchamp, Samuel (Butch), 133, 140, 141, 146

Beauchamp, Sophonsiba (Miss), 133, 143

Beck, Warren, 174 n. 3, 175 nn. 6 and 7

Benson, Carl, 162 n. 11

Bergson, Henri, 22, 52–59, 159–60 n. 1; Bergson's influence on Faulkner, 10, 20, 24, 35–39, 49–51, 52–73, 87–88, 102, 104, 118, 136; on the divided mind, time, self, and language, 53–56, 59; the final act in narrative, 57, 73; freedom and volition arise from deeper mind, 57, 68; language of duration in images and tropes, 55–56; paradox in, and Faulkner, 29, 56–57; on structure of disjunct narrative, 56–57; on "true" or "real duration," 19–20, 52–53, 54–57. *See*

193